Field and Forest

Field and Forest

Classic Hunting Stories

Edited by
Stephen J. Bodio

LYONS PRESS
Guilford, Connecticut
An imprint of Globe Pequot Press

Lyons Press is an imprint of Globe Pequot Press.

Project editor: Meredith Dias
Layout: Sue Murray

Library of Congress Cataloging-in-Publication Data is available on file.

ISBN 978-0-7627-9288-7

Printed in the United States of America

10 9 8 7 6 5 4 3 2 1

Contents

Introduction
By Stephen Bodio

This is a collection of tales written in the late nineteenth and early twentieth centuries, from the Civil War to around 1930: the time that some historically minded outdoorsmen wistfully call the Golden Age. For hunters it was a great time to be alive, maybe the best; I must admit I would have loved it. Almost any corner of the globe was open to someone with a little money and a lot of determination. All the great gun designs had assumed their final form, from lever-action Winchesters, through bolt actions like the Mannlicher-Schoenauer '03 and the Mauser '98, up to the finest hammerless double-barreled shotguns from London's bespoke shops. These were the glory years of paper journalism, when print was king, and the standard of everyday "disposable" writing was higher than it has been since. Hunting was still prestigious, and expeditions to track game by the likes of Teddy Roosevelt or New York socialite Suydam Cutting attracted the sponsorship of great museums. Such popular writers as Zane Grey and Ernest Thompson Seton shared space in magazines with scientists Roy Chapman Andrews, William Beebe, and William T. Hornaday, and even former-president Teddy Roosevelt.

Although I said "men," this was also the first era when wealthy adventurous women went hunting on safari in Africa, even bought plantations there, and wrote as knowledgeably as their male peers. At home they shot quail or went to the plains for prairie chickens in the fall; some, unlike most of their male companions, were not embarrassed to tell you how to cook your quarry as well.

I have left out the kind of tales that a contemporary writer calls "I knew an old dog who died" stories and cute ones where the hunter dies in the last sentence or wakes up in a heaven (or hell) full of grouse. I *have* added one sentimental but factual story, Seton's "Lobo," a good tale and a historical marker: The first two pro-wolf writings anywhere are by "reformed" American wolf trappers, Seton and Aldo Leopold, and the story itself lives on with the current wolf wars. A Korean publisher recently published the tale as a book!

Instead, *Field and Forest* is for the most part a collection of true chronicles, pieces that celebrate a time when the entire world was a sportsman's playground, when literate people might use one of the world's finest double guns to shoot quail as guests on a private plantation or raise a sporting rifle to dutifully kill two man-eating lions that raided the Empire's construction camp on the Uganda Railway. It was a more innocent time, one that unquestioningly accepted the existence of blood sports but was more playful; the head scientist of a Mongolian paleontological expedition could chase antelope and wolves across the steppes with his car and then write gleefully about it in a popular magazine. If chasing wolves with packs of borzois on an Imperial

Russian estate seemed exotic to its Western chroniclers, remember that similar hunts, minus only the lines of serfs, were and still are taking place on the North American plains. Custer and Roosevelt both ran wolfhounds.

Some of the stories in this collection are about practices still popular in the unreconstructed West where I live. I have more than a few neighbors who run packs of lion and bear hounds; at least one family is also well known for its activism in conservation circles. But in the late 1990s, when Arizona rancher and guide Warner Glenn rediscovered the American jaguar with his pack of hounds (he photographed it, let it go, and started an organization to preserve its kind), modern journalism seems to have collectively decided to ignore the hunter and the wandering American jaguar. The only popular magazine article about the discovery I ever saw appeared in the Moscow-based hunting and fishing magazine *Oxota,* in Russian! Such stories were commonplace on the newsstands of my youth, as late as the 1950s; today, in several states hunting with hounds is against the law. In this book we have one of the tales that invented the fast-disappearing genre: Zane Grey's "Tige's Lion."

There is a gentler side to *Field and Forest* as well. "The Forest and the Steppe" by Ivan Turgenev is like an impressionist painting or a tone poem, evoking in a distant place and time Russia's most beautiful landscapes and seasons. It is so evocative and moving in its melancholy that I try to read it at least a couple times a year; I suspect you will too. Grace Gallatin Thompson Seton's piece on hunting an antelope prefigures today's thoughtful hunting stories as, having killed her first antelope, she both rejoices in her shot and allows herself to mourn the death of her quarry.

If you hunt, and read, these stories will resonate with you. If you don't hunt, they may at the very least entertain you—and make you feel, dream, think, and realize that progress is not always what it seems.

Steve Bodio
Magdalena, New Mexico
March 2013

Field and Forest: Classic Hunting Stories

The Prairie Chicken

The Pinnated Grouse. The Sharp-Tailed Grouse
From* Game Bird Shooting, *1931
Capt. Charles Askins

My first real chicken hunt occurred in the Osage Nation of the Indian Territory in the late eighties. There were three of us, with a team, a wagon and a pair of dogs.

The dogs were ranging ahead and we followed in the wagon. Nothing had stirred from the tall prairie grass.

I noticed that some dwarf postoaks well ahead of us seemed to be conspicuously filled with birds' nests, fifty to the tree and many trees loaded. "What are they?" I asked.

The driver said "Chickens," and I whipped out and on ahead with my dogs. Soon the chickens flew out of the trees, hundreds of them; but there were others on the ground that didn't fly. The dog pointed, and I shot at a chicken, missing with both barrels at about thirty yards.

All around me the chickens climbed out, cackling. They didn't fly far, and they put up three bevies of quail in their flight.

Getting out the empty brass shells and reloading as fast as I could, I was interrupted by a shout from the wagon. Looking back, I saw eleven deer, coming from the timber, crossing an opening within a hundred yards of me, the does in front, bucks behind, galloping slowly, unafraid.

The driver grabbed his old Sharps rifle, but couldn't find his cartridges in time. He finally shot and missed.

As the deer entered the next clump of oaks, a great flock of large black colored birds, looking not unlike crows in the distance, took wing and went into the timber with the deer.

We estimated that bunch of wild turkeys as containing three hundred birds, and I never since have seen another such flock.

The driver tied his team and followed the deer. The oldtimer took his shotgun and followed the turkeys. Taking the dogs, I went on down into a lush grassy valley, along a branch, where the chickens and the quail had gone.

The dogs pointed, now chickens, now quail, and along with what I bagged of them I killed one turkey and five mallard ducks. I couldn't carry all the birds; they were piled under a tree until the wagon camp up.

The driver got no deer, the oldtimer killed two turkeys, and I emptied all the shells I had.

The Osage Indian has become rich since that day, his race is the richest people in the world; but if he had only known it he was nearer to Indian heaven in those days than he ever will be again.

That night I myself felt that I was surely in a hunters' paradise as I loaded shells by lantern light and listened to the coyotes howling as they ringed the camp. Today I know all too well that it was nothing less.

All Chickens Are Chickens

We are classing all the birds in this chapter as prairie chickens, though there are minor differences or varieties of the true chicken, besides the sharptail, quite a different bird. All prairie chickens look alike, from those found on the Atlantic Coast to the chicken of the Panhandle of Texas, though they bear different Latin names. The Eastern variety is practically extinct.

The pinnated grouse is strictly a prairie bird, though sometimes driven to the woods by stress of weather or for forage. He is the only prairie grouse in this country, or perhaps in any other country, grouse in general being "woods Indians." The willow grouse is more or less a bird of the open, but he is really a ptarmigan, with a range extending across British America and the North of Europe.

Our pinnated grouse is said to have an unconquerable aversion to civilization, refusing to nest in a cultivated field or anywhere except the unbroken sod. This may be only relatively true; possibly we have accepted a conclusion without testing it. No game bird was wilder than the turkey, yet he was domesticated; because there was real need of him—he fitted splendidly into a domestic niche not previously occupied.

The prairie chicken cannot replace or displace the universal domestic hen—man can live without him, have as much to eat, make as much money. He is of interest only to the sportsman, who should have protected him and perpetuated his race. If it had been the business of the poultryman to breed prairie chickens, we should have had them by the millions; but it being the business of the shooting man, our finest grouse may become extinct.

When the Cherokee Strip of the Indian Territory was opened to settlement, in 1893, the land was alive with prairie chickens. They came in from the prairie to feed with the tame hens, alighted on the roof of the shack before daylight, followed the plow and dusted in the furrow, watered at the horse-trough, and scratched in the garden like veritable brown leghorns. In six years they were all gone, not a bird left east of the Cimarron River.

People said the chicken had gone west, migrated through dislike of civilization, of the plow and the reaper. As a matter of fact they were all dead.

It was difficult for the settler to understand that. Of the million chickens which were there when he came, shooting winter and summer, spring and fall, he had killed no more than a thousand a year. He failed to consider that his nearest neighbor, most distant neighbor as well, had also killed a thousand, and that just so the thousands made a million.

The birds were trapped in the barnyard, tolled under the traps by domestic chickens. In the spring the farmer carried his gun at his work in the fields in order that no frying-size chicken might be lost. In summer his wheat shocks needed protection and got it. In the fall he hunted for sport, in the winter for the market. I have heard more than a few Oklahoma "sooners" tell of knocking the birds over with a plow wrench when they became too tame and there was no gun at hand. And so inevitably the prairie chickens were literally exterminated.

Such is the history of the great prairie grouse in every new land all the way from the Alleghenies to the Rocky Mountains.

They were killed in season and out because they represented food easily procured. The big chicken was helpless; child of the open prairies, he had nowhere to hide his head. Though strong of wing and bold of flight, he could not leave the country to find another beyond danger, as do the waterfowl. Like every other non-migrant, where he was born and raised, there he lived and died.

Had our bob-white quail weighed a pound instead of a short eight ounces, had he, too, been strictly a bird of the open, he surely would have "gone west" with the chicken. One salvation of the quail was that it often cost more to kill him than he was worth, whereas just about as often, a two-cent cartridge fired at a chicken meant a meal for the family.

When all is said, the passing of the prairie chicken is not to be laid to the market shooter or the sportsman, but to the farmer, the man who lived in a cabin and broke the sod.

For another thing, I believe it a fair statement to assert that four-fifths of the prairie chickens killed in this country, from the time the first bird was shot on the moors of Massachusetts until today, have been slaughtered when no more than two-thirds grown. For thirty years, wherever there have been chickens early shooting by "sooners" on the farms has gone on in spite of more and more game laws. When the young chickens reached a weight of a pound or more, able to fly a hundred yards, getting up at the shooter's feet, winging slow and straight, a dainty on the table, they have been killed. And every "sooner," man and boy, considered himself a great chicken shot, though he could hit no other game bird whatever. No, the farmer has never been a friend of the chicken, even though today he is of the quail.

In the year 1929, after many complaints had reached the Game Department of Oklahoma concerning the alleged depredations of the prairie chicken in a few counties, a three-days open season was declared on the birds. Chickens were to be shot only by residents of the state, under the usual resident license fee of one dollar and twenty-five cents. The day before the opening, it seemed as if all the small-game hunters of the state were ready to make war on the few remaining chickens. The shooters came from every section, and it was estimated that thirty thousand passed through the little city of Enid on the way to the chicken grounds on that day. A garage man of Fairview counted two thousand cars passing his station in two hours. All the careful protection of the Oklahoma game authorities, over a period of twenty years, was undone in those three days. Most of the hunters camped in the fields, ready to start work at peep-o'-day. Some of them got a chicken and some did not, there being three hunters to every grouse. Some of the farmers charged five dollars a day for permission to cross their places, but most of them went down into storm cellars to keep from being shot.

That was all primarily the work of the automobile, which is chiefly what modern game conservation has to contend with.

Today, there are more grouse in Canada, odds over, than in the United States. Some Americans say that Alberta can now make the same showing of chickens that Iowa did forty years ago. This is decidedly optimistic, and not borne out by the Canadian game authorities. Furthermore, to many of us the prairie of western Canada is a far cry, and it costs fifty dollars for a license when we get there. However, to those who can afford it, the trip is well worth while, not only for the experience of hunting prairie chickens where there actually are more chickens than hunters, but also for the unexcelled waterfowl shooting.

In the United States, up to the beginning of the World War the Dakotas were the last stronghold of the prairie grouse. There were chickens or sharp-tailed grouse, one or the other, pretty much all over both North and South Dakota. Wheat prices were high during the war, and the sod largely disappeared, together with the chicken. In the dual interest of sport and conservation, the introduced Old World pheasant, an inferior game bird, has now in a great measure displaced the chicken. Not that the native grouse cannot be bred like the pheasant, in captivity; fully as much because the pheasant is a runner and better adapted to withstand continual persecution. Some grouse remain in the rougher country west of the Missouri River. That river used to be the dividing line between the prairie chicken country and that of the sharp-tailed grouse, but now the two birds are found in the same territory—all rough country where cultivation is difficult.

In the "sandhills" of Nebraska the chicken should linger longer than elsewhere in the prairie states, for the simple reason that for years to come there should be more birds than the sparse population can eat. The Nebraska hills, under the Kincaid Law, have a settler to every square mile, theoretically. In reality many of the homestead claims have been abandoned, and houses may be several miles apart. If the farmers' lot is harder anywhere than in these hills, I don't know of it.

The elevation of this hill country is from 2000 to 4000 feet, with air sharp and bracing. The rivers, like the Loup, Niobrara, and Elkhorn, are clear, cold and swift. Over all this section are beautiful lakes, from mere ponds to lakes a mile wide and three times as long, where black bass are caught and the wildfowl remain until ice and snow drive them southward. Grouse grow fat on the sand-cherries, rosebuds and grasshoppers, while men become lean, starve out—which is as it should be, so far as I am concerned.

In the days of market hunting, Kansas was noted for its chickens. Incidentally, Kansas chicken shooters hitched a wire between two wagons, and with these driving across the prairie 300 yards apart, the gunners walked back of the wire, taking the grouse as they arose until the wagon was filled.

To the oldtimer no other bird can quite take the place of the prairie chicken. Perhaps the first bird he ever killed on the wing was a chicken. Perhaps the last bird he ever killed on the wing was a chicken, too; and then the birds were found far apart. Country doctor, county-seat lawyer, well-to-do farmer, or retired market shooter, bearing in mind the days of his youth, August first found him migrating west after the chickens. On the prairies of Iowa, Minnesota or beyond, he found them. All the year he had lived frugally and saved carefully for that. Once again the big grouse climbed from the yellow grass, cackling, defiant; and brave old days were lived over again. And so till the gun was laid aside for the last time, when there were no more chickens and instead a long-tailed alien bird scampered before the dog.

There were supposed to be three varieties of the pinnated grouse. The Eastern variety (*Tympanuchus cupido*) was generally known as the heath hen. Some years ago the last survivors were perpetually protected on Martha's Vineyard. They too may all be gone by now. The habitat of the common variety extended from Indiana across Illinois, throughout Wisconsin, thence west across lower Minnesota and the plains. The third variety was found in the Panhandle of Texas, in western Oklahoma, and in western Kansas. All of these birds were and where still found are much alike, the Texas variety apparently slightly smaller and perhaps more rapid in flight.

The sharp-tailed grouse, universally called "grouse" in the West, is a different bird from the true chicken. He is lighter in color, with a sharper tail, and more like the quail in his habits. He packs less, if at all, and takes less kindly to settlements. The pinnated grouse, or true prairie chicken, is very fond of cultivated fields, of wheat, kaffir, and corn, but the sharptail clings to his native hills, living today as he did when he and the buffalo had a common range in the Northwest. The sharptail lies better to a dog than the chicken, doesn't rise so wild in cold weather, and his flights are not so long. An old "grouse" is a better table bird than an old chicken, being more like a quail about this. His wingbeats are slightly more rapid than those of a chicken, and his flight steadier, though he towers higher. He is a splendid game bird, from his topknot to his feathered toes.

The chicken, or today's remaining Dakota pinnated grouse, packs in the fall, about the first of October, and thereafter tends to migrate to the southeastward. Probably this tendency to migrate is not a natural habit but one acquired. In the life of the chicken of the upper Mississippi Valley, as settlements encroached his breeding grounds would lie to the northwest, but in winter the best foraging grounds would be found to the southeast, in the great fields of standing corn, and that was where he went. In the same way the chickens of Kansas moved south and east into the Indian Territory, and Missouri, where they could find acorns and more or less protection from winter storms.*

Having spent many years among the chickens, I may be prejudiced. However, that I have given the pinnated grouse first place and the place of honor in this book is solely for what he was. I am confident of making no error in saying that in America one hundred years ago there were more prairie chickens than all other grouse combined. It was a prairie grouse empire, all the way from the Atlantic Coast to beyond the Rockies, from the Gulf of Mexico almost to the Arctic Circle.

In Indian Territory days of beloved memory, I have more than once sat with my back to boulder and watched a flock of fifty chickens for hours. They would be collected, cocks and hens, on a bare spot of ground on the bald prairie. Perfectly aware of my presence, yet, since I made no effort to molest them and kept still, they treated me with supreme indifference. The hens crept about coyly, pretending to scratch for food, while the cocks crowed with upstretched necks, precisely like a rooster of the barnyard, or, again, strutted like miniature turkey gobblers. Now and then all of them set up a cackle, while from far and near

---

* Sharptails do not migrate to the same extent. Nor have the sharptails of Manitoba "retreated" eastward into the vast newly opened scrub and muskeg country toward James Bay, as is erroneously reported by sportsmen. They always have been there. The northern or dark variety is found from the eastern shores of James Bay to central Alaska and south to Lake Winnipeg, but not in the United States.

came the booming of bachelor cocks, which may have been shut out from this community gathering.

While watching a flock of chickens, in the early morning of a mellow spring day, I saw two cocks fight an unforgettable battle. The weaker bird didn't know enough to quit, and the stronger never meant to. At last I went to the conquering bird and "shooed" him off. At that he wouldn't fly, but ran a short distance and stood waiting for me to depart, that he might finish his job. I picked up the vanquished bird, too far gone to attempt to escape, and carried him fifty yards out into the tall grass. Shortly he showed signs of recovering, and as soon as able to walk went directly back to the mound and renewed the fight. When again too far spent to escape, I caught him a second time, carrying him nearly to the house where I lived, a mile distant. By and by he got on his feet, staggering off in the direction of the fighting ground, and while I never saw him again, I have always been sure that he went directly back and was killed.

The cock prairie chicken is a wonderfully plucky chap, and he who has once seen them fight will no longer marvel that they sometimes carry off a heavy load of shot.

That there are still some chickens left to shoot is as much due to climatic conditions as to other reasons. In the semiarid regions of the Rocky Mountain tablelands, where it rains only at unexpected times, where wheat will not grow, nor corn, where people exist rather than live, the prairie chickens find sanctuary. Where the winds blow and the sands drift, and the ridges of hills rise broken-toothed above the deep valleys, the brown grouse boom away over the grassland, coveys in summer, great packs in winter.

Draw a straight line from the northeast corner of the Panhandle of Texas to the Bad Lands of South Dakota, and it passes through the best chicken grounds that remain today, south of Canada.

Just how far the flight of a chicken might extend I do not know. When duck shooting on Trappers Lake in western Minnesota, I have seen packs of chickens cross the lake like waterfowl, a hundred feet in the air, their approach noted for a mile before they reached me, in sight for two miles after they had gone by. Doubtless these birds were on migration, bent for the corn fields of Iowa, a hundred miles distant. Perhaps no other grouse makes such extended flights, except the willow ptarmigan of the Barren Grounds.

Not all the pleasure of chicken shooting is due to the birds killed. The prairie wilderness is no less attractive than the wilderness of the woods. In association with the pinnated grouse, not to be severed, are the wide, open prairies, with wind-swept grass rolling like the sea. Roads were rarely followed in the old days; the team was headed across an unmarked prairie, hill and valley.

Blue in the distance, a cottonwood grove marks the borders of a lake. Hay flats may have been mowed, but the wild grass, undefeated, will not down, and again has reached the height of a foot. On the hillsides the sedge and redtop bend as the wagon passes over, then rise again until none but an Indian could mark the passage. It is early October, yet on the tablelands there is an icy tonic in the rarefied morning air. On the hilltops the frost opens sparkling eyes for one peep at the day, then is gone. Deep in the valleys, shaded by the ridge hills now rosebud-tinted in red, it still glares in white defiance.

The red setter and the white pointer swing and sweep across the hills and disappear into the valley. Away off the flat, near a stack of hay, the setter stops uncertain, while two dog-like animals trot up to him. The wild dogs and the tame one spar about for a minute, but nothing comes of it, and the setter gallops off about his business of finding chickens. The coyotes, catching sight of the hunting rig, prance away with stiff-legged jumps, then strike an easy lope for the purple hills in the distance.

In the swale, where the grass is thick but not tall, where the lingering frost is turning to dew, the dogs stop. The team of broncs is sent forward at a gallop; but when a hundred yards back the more nervous gunner insists that the team stop and the shooters go ahead on foot. Our old chicken hunter is anxious about this first shot of the season, meaning to take no unnecessary risk of the birds rising wild. A hard man on even bachelor chickens.

Carefully, from right and left, they stalk the standing dogs. No chickens break cover. In front of the red dog are round, well-padded spots, a dozen of them, where the grouse have roosted. Toward the adjacent ridge are trails plainly written in the dewy grass, twisting, criss-crossing, wandering apparently anywhere, yet always drifting towards the sun-crowned hill.

"That is where they roosted," says the oldtimer. "They have gone to the ridge now, where the sun has started the hoppers to moving."

Carefully and stiffly, with keen, cautious noses, and the wisdom of much experience, the dogs follow the trail up the hill, around the brow of the ridge and into a deep depression. The two men might have pressed on faster had they wished, for everywhere the wet grass betrayed the meandering footsteps of the fowl.

In the valley they have just left, skirting the foot of the ridge, bent on seeing as much of the sport as he can, the driver of the wagon has kept even progress with the hunters. Suddenly he gives a loud whoop.

Dashing back to the brow of the ridge, the hunters can see what has happened. The wise birds, having seen the hunters coming in pursuit, have doubled back, returning to the swale, where the wagon has driven into the very midst of them. Climbing, cackling, towering, curving, whipping the grass with powerful wings, the chickens are rising on every side, while the driver points his whip at first one bird and then another, until fifty great grouse are up and gone.

From their vantage on the hilltop, the hunters have anyhow marked the pack accurately. Soon they will be among the scattered grouse. Here we shall leave them, assured that veteran shots will give a good account of themselves.

In northern Nebraska, in the "hay country" where in the year 1900 very little land had even been touched by the plow, we were located for two weeks on Lake Creek, a tributary of the Elkhorn River. Lake Creek swept in a wide horseshoe bend about the ranchhouse where we stayed. The valley, inside the half circle, was as level as a floor, three miles across, hedged in by towering sand-hills, bases clothed in bunch grass, the wind cutting steadily at their bare tops. It was all unfenced prairie, just as the Pawnee Indians and the buffalo had left it years before. The chickens would be there, we knew, with perhaps mallards along the creek and snipe in the overflows. We hunted on horseback, mounted on steady old cow-ponies.

There comes a time in the fall when the bevies of chickens break up, the old hen and her brood separating, every bird for itself. Later they collect in packs, then becoming wild. We had happened on such a time; the fowl like a great pack that had been scattered. It was October, nights frosty, but the sun beating down on the yellow grass with mellow force. We felt lazy and content, the horses were lazy, the chickens were lazy. Not even the mallards under the creek bank had a worry in the world.

I had never before seen chickens in such numbers. After the first few hours we did not shoot many birds—nothing could be done with them. We did not feel like eating fried chicken day after day, for dinner, breakfast and supper. Our three neighbors accepted but few, through courtesy, chicken having palled on them long since. Game has to be scarce in order to be appreciated, but we understood then how a market shooting gang a few years before might have killed five hundred chickens in a day. For honest wing-shooting we went to a snipe slash, a little distance from the house; again breaking the monotony by chasing coyotes with a pair of wolfhounds. I did try out a gun which my shooting chum owned, a little 28 gauge single-barrel, with which I killed twenty-eight chickens straight in two days' shooting. I subsequently bought a 28 double, and used it for four years with much satisfaction on chickens and quail.

And so to conclude, a further word about chicken guns, since I have promised to write of guns. In the old days any kind of gun would kill chickens, and did. Today chicken seasons are set much later, the birds are strong and wary. Shots must be taken to the utmost limits of shotgun range. The best chicken gun is simply a duck gun which will drop the birds at a good sixty yards.

Any grouse that gets up within fifty yards is to be taken. There is no need for special instruction in gun handling. It is all very much like jumping ducks, the fowl climbing, the shot sent high, the lead on a passing bird about the same as that on a mallard. With luck, in the standing corn and kaffir, a few birds may be killed. The best chance is to catch the big grouse as they come into the corn field; or post a gun or two where it is known the chickens will go out, and then have another gun and the dogs drive the field.

De Shootin'est Gent'man

Nash Buckingham

Supper was a delicious memory. In the matter of a certain goose stew, Aunt Molly had fairly outdone herself. And we, in turn, had jolly well done her out of practically all the goose. It may not come amiss to explain frankly and aboveboard the entire transaction with reference to said goose. Its breast had been deftly detached, lightly grilled and sliced into ordinary "mouth-size" portions. The remainder of the dismembered bird, back, limbs and all parts of the first part thereunto pertaining were put into an iron pot. Keeping company with the martyred fowl, in due proportion of culinary wizardry, were sundry bell peppers, two cans of mock turtle soup, diced roast pork, scrambled ham rinds, peas, potatoes, some corn and dried garden okra, shredded onions and pretty much anything and everything that wasn't tied down or that Molly had lying loose around her kitchen. This stew, served right royally, and attended by outriders of "cracklin' bread," was flanked by a man-at-arms in the form of a saucily flavored brown gravy. I recall a dish of broiled teal and some country puddin' with ginger pour-over, but merely mention these in passing.

So the Judge and I, in rare good humor (I forgot to add that there had been a dusty bottle of the Judge's famous port), as becomes sportsmen blessed with a perfect day's imperfect duck shooting, had discussed each individual bird brought to bag, with reasons, pro and con, why an undeniably large quota had escaped uninjured. We bordered upon that indecisive moment when bedtime should be imminent, were it not for the delightful trouble of getting started in that direction. As I recollect it, ruminating upon our sumptuous repast, the Judge had just countered upon my remark that I had never gotten enough hot turkey hash and beaten biscuits, by stating decisively that his craving for smothered quail remained inviolate, when the door opened softly and in slid "Ho'ace"! He had come, following a custom of many years, to tale final breakfast instructions before packing the embers in "Steamboat Bill," the stove, and dousing our glim.

Seeing upon the center table, t'wixt the Judge and me, a bottle and the unmistakable ingredients and tools of the former's ironclad rule for a hunter's nightcap, Ho'ace paused in embarrassed hesitation and seated himself quickly upon an empty shell case. His attitude was a cross between that of a timid gazelle's scenting danger and a wary hunter's sighting game and effacing himself gently from the landscape.

Long experience in the imperative issue of securing an invitation to "get his'n" had taught Ho'ace that it were ever best to appear humbly disinterested and thoroughly foreign to the subject until negotiations, if need be even much later, were opened with him directly or indirectly. With old-time members he steered along the above lines. But with newer ones or their uninitiated guests, he believed in quicker campaigning, or, conditions warranting, higher pressure sales methods. The Judge, reaching for the sugar bowl, mixed his sweetening water with adroit twirl and careful scrutiny as to texture; fastening upon Ho'ace meanwhile a melting look of liquid mercy. In a twinkling, however, his humor changed and the darky found himself in the glare of a forbidding menace, creditable in his palmiest days to the late Mister Chief Justice Jeffries himself.

"Ho'ace," demanded the Judge, tilting into his now ready receptacle a gurgling, man-size libation, "who is the best shot—the best duck-shot—you have ever paddled on this lake—barring—of course—a-h-e-m-m—myself?" Surveying himself with the coyness of a juvenile, the Judge stirred his now beading toddy dreamily and awaited the encore. Ho'ace squirmed a bit as the closing words of the Judge's query struck home with appalling menace upon his ears. He plucked nervously at his battered headpiece. His eyes, exhibiting a vast expanse of white, roamed pictured walls and smoke-dimmed ceiling in furtive, reflective, helpless quandary. Then speaking slowly and gradually warming to his subject, he fashioned the following alibi.

"Jedge, y' know, suh, us all has ouh good an' ouh bad days wid de ducks. Yes, my Lawdy, us sho' do. Dey's times whin de ducks flies all ovah ev'ything an' ev'ybody, an' still us kain't none o' us hit nuthin'—lak me an' you wuz dis mawnin'." At this juncture the Judge interrupted, reminding Ho'ace that he meant when the Judge—and not the Judge and Ho'ace—was shooting.

"An' den deys times whin h'it look lak dey ain't no shot too hard nur nary a duck too far not t'be kilt. But Mister Buckin'ham yonder—Mister Nash—he brung down de shootin'est gent'man what took all de cake. H'it's lots o' d' members here whut's darin' shooters, but dat fren' o' Mister Nash's—uummppphhh—don't never talk t' me 'bout him whur de ducks kin hear. 'Cause dey'll leave de laik ef dey hears he's even comin' dis way.

"Dat gent'man rode me jes' lak I wuz' er saddle, an' he done had on rooster spurs. Mister Nash he brung him on down here an' say, 'Ho'ace,' he say, 'here's a gent'man frum Englan',' he say, 'Mister Money—Mister Harol' Money—an' say I wants you t' paddle him tomorrow an' see dat he gits er gran' shoot—unnerstan'?' I say, 'Yaas, suh, Mister Nash,' I say, 'dat I'll sho'ly do, suh. Mister Money gwi' hav' er fine picnic ef I has t' see dat he do my sef—but kin he shoot, suh?'

"Mister Nash, he say, 'Uh—why—uh—yaas, Ho'ace, Mister Money he's—uh—ve'y fair shot—'bout lak Mister Immitt Joyner or Mister Hal Howard.' I say t' mysef, I say, 'Uuummmpphhh—huuummmmppphhh—well—he'ah now—ef dats d' case, me an' Mister Money gwi' do some shootin' in d' mawnin.'

"Mister Money he talk so kin'er queer an' brief like, dat I hadda pay clos't inspection t' whut he all de time asayin'. But nex' mawnin', whin me an' him goes out in de bote, I seen he had a gre't big ol' happy bottle o' Brooklyn Handicap in dat shell box so I say t' m'sef, I say, 'W-e-l-l-l—me an' Mister Money gwi' got erlong someway, us is.'

"I paddles him on up de laik an' he say t' me, say, 'Hawrice—uh—hav yo'—er—got anny wager,' he say, 'or proposition t' mek t' me, as regards," he say, 't' shootin' dem dar eloosive wil'fowls?' he say.

"I kinder studies a minit, 'cause, lak I done say, he talk so brief. Den I says, 'I guess you is right 'bout dat, suh.'

"He say, 'Does you follow me, Hawrice, or is I alone?' he say.

"I says, 'Naw, suh, Mister, I'm right wid you in dis bote.'

"'You has no proposition t' mek wid me den?' he say.

"S' I, 'Naw, suh, Boss, I leaves all dat wid you, suh, trustin' t' yo' gin'rosity, suh.'

"'Ve'y good, Hawrice,' he say, 'I sees you doan grasp de principul. Now I will mek you de proposition,' he say. I jes' kep' on paddlin'. He say, 'Ev'y time I miss er duck you gits er dram frum dis hu'ah bottle—ev'y time I kills er duck—I gits de drink—which is h'it—come—come—speak up, my man.'

"I didn' b'lieve I done heard Mister Money rightly, an' I say, 'Uh—Mister Money,' I say, 'suh, does you mean dat I kin d' chice whedder you misses or kills ev'y time an' gits er drink?'

"He say, 'Dat's my defi',' he say.

"I says, 'Well, den—w-e-l-l—den—ef dat's de case, I gwi' choose ev'y time yo' misses, suh.' Den I say t'm'sef, I say, 'Ho'ace, right hu'ah whar you gotta be keerful, 'ginst you fall outa d' bote an' git fired frum d' lodge; 'cause ef'n you gits er drink ev'y time dis gent'man misses an' he shoot lak Mister Hal Howard, you an' him sho' gwi' drink er worl' o' liquah—er worl' o' liquah.'

"I pushes on up nurly to de Han'werker stan', an' I peeks in back by da li'l pocket whut shallers off'n de laik, an' sees some sev'ul blackjacks—four on 'em—settin' in dar. Dey done seen us, too. An' up come dey haids. I spy 'em twis'in', an' turnin'—gittin' raidy t' pull dey freight frum dar. I says, 'Mister Money,' I says, 'yawnder sets some ducks—look out now, suh, 'cause dey gwi' try t' rush on out pas' us whin dey come outa dat pocket.' Den I think, 'W-e-l-l-l, hu'ah whar I knocks d' gol' fillin' outa d' mouf' o' Mister Money's bottle o' Brooklyn Handicap!'

"I raised de lid o' d' shell box an' dar laid dat ol' bottle—still dar. I say, 'Uuummmppphhh—hummmph.' Jus''bout dat time up goes dem black-haids an' outa dar dey come—dey did—flyin' low t' d' watah—an' sorta raisin' lak—y' knows how dey does h'it, Jedge?'

"Mister Money he jus' pick up dat fas' feedin' gun—t'war er pump—not one o' dese hu'ah new afromatics—an' whin he did, I done reach f' d' bottle, 'cause I jes' natcherly know'd dat my time had done come. Mister Money he swings down on dem bullies. Ker-py—ker-py-powie-powie—splamp-splamp-splamp—ker-splash—Lawdy mussy—gent'mans—fo' times, right in d' same place, h'it sounded lak—an' d' las' duck fell ker-flop almos' in ouh bote.

"I done let go d' bottle, an' Mister Money say—mighty cool lak—say, 'Hawrice, say, kin'ly to examine dat las' chap clos'ly,' he say, 'an' obsurve,' he say, 'ef'n he ain' shot thru de eye.'

"I rakes in dat blackjack, an' sho' nuff—bofe eyes done shot plum out—yaas, suh, bofe on 'em right on out. Mister Money say, 'I wuz—er—slightly afraid,' he say, 'dat I had unknowin'ly struck dat fella er trifle too far t' win'ward,' he say. 'A ve'y fair start, Hawrice,' he say. 'You'd bettah place me in my station, so we may continue on wid'out interruption,' he say.

"'Yaas, suh,' I say. 'I'm on my way right dar now, suh,' an I say t' m'sef, I say, 'Mek haste, Man, an' put dis gent'man in his bline an' giv' him er proper chanc't to miss er duck. I didn' hones'ly b'lieve but whut killin' all four o' dem other ducks so peart lak wuz er sorter accident. So I put him on de Han' werker bline. He seen I kep' de main shell bucket an' d' liquah, but he never said nuthin'. I put out d' m 'coys an' den creep back wid d' bote into d' willows t' watch.

"Pretty soon, hu'ah come er big ole drake flyin' mighty high. Ouh ole hen bird she holler t' him, an' d' drake he sorter twis' his haid an' look down. 'Warn't figurin' nuthin' but whut Mister Money gwi' let dat drake circle an' come 'mongst d' m 'coys—but—aw—aw! All uv er sudden he jus' raise up sharp lak an'—kerzowie! Dat ole drake jus' throw his haid on his back an' ride on down—looked t' me lak he fell er mile—an' whin he hit he thow'd watah fo' feet. Mister Money he nuvver said er word—jus' sot dar!

"Hu'ah come another drake—way off t' d' lef'—up over back o' me. He turn eroun'—quick lak—he did an'—kerzowie—he cut him on down, too. Dat drake fall way back in d' willows an' cose I hadda wade after 'im.

"Whilst I wuz gone, Mister Money shoot twice. An' whin I come stumblin' back, dar laid two mo' ducks wid dey feets in de air. Befo' I hav' time t' git in de bote again he done knock down er hen away off in d' elbow brush.

"I say, 'Mister Money, suh, I hav' behin' some far-knockin' guns in my time an' I'se er willin' worker, shoe—but ef you doan, please suh, kill dem ducks closer lak, you gwi' kill yo' willin' supporter Ho'ace in de mud.' He say, 'Da's all right 'bout dat,' he say. 'Go git d' bird—he kain't git er-way 'cause h'its dead ez er wedge.'

"Whin I crawls back t' d' bote dat las' time—it done got mighty col'. Dar us set—me in one en' ashiverin' an' dat ole big bottle wid de gol' haid in de far en'. Might jus' ez well bin ten miles so far ez my chances had done gone.

"Five mo' ducks come in—three singles an' er pair o' sprigs. An' Mister Money he chewed 'em all up lak good eatin'. One time, tho' he had t' shoot one o' them high-flyin' sprigs twice, an' I done got halfway in de bote reachin' fer dat bottle—but de las' shot got 'im. Aftah while, Mister Money say—'Hawrice,' he say, 'how is you hittin' off—my man?'

"'Mister Money,' I say, 'I'se pow'ful col', suh, an' ef you wants er 'umble, no 'count paddler t' tell you d' truth, suh, I b'lieves I done made er pow'ful po' bet.' He say 'Poss'bly so, Hawrice, poss'bly so.' But dat 'poss'bly' didn' git me nuthin'.

"Jedge, y' Honor, you know dat gent'man sot dar an' kill ev'ry duck come in, an' had his limit long befo' de eight-o'clock train runned. I done gone t' watchin' an' de las' duck whut come by wuz one o' dem lightnin'-express teals. Hu'ah he come—er greenwing drake—look lak' somebody done blowed er buckshot pas' us. I riz' up an' hollered, 'Fly fas', ole teal, do yo' bes'—caus' Ho'ace needs er drink.' But Mister Money jus' jumped up an' thow'd him forty feet—skippin' 'long d' watah. I say, 'Hol' on, Mister Money, hol' on—you done kilt d' limit.'

"'Oh,' he say, 'I hav'—hav' I?'

"I say, 'Yaas, suh, an' you ain't bin long 'bout h'it—neither.'

"He say, 'What are you doin' gittin' so col' then?'

"I say, 'I spec' findin' out dat I hav' done made er bad bet had er lot t' do wid d' air.'

"An' dar laid dat Brooklyn Handicap all dat time—he nuvver touched none—an' me neither. I paddles him on back to de house, an' he comes er stalkin' on in hu'ah, he did—lookin' kinda mad lak—never said nuthin' 'bout no drink. Finally he say,

'Hawrice,' he say, 'git me a bucket o' col' watah.' I say t' m'sef, I say, 'W-e-l-l-l, das mo' lak h'it—ef he wants er bucket o' watah. Boy—you gwi' see some real drinkin' now.'

"Whin I come in wid d' pail, Mister Money took offin all his clothes an' step out onto d' side po'ch an' say, 'Th'ow dat watah ovah me, Hawrice. I am lit'rully compel,' he say, 't' have my col' tub ev'y mawnin'.' M-a-n-n-n-n! I sho' tow'd dat ice col' watah onto him wid all my heart an' soul. But he jus' gasp an' hollah, an' jump up an' down an' slap hisse'f. Den he had me rub him red wid er big rough towel. I sho' rubbed him, too. Come on in d' clubroom hu'ah, he did, an' mek hisse'f comfort'ble in dat big ol' rockin' chair yonder—an' went t' readin'. I brought in his shell bucket an' begin cleanin' his gun. But I seen him kinder smilin' t' hisse'f. Atta while, he says 'Hawrice,' he say, 'you hav' done los' yo' bet?'

"I kinder hang my haid lak, an''low, 'Yaas, suh, Mister Money, I don' said farewell t' d' liquah!'

"He say, 'Yo' admits den dat you hav' done los' fair an' square—an' dat yo' realizes h'it?'

"'Yaas, suh!'

"He say, 'Yo' judgmint,' he say, 'wuz ve'y fair, considerin',' he say, 'de great law uv' av'ridge—but circumstance,' he say, 'has done render de ult'mate outcome subjec' t' d' mighty whims o' chance?'

"I say, 'Yaas, suh,' ve'y mournful lak.

"He say, 'In so far as realizin' on anything 'ceptin' de mercy o' d' Cote—say—you is absolutely non-est—eh, my man?'

"I say, 'Yaas, suh, barrin' yo' mercy, suh.'

"Den he think er moment, an' say, 'Verrree—verree—good!'

"Den he 'low,' Sence you acknowledges d' cawn, an' admits dat you hav' done got grabbed,' he say, 'step up,' he say, 'an' git you a tumbler—po' yo'sef er drink—po' er big one, too.'

"I never stopped f' nuthin' den—jes' runned an' got me a glass outa de kitchen. Ole Molly, she say, 'Whur you goin' so fas'?' I say, 'Doan stop me now ole 'ooman—I got business—p'ticler business—an' I sho' poh'd me er big bait o' liquah—er whole sloo' o' liquah. Mister Money say, 'Hawrice—de size o' yo' po'tion,' he say, 'is primus facious ev'dence,' he say, 'dat you gwi' spout er toast in honor,' he say, 'o' d' occasion.'

"I say, 'Mister Money, suh,' I say, 'all I got t' say, suh, is dat you is de kingpin, champeen duck shotter so far as I hav' done bin' in dis life—an' ve'y prob'ly as far as I'se likely t' keep on goin', too.' He sorter smile t' hisse'f!

"'Now, suh, please, suh, tell me dis—is you ever missed er duck—anywhar'—anytime—anyhow—suh?'

"He say 'Really, Hawrice,' he say, 'you embarrasses me,' he say, 'so hav' another snifter—there is mo', considerably mo',' he say, 'in yo' system what demands utt'rance,' he say.

"I done poh'd me another slug o' Brooklyn Handicap an' say, 'Mister Money,' I say, 'does you expec' t' ever miss another duck ez long ez you lives, suh?'

"He say, 'Hawrice,' he say, 'you embarrasses me,' he say, 'beyon' words—you overwhelms me,' he say. 'Git t' hell outa hu'ah befo' you gits us bofe drunk.'"

The First Gun

From **The Amateur Poacher,** *1879*

Richard Jefferies

THEY BURNED THE OLD GUN THAT USED TO STAND IN THE DARK corner up in the garret, close to the stuffed fox that always grinned so fiercely. Perhaps the reason why he seemed in such a ghastly rage was that he did not come by his death fairly. Otherwise his pelt would not have been so perfect. And why else was he put away up there out of sight?—and so magnificent a brush as he had too. But there he stood, and mounted guard over the old flintlock that was so powerful a magnet to us in those days. Though to go up there alone was no slight trial of moral courage after listening to the horrible tales of the carters in the stable or the old women who used to sit under the hedge in the shade, on an armful of hay, munching their crusts at luncheon time.

The great cavernous place was full of shadows in the brightest summer day; for the light came only through the chinks in the shutters. These were flush with the floor and bolted firmly. The silence was intense, it being so near the roof and so far away from the inhabited parts of the house. Yet there were sometimes strange acoustical effects—as when there came a low tapping at the shutters, enough to make your heart stand still. There was then nothing for it but to dash through the doorway into the empty cheese-room adjoining, which was better lighted. No doubt it was nothing but the labourers knocking the stakes in for the railing round the rickyard, but why did it sound just exactly outside the shutters? When that ceased the staircase creaked, or the pear-tree boughs rustled against the window. The staircase always waited till you had forgotten all about it before the loose worm-eaten planks sprang back to their place.

Had it not been for the merry whistling of the starlings on the thatch above, it would not have been possible to face the gloom and the teeth of Reynard, ever in the act to snap, and the mystic noises, and the sense of guilt—for the gun was forbidden. Besides which there was the black mouth of the open trapdoor overhead yawning fearfully—a standing terror and temptation; for there was a legend of a pair of pistols thrown up there out of the way—a treasure-trove tempting enough to make us face anything. But Orion must have the credit of the courage; I call him Orion because he was a hunter and had a famous dog. The last I heard of him he had just ridden through a prairie fire, and says the people out there think nothing of it.

We dragged an ancient linen-press under the trapdoor, and put some boxes on that, and finally a straight-backed oaken chair. One or two of those chairs were split up and helped to do the roasting on the kitchen hearth. So, climbing the pile, we emerged under the rafters, and could see daylight faintly in several places coming through the starlings' holes. One or two bats fluttered to and fro as we groped among the lumber, but no pistols could be discovered; nothing but a cannon-ball, rusty enough and about as big as an orange, which they say was found in the wood, where there was a brush in Oliver's time.

In the middle of our expedition there came the well-known whistle, echoing about the chimneys with which it was the custom to recall us to dinner. How else could you make people hear who might be cutting a knobbed stick in the copse half a mile away or bathing in the lake? We had to jump down with a run; and then came the difficulty; for black dusty cobwebs, the growth of fifty years, clothed us from head to foot. There was no brushing or picking them off, with that loud whistle repeated every two minutes.

The fact where we had been was patent to all; and so the chairs got burned—but one, which was rickety. After which a story crept out, of a disjointed skeleton lying in a corner under the thatch. Though just a little suspicious that this might be a *ruse* to frighten us from a second attempt, we yet could not deny the possibility of its being true. Sometimes in the dusk, when I sat poring over "Koenigsmark, the Robber," by the little window in the cheese-room, a skull seemed to peer down the trapdoor. But then I had the flintlock by me for protection.

There were giants in the days when that gun was made; for surely no modern mortal could have held that mass of metal steady to his shoulder. The linen-press and a chest on the top of it formed, however, a very good gun-carriage; and, thus mounted, aim could be taken out of the window at the old mare feeding in the meadow below by the brook, and a "bead" could be drawn upon Molly, the dairymaid, kissing the fogger behind the hedge, little dreaming that the deadly tube was levelled at them. At least this practice and drill had one useful effect—the eye got accustomed to the flash from the pan, instead of blinking the discharge, which ruins the shooting. Almost everybody and everything on the place got shot dead in this way without knowing it.

It was not so easy as might be supposed to find proper flints. The best time to look for them was after a heavy storm of rain had washed a shallow channel beside the road, when you might select some handy splinters which had lain hidden under the dust. How we were found out is not quite clear; perhaps the powder left a smell of sulphur for any one who chanced to go up in the garret.

But, however that may be, one day, as we came in unexpectedly from a voyage in the punt, something was discovered burning among the logs on the kitchen hearth; and, though a desperate rescue was attempted, nothing was left but the barrel of our precious gun and some crooked iron representing the remains of the lock. There are things that are never entirely forgiven, though the impression may become fainter as years go by. The sense of the cruel injustice of that act will never quite depart.

But they could not burn the barrel, and we almost succeeded in fitting it to a stock of elder. Elder has a thick pith running down the centre; by removing that the gouge and chisel had not much work to do to make a groove for the old bell-mouthed barrel to lie in. The matchlock, for as such it was intended, was nearly finished when our hopes were dashed to the ground by a piece of unnatural cunning. One morning the breechpiece that screwed in was missing. This was fatal. A barrel without a breechpiece is like a cup without a bottom. It was all over.

There are days in spring when the white clouds go swiftly past, with occasional breaks of bright sunshine lighting up a spot in the landscape. That is like the memory of one's youth. There is a long dull blank, and then a brilliant streak of recollection. Doubtless it was a year or two afterwards when, seeing that the natural instinct could not be suppressed but had better be recognised, they produced a real gun (single-barrel) for me from the clock-case.

It stood on the landing just at the bottom of the dark flight that led to the garret. An oaken case six feet high or more, and a vast dial, with a mysterious picture of a full moon and a ship in full sail that somehow indicated the quarters of the year, if you had been imitating Rip Van Winkle and after a sleep of six months wanted to know whether it was spring or autumn. But only to think that all the while we were puzzling over the moon and the ship and the queer signs on the dial a gun was hidden inside! The case was locked, it is true; but there are ways of opening locks, and we were always handy with tools.

This gun was almost, but not quite so long as the other. That dated from the time between Stuart and Hanover; this might not have been more than seventy years old. And a beautiful piece of workmanship it was; my new double breech-loader is a coarse common thing to compare with it. Long and slender and light as a feather, it came to the shoulder with wonderful ease. Then there was a groove on the barrel at the breech and for some inches up which caught the eye and guided the glance like a trough to the sight at the muzzle and thence to the bird. The stock was shod with brass, and the trigger-guard was of brass, with a kind of flange stretching half-way down to the butt and inserted in the wood. After a few minutes' polishing it shone like gold, and to see the sunlight flash on it was a joy.

You might note the grain of the barrel, for it had not been browned; and it took a good deal of sand to get the rust off. By aid of a little oil and careful wiping after a shower it was easy to keep it bright. Those browned barrels only encourage idleness. The lock was a trifle dull at first, simply from lack of use. A small screwdriver soon laid it to pieces, and it speedily clicked again sweet as a flute. If the hammer came back rather far when at full-cock, that was because the lock had been converted from a flint, and you could not expect it to be absolutely perfect. Besides which, as the fall was longer the blow was heavier, and the cap was sure to explode.

By old farmhouses, mostly in exposed places (for which there is a reason), one or more huge walnut trees may be found. The provident folk of those days planted them with the purpose of having their own gunstocks cut out of the wood when the tree was thrown. They could then be sure it was really walnut, and a choice piece of timber thoroughly well seasoned. I like to think of those times, when men settled themselves down, and planted and planned and laid out their gardens and orchards and woods, as if they and their sons and sons' sons, to the twentieth generation, were sure to enjoy the fruit of their labour.

The reason why the walnuts are put in exposed places, on the slope of a rise, with open aspect to the east and north, is because the walnut is a foolish tree that will not learn by experience. If it feels the warmth of a few genial days in early spring, it immediately protrudes its buds; and the next morning a bitter frost cuts down every hope of fruit for that year, leaving the leaf as black as may be. Wherefore the east wind is desirable to keep it as backward as possible.

There was a story that the stock of this gun had been cut out of a walnut tree that was thrown on the place by my great-grandfather, who saw it well seasoned, being a connoisseur of timber, which is, indeed, a sort of instinct in all his descendants. And a vast store of philosophy there is in timber if you study it aright.

After cleaning the gun and trying it at a mark, the next thing was to get a good shot with it. Now there was an elm that stood out from the hedge a little, almost at the top of the meadow, not above five-and-twenty yards from the other hedge that bounded the field. Two mounds could therefore be commanded by any one in ambush behind the elm, and all the angular corner of the mead was within range.

It was not far from the house; but the ground sank into a depression there, and the ridge of it behind shut out everything except just the roof of the tallest hayrick. As one sat on the sward behind the elm, with the back turned on the rick and nothing in front but the tall elms and the oaks in the other hedge, it was quite easy to fancy it the verge of the prairie with the backwoods close by.

The rabbits had scratched the yellow sand right out into the grass—it is always very much brighter in colour where they have just been at work—and the fern, already almost yellow too, shaded the mouths of their buries. Thick bramble bushes grew out from the mound and filled the space between it and the elm; there were a few late flowers on them still, but the rest were hardening into red sour berries. Westwards, the afternoon sun, with all his autumn heat, shone full against the hedge and into the recess, and there was not the shadow of a leaf for shelter on that side.

The gun was on the turf, and the little hoppers kept jumping out of the grass on to the stock; once their king, a grasshopper, alighted on it and rested, his green limbs tipped with red rising above his back. About the distant wood and the hills there was a soft faint haze, which is what Nature finishes her pictures with. Something in the atmosphere which made it almost visible; all the trees seemed to stand in a liquid light—the sunbeams were suspended in the air instead of passing through. The butterflies even were very idle in the slumberous warmth; and the great green dragon-fly rested on a leaf, his tail arched a little downwards, just as he puts it when he wishes to stop suddenly in his flight.

The broad glittering trigger-guard got quite hot in the sun, and the stock was warm when I felt it every now and then. The grain of the walnut-wood showed plainly through the light polish; it was not varnished like the stock of the double-barrel they kept padlocked to the rack over the high mantelpiece indoors. Still you could see the varnish. It was of a rich dark horse-chestnut colour, and yet so bright and clear that if held close you could see your face in it. Behind it the grain of the wood was just perceptible; especially at the grip, where hard hands had worn it away somewhat. The secret of that varnish is lost—like that of the varnish on the priceless old violins.

But you could feel the wood more in my gun; so that it was difficult to keep the hand off it, though the rabbits would not come out; and the shadowless recess grew like a furnace, for it focused the rays of the sun. The heat on the sunny side of a thick hedge between three and four in the afternoon is almost tropical if you remain still, because the air is motionless; the only relief is to hold your hat loose; or tilt it against your head, the other edge of the brim on the ground. Then the grass-blades rise up level with the forehead. There is a delicious smell in growing grass, and a sweetness comes up from the earth.

Still it got hotter and hotter; and it was not possible to move in the least degree, lest a brown creature sitting on the sand at the mouth of his hole, and hidden himself by the fern, should immediately note it. And Orion was waiting in the rickyard for the sound of the report, and very likely the shepherd too. We knew that men in Africa, watched by lions, had kept still in the sunshine till, reflected from the rock, it literally scorched them, not daring to move; and we knew all about the stoicism of the

Red Indians. But Ulysses was ever my pattern and model; that man of infinite patience and resource.

So, though the sun might burn and the air become suffocating in that close corner, and the quivering line of heat across the meadow make the eyes dizzy to watch, yet not a limb must be moved. The black flies came in crowds; but they are not so tormenting if you plunge your face in the grass, though they titillate the back of the hand as they run over it. Under the bramble bush was a bury that did not look much used; and once or twice a great blue fly came out of it, the buzz at first sounding hollow and afar off and becoming clearer as it approached the mouth of the hole. There was the carcass of a dead rabbit inside no doubt.

A humble-bee wandering along—they are restless things—buzzed right under my hat, and became entangled in the grass by my ear. Now we knew by experience in taking their honey that they could sting sharply if irritated, though good-tempered by nature. How he "burred" and buzzed and droned!—till by-and-by, crawling up the back of my head, he found an open space and sailed away. Then, looking out again, there was a pair of ears in the grass not ten yards distant: a rabbit had come out at last. But the first delight was quickly over: the ears were short and sharply pointed, and almost pinkly transparent.

What would the shepherd say if I brought home one of his hated enemies no bigger than a rat? The young rabbit made waiting still more painful, being far enough from the hedge to get a clear view into the recess if anything attracted his notice. Why the shepherd hated rabbits was because the sheep would not feed where they had worn their runs in the grass. Not the least movement was possible now—not even that little shifting which makes a position just endurable: the heat seemed to increase; the thought of Ulysses could hardly restrain the almost irresistible desire to stir.

When, suddenly, there was a slight rustling among the boughs of an oak in the other hedge, as of wings against twigs: it was a woodpigeon, better game than a rabbit. He would, I knew, first look round before he settled himself to preen his feathers on the branch, and, if everything was still while that keen inspection lasted, would never notice me. This is their habit—and the closer you are underneath them the less chance of their perceiving you: for a pigeon perched rarely looks straight downwards. If flying, it is just the reverse; for then they seem to see under them quicker than in any other direction.

Slowly lifting the long barrel of the gun—it was fortunate the sunlight glancing on the bright barrel was not reflected towards the oak—I got it to bear upon the bird; but then came a doubt. It was all eight-and-twenty yards across the angle of the meadow to the oak—a tremendous long shot under the circumstances. For they would not trust us with the large copper powder-flask, but only with a little pistol-flask (it had belonged to the pair of pistols we tried to find), and we were ordered not to use more than a charge and a half at a time. That was quite enough to kill blackbirds. (The noise of the report was always a check in this way; such a trifle of powder only made a slight puff.)

Shot there was in plenty—a whole tobacco-pipe bowl full, carefully measured out of the old yellow canvas money-bag that did for a shot belt. A starling could be knocked off the chimney with this charge easily, and so could a blackbird roosting in a bush at night. But a woodpigeon nearly thirty yards distant was another matter; for the old folk (and the birdkeepers too) said that their quills were so hard the shot would glance aside unless it came with great force. Very likely the pigeon would escape, and all the rabbits in the buries would be too frightened to come out at all.

A beautiful bird he was on the bough, perched well in view and clearly defined against the sky behind; and my eye travelled along the groove on the breech and up the barrel, and so to the sight and across to him; and the finger, which always would keep time with the eye, pulled at the trigger.

A mere puff of a report, and then a desperate fluttering in the tree and a cloud of white feathers floating above the hedge, and a heavy fall among the bushes. He was down, and Orion's spaniel (that came racing like mad from the rickyard the instant he heard the discharge) had him in a moment. Orion followed quickly. Then the shepherd came up, rather stiff on his legs from rheumatism, and stepped the distance, declaring it was thirty yards good; after which we all walked home in triumph.

Molly the dairymaid came a little way from the rickyard, and said she would pluck the pigeon that very night after work. She was always ready to do anything for us boys; and we could never quite make out why they scolded her so for an idle hussy indoors. It seemed so unjust. Looking back, I recollect she had very beautiful brown eyes.

"You mind you chaws the shot well, measter," said the shepherd, "afore you loads th' gun. The more your chaws it the better it sticks thegither, an' the furder it kills um:" a theory of gunnery that which was devoutly believed in in his time and long anticipated the wire cartridges. And the old soldiers that used to come round to haymaking, glad of a job to supplement their pensions, were very positive that if you bit the bullet and indented it with your teeth, it was perfectly fatal, no matter to what part of the body its billet took it.

In the midst of this talk as we moved on, I carrying the gun at the trail with the muzzle downwards, the old ramrod, long disused and shrunken, slipped half out; the end caught the ground, and it snapped short off in a second. A terrible disaster this, turning everything to bitterness: Orion was especially wroth, for it was his right next to shoot. However, we went down to the smithy at the inn, to take counsel of the blacksmith, a man of knowledge and a trusty friend. "Aha!" said he, "it's not the first time I've made a ramrod. There's a piece of lancewood in the store overhead which I keep on purpose; it's as tough as a bow—they make carriage-shafts of it; you shall have a better rod than was ever fitted to a Joe Manton." So we took him down some pippins, and he set to work on it that evening.

That Twenty-Five-Pound Gobbler

Archibald Rutledge

I SUPPOSE THAT THERE ARE OTHER THINGS WHICH MAKE A hunter uneasy, but of one thing I am very sure: that is to locate and to begin to stalk a deer or a turkey, only to find that another hunter is doing precisely the same thing at the same time. The feeling I had was worse than uneasy. It is, in fact, as inaccurate as if a man should say, after listening to a comrade swearing roundly, "Bill is expressing himself uneasily."

To be frank, I was jealous; and all the more so because I knew that Dade Saunders was just as good a turkey-hunter as I am—and maybe a good deal better. At any rate, both of us got after the same whopping gobbler. We knew this turkey and we knew each other; and I am positive that the wise old bird knew both of us far better than we knew him.

But we hunters have ways of improving our acquaintance with creatures that are over-wild and shy. Both Dade and I saw him, I suppose, a dozen times; and twice Dade shot at him. I had never fired at him, for I did not want to cripple, but to kill; and he never came within a hundred yards of me. Yet I felt that the gobbler ought to be mine; and for the simple reason that Dade Saunders was a shameless poacher and a hunter-out-of-season.

I have in mind the day when I came upon him in the pinelands in mid-July, when he had in his wagon *five* bucks in the velvet, all killed that morning. Now, this isn't a fiction story; this is fact. And after I have told you of those bucks, I think you'll want me to beat Dade to the great American bird.

This wild turkey had the oddest range that you could imagine. You hear of turkeys ranging "original forests," "timbered wilds," and the like. Make up your mind that if wild turkeys have a chance they are going to come near civilization. The closer they are to man, the farther they are away from their other enemies. Near civilization they at least have (but for the likes of Dade Saunders) the protection of the law. But in the wilds what protection do they have from wildcats, from eagles, from weasels (I am thinking of young turkeys as well as old), and from all their other predatory persecutors?

Well, as I say, time and again I have known wild turkeys to come, and to seem to enjoy coming, close to houses. I have stood on the porch of my plantation home and have watched a wild flock feeding under the great live-oaks there. I have repeatedly flushed wild turkeys in an autumn cornfield. I have shot them in rice stubble.

Of course they do not come for sentiment. They are after grain. And if there is any better wild game than a rice-field wild turkey, stuffed with peanuts, circled with browned sweet potatoes, and fragrant with a rich gravy that plantation cooks know how to make, I'll follow you to it.

The gobbler I was after was a haunter of the edges of civilization. He didn't seem to like the wild woods. I think he got hungry there. But on the margins of fields that had been planted he could get all he wanted to eat of the things he most enjoyed. He particularly liked the edges of cultivated fields that bordered either on the pinewoods or else on the marshy rice-lands.

One day I spent three hours in the gaunt chimney of a burned rice-mill, watching this gobbler feeding on such edges. Although I was sure that sooner or later he would pass the mouth of the chimney, giving me a chance for a shot, he kept just that distance between us that makes a gun a vain thing in a man's hands. But though he did not give me my chance, he let me watch him all I pleased. This I did through certain dusty crevices between the bricks of the old chimney.

If I had been taking a post-graduate course in caution, this wise old bird would have been my teacher. Whatever he happened to be doing, his eyes and his ears were wide with vigilance. I saw him first standing beside a fallen pine log on the brow of a little hill where peanuts had been planted. I made the shelter of the chimney before he recognized me. But he must have seen the move I made.

I have hunted turkeys long enough to be thoroughly rid of the idea that a human being can make a motion that a wild turkey cannot see. One of my woodsman friends said to me, "Why, a gobbler can see anything. He can see a jaybird turn a somersault on the verge of the horizon." He was right.

Watching from my cover I saw this gobbler scratching for peanuts. He was very deliberate about this. Often he would draw back one huge handful (or footful) of viney soil, only to leave it there while he looked and listened. I have seen a turkey do the same thing while scratching in leaves. Now, a buck while feeding will alternately keep his head up and down; but a turkey gobbler keeps his down very little. That bright black eye of his, set in that sharp bluish head, is keeping its vision on every object on the landscape.

My gobbler (I called him mine from the first time I saw him) found many peanuts, and he relished them. From that feast he walked over into a patch of autumn-dried crabgrass. The long pendulous heads of this grass, full of seeds, he stripped skillfully. When satisfied with this food, he dusted himself beside an old stump. It was interesting to watch this; and while he was doing it I wondered if it was not my chance to leave the chimney, make a detour, and come up behind the stump. But of course just as I decided to do this, he got up, shook a small cloud of dust from his feathers, stepped off into the open, and there began to preen himself.

A short while thereafter he went down to a marshy edge, there finding a warm sandy hole on the sunny side of a briar patch, where he continued his dusting and loafing. I believe that he knew the stump, which shut off his view of what was behind it, was no place to choose for a midday rest.

All this time I waited patiently; interested, to be sure, but I would have been vastly more so if the lordly old fellow had turned my way. This I expected him to do when he got tired of loafing. Instead, he deliberately walked into the tall ranks of the marsh, which extended riverward for half a mile. At that I hurried forward, hoping to flush him on the margin; but he had vanished for that day. But though he had escaped me, the sight of him had made me keen to follow him until he expressed a willingness to accompany me home.

Just as I was turning away from the marsh I heard a turkey call from the shelter of a big live-oak beside the old chimney. I knew that it was Dade Saunders, and that he was after my gobbler. I walked over to where he was making his box-call plead. He expressed no surprise on seeing me. We greeted each other as two hunters, who are not over-friendly, greet when they find themselves after the same game.

"I seen his tracks," said Dade. "I believe he limps in the one foot since I shot him last Sunday will be a week."

"He must be a big bird," I said; "you were lucky to have a shot."

Dade's eyes grew hungrily bright.

"He's the biggest in these woods, and I'll git him yet. You jest watch me."

"I suppose you will, Dade. You are the best turkey-hunter of these parts."

I hoped to make him overconfident; and praise is a great corrupter of mankind. It is not unlikely to make a hunter miss a shot. I remember that a friend of mine once said laughingly: "If a man tells me I am a good shot, I will miss my next chance, as sure as guns; but if he cusses me and tells me I'm not worth a darn, then watch me shoot!"

Dade and I parted for the time. I went off toward the marsh, whistling an old song. I wanted to have the gobbler put a little more distance between himself and the poacher. Besides, I felt that it was right of me to do this: for while I was on my own land, my visitor was trespassing. I hung around in the scrub-oak thickets for a while; but no gun spoke out, I knew that the old gobbler's intelligence plus my whistling game had "foiled the relentless" Dade. It was a week later that the three of us met again.

Not far from the peanut field there is a plantation corner. Now, most plantation corners are graveyards; that is, cemeteries of the old days, where slaves were buried. Occasionally now Negroes are buried there, but pathways have to be cut through the jungle-like growths to enable the cortege to enter.

Such a place is a wilderness for sure. Here grow towering pines, mournful and moss-draped. Here are hollies, canopied with jasmine-vines; here are thickets of myrtle, sweet gum, and young pines. If a covey of quail goes into such a place, you might as well whistle your dog off and go after another lot of birds.

Here deer love to come in the summer, where they can hide from the heat and the gauze-winged flies. Here in the winter is a haunt for woodcock, a good range (for great live-oaks drop their sweet acorns) for wild turkeys, and a harbor for foxes. In those great pines and oaks turkeys love to roost. It was on the borders of just such a corner that I roosted the splendid gobbler.

It was a glowing December sunset. I had left the house an hour before to stroll the plantation roads, counting (as I always do) the number of deer and turkey tracks that had recently been made in the soft damp sand. Coming near the dense corner, I sat against the bole of a monster pine. I love to be a mere watcher in woodlands as well as a hunter.

About two hundred yards away there was a little sunny hill, grown to scrub-oaks. They stood sparsely; that enabled me to see well what I now saw. Into my vision, with the rays of the sinking sun gleaming softly on the bronze of his neck and shoulders, the great gobbler stepped with superb beauty. Though he deigned to scratch once or twice in the leaves, and peck indifferently at what he thus uncovered, I knew he was bent on roosting; for not only was it nearly his bedtime, but he seemed to be examining with critical judgment every tall tree in his neighborhood.

He remained in my sight ten minutes; then he stepped into a patch of gallberries. I sat where I was. I tried my best to be as silent and as motionless as the bodies lying in the ancient graves behind me. The big fellow kept me on the anxious bench for five minutes. Then he shot his great bulk into the air, beating his ponderous way into the huge pine that seemed to sentry that whole wild tract of woodland.

I marked him when he came to his limb. He sailed up to it and alighted with much scraping of bark with his No. 10 shoes. There was my gobbler poised against the warm red sky of that winter twilight. It was hard to take my sight from him; but I did so in order to get my bearings in relation to his position. His flight had brought him nearer to me than he had been on the ground. But he was still far out of gun-range.

There was no use for me to look into the graveyard, for a man cannot see a foot into such a place. I glanced down the dim pinewood road. A moving object along its edge attracted my attention. It skulked. It seemed to flit like a ghostly thing from pine to pine. But, though I was near a cemetery, I knew I was looking at no "haunt." It was Dade Saunders.

He had roosted the gobbler, and he was trying to get up to him. Moreover, he was at least fifty yards closer to him than I was. I felt like shouting to him to get off my land; but then a better thought came. I pulled out my turkey call.

The first note was good, as was intended. But after that there came some heart-stilling squeaks and shrills. In the dusk I noted two things; I saw Dade make a furious gesture, and at almost the same instant the old gobbler launched out from the pine, winging a lordly way far across the graveyard thicket. I walked down slowly and peeringly to meet Dade.

"Your call's broke," he announced.

"What makes you think so?" I asked.

"Sounds awful funny to me," he said; "more than likely it might scare a turkey. Seen him lately?" he asked.

"You are better at seeing that old bird than I am, Dade."

Thus I put him off; and shortly thereafter we parted. He was sure that I had not seen the gobbler; and that suited me all right.

Then came the day of days. I was up at dawn, and when certain red lights between the stems of the pines announced daybreak, I was at the far southern end of the plantation, on a road on either side of which were good turkey woods. I just had a notion that my gobbler might be found there, as he had of late taken to roosting in a tupelo swamp near the river, and adjacent to these woodlands.

Where some lumbermen had cut away the big timber, sawing the huge short-leaf pines close to the ground, I took my stand (or my seat) on one of these big stumps. Before me was a tangle of undergrowth; but it was not very thick or high. It gave me the screen I wanted; but if my turkey came out through it, I could see to shoot.

It was just before sunrise that I began to call. It was a little early in the year (then the end of February) to lure a solitary gobbler by a call; but otherwise the chance looked good. And I am vain enough to say that my willow box was not broken that morning. Yet it was not I but two Cooper's hawks that got the old wily rascal excited.

They were circling high and crying shrilly over a certain stretch of deep woodland; and the gobbler, undoubtedly irritated by the sounds, or at least not to be outdone by two mere marauders on a domain which he felt to be his own, would gobble fiercely every time one of the hawks would cry. The hawks had their eye on a building site; wherefore their excited maneuvering and shrilling continued; and as long as they kept up their screaming, so long did the wild gobbler answer in rivalry or provoked superiority, until his wattles must have been fiery red and near to bursting.

I had an idea that the hawks were directing some of their crying at the turkey, in which case the performance was a genuine scolding match of the wilderness. And before it was over, several gray squirrels had added to the already raucous debate their impatient coughing barks. This business lasted nearly an hour, until the sun had begun to make the thickets "smoke off" their shining burden of morning dew.

I had let up on my calling for a while; but when the hawks had at last been silenced by the distance, I began once more to plead. Had I had a gobbler-call, the now enraged turkey would have come to me as straight as a surveyor runs a line. But I did my best with the one I had. I had answered by one short gobble, then by silence.

I laid down my call on the stump and took up my gun. It was in such a position that I could shoot quickly without much further motion. It is a genuine feat to shoot a turkey on the ground *after* he has made you out. I felt that a great moment was coming.

But you know how hunter's luck sometimes turns. Just as I thought it was about time for him to be in the pine thicket ahead of me, when, indeed, I thought I had heard his heavy but cautious step, from across the road, where lay the companion tract of turkey-woods to the one I was in, came a delicately pleading call from a hen turkey. The thing was irresistible to the gobbler; but I knew it to be Dade Saunders. What should I do?

At such a time a man has to use all the headwork he has. And in hunting I had long since learned that that often means not to do a darn thing but to sit tight. All I did was to put my gun to my face. If the gobbler was going to Dade, he might pass me. I had started him coming; if Dade kept him going, he might run within hailing distance. Dade was farther back in the woods than I was. I waited.

No step was heard. No twig was snapped. But suddenly, fifty yards ahead of me, the great bird emerged from the thicket of pines. For an instant the sun gleamed on his royal plumage. My gun was on him, but the glint of the sun along the barrel dazzled me. I stayed my finger on the trigger. At that instant he made me out. What he did was smart. He made himself so small that I believed it to be a second turkey. Then he ran crouching through the vines and huckleberry bushes.

Four times I thought I had my gun on him, but his dodging was that of an expert. He was getting away; moreover, he was making straight for Dade. There was a small gap in the bushes sixty yards from me, off to my left. He had not yet crossed that. I threw my gun in the opening. In a moment he flashed into it, running like a racehorse. I let him have it. And I saw him go down.

Five minutes later, when I had hung him on a scrub-oak, and was admiring the entire beauty of him, a knowing, cat-like step sounded behind me.

"Well, sir," said Dade, a generous admiration for the beauty of the great bird overcoming other less kindly emotions, "so you beat me to him."

There was nothing for me to do but to agree. I then asked Dade to walk home with me so that we might weigh him. He carried the scales well down at the 25-pound mark. An extraordinary feature of his manly equipment was the presence of three separate beards, one beneath the other, no two connected. And his spurs were respectable rapiers.

"Dade," I said, "what am I gong to do with this gobbler? I am alone here on the plantation."

The pineland poacher did not solve my problem for me.

"I tell you," said I, trying to forget the matter of the five velveted bucks, "some of the boys from down the river are going to come up on Sunday to see how he tastes. Will you join us?"

You know Dade Saunders' answer; for when a hunter refuses an invitation to help eat a wild turkey, he can be sold to a circus.

Bear Hunting in the Smokies

Horace Kephart

Git up, pup! You've scrounged right in hyur in front of the far [fire]. You Dred! Whut makes you so blamed contentious?"

Little John shoved both dogs into a corner, and strove to scrape some coals from under a beech forestick that glowed almost hot enough to melt brass.

"This is the wust coggled-up far I ever seen, to fry by. Bill, hand me some Old Ned from that suggin' o' mine."

A bearded hunchback reached his long arm to a sack that hung under our rifles, drew out a chunk of salt pork, and began slicing it with his jackknife. On inquiry I learned that "Old Ned" is merely slang for fat pork, but that "suggin" or "sujjit" (the *u* pronounced like *oo* in look) is true mountain dialect for a bag, valise or carryall, its etymology being something to puzzle over.

Four dogs growled at each other under a long bunk of poles and hay that spanned one side of our cabin. The fire glared out upon the middle of an unfloored and windowless room. Deep shadows clung to the walls and benches, charitably concealing much dirt and disorder left by previous occupants, much litter of our own contributing.

We were on a saddle of the divide, a mile above sea level, in a hut built years ago for temporary lodgment of cattlemen herding on the grassy "balds" of the Smokies. A sagging "shake" roof covered its two rooms and the open space between them that we called our "entry." The state line between North Carolina and Tennessee ran through this unenclosed hallway. The Carolina room had a puncheon floor and a clapboard table, also better bunks than its mate; but there had risen a stiff southerly gale that made the chimney smoke so abominably that we were forced to take quarters in the neighbor state.

Granville lifted the lid from a big Dutch oven and reported "Bread's done."

There was a flash in the frying-pan, a curse and a puff from Little John. The coffee-pot boiled over. We gathered about the hewn benches that served for tables, and sat *à la Turc* upon the ground. For some time there was no sound but the gale without and the munching of ravenous men.

"If this wind'll only cease afore mornin', we'll git us a bear tomorrow."

A powerful gust struck the cabin, by way of answer; a great roaring surged up from the gulf of Defeat, from Desolation, and from the other forks of Bone Valley—clamor of ten thousand trees struggling with the blast.

"Hit's gittin' wusser."

"Any danger of this roost being blown off the mountain?" I inquired.

"Hit's stood hyur twenty year through all the storms; I reckon it can stand one more night of it."

"A man couldn't walk upright outside the cabin," I asserted, thinking of the St. Louis tornado, in which I had lain flat on my belly, clinging to an iron post.

The hunchback turned to me with a grave face. "I've seed hit blow, here on top o' Smoky, till a hoss couldn't stand up agin it. You'll spy, tomorrow, that several trees has been wind-throwed and busted to kindlin'."

I recalled that "several," in the South, means many—"a good many," as our own tongues phrase it.

"Oh shucks, Bill Cope," put in "Doc" Jones, "whut do you-uns know about windstorms? Now, *I've* hed some experiencin' up hyur that'll do to tell about. You remember the big storm three year ago, come grass, when the cattle all huddled up atop o' each other and friz in one pile, solid."

Bill grunted an affirmative.

"Wal, sir, I was a-herdin', over at the Spencer Place, and was out on Thunderhead when the wind sprung up. There come one turrible vyg'rous blow that jest nacherally lifted the ground. I went up in the sky, my coat ripped off, and I went a-sailin' end-over-end."

"Yes?"

"Yes. About half an hour later, I lit spang in the mud way down yander in Tuckaleechee Cove—yes, sir; ten mile as the crow flies, and a mile deeper'n trout-fish swim."

There was silence for a moment. Then Little John spoke up: "I mind about that time, Doc, but I disremember which buryin'-ground they-all planted ye in."

"Planted! *Me*? Huh! But I had one tormentin' time findin' my hat!"

The cabin shook under a heavier blast.

"Old Wind-maker's blowin' liars out o' North Car'lina. Hang on to yer hat, Doc! Whoop! Hear 'em a-comin'"

"Durn this blow, anyhow! No bear'll cross the mountain sich a night as this."

"Can't we hunt down on the Carolina side?" I asked.

"That's whar we're goin' to drive; but hit's no use if the bear don't come over."

"How is that? Do they sleep in one state and eat in the other?"

"Yes. You see, the Tennessee side of the mountain is powerful steep and laurely, so man nor dog cain't git over it in lots o' places: that's whar the bears den. But the mast, sich as acorns and beech and hickory nuts, is mostly on the Car'lina side; that's whar they hafter come to feed. So, when its blows like this, they stay at home and suck their paws."

"So we'll have to do, at this rate."

"I'll go see whut the el-e-ments looks like."

We arose from our squatting postures. John opened the little shake door, which swung violently backward as another gust of wind boomed against the cabin. Dust and hot ashes scattered in every direction. The dogs sprang up, one encroached upon another, and they flew at each other's throats. They were powerful beasts, dangerous to man as well as to the brutes they were trained to fight; but John was their master, and he soon booted them into surly subjection.

"The older dog don't ginerally raise no ruction; hit's the younger one that's ill," by which he meant vicious. "You Coaly, you'll git some o' that meanness shuck outen you if you tackle an old she-bear tomorrow!"

"Has the young dog ever fought a bear?"

"No, he don't know nothin'. But I reckon he'll pick up some larnin' in the next two, three days."

"Have those dogs got the Plott strain? I've been told that the Plott hounds are the best bear dogs in the country."

"'Tain't so," snorted John. "The Plott curs are the best; that is, half hound, half cur—though what weuns call the cur, in this case, really comes from a big furrin dog that I don't rightly know the breed of. Fellers, you can talk as you please about a streak o' the cur spilin' a dog; but I know hit ain't so—not for bear fightin' in these mountains, whar you cain't foller up on hossback, but hafter do your own runnin'."

"What is the reason, John?"

"Wal, hit's like this: a plumb cur, of course, cain't foller a cold track—he jest runs by sight; and he won't hang—he quits. But, t'other way, no hound'll really fight a bear—hit takes a big severe dog to do that. Hounds has the best noses, and they'll run a bear all day and night, and the next day, too; but they won't never tree—they're afeared to close in. Now look at them dogs o' mine. A cur ain't got no dew-claws—them dogs has. My dogs can foller ary trail, same's hound; but they'll run right in on the varmint, snappin' and chawin' and worryin' him till he gits so mad you can hear his tuches pop half a mile. He cain't run away—he haster stop every bit and fight. Finally he gits so tarred [tired] and het up that he trees to rest hisself. Then we-uns ketches up and finishes him."

"Mebbe you-uns don't know that a dewclawed dog is snakeproof—"

But somebody, thinking that dog talk had gone far enough, produced a bottle of soothing-syrup that was too new to have paid tax. Then we discovered that there was musical talent, of a sort, in Little John. He cut a pigeon-wing, twirled around with an imaginary banjo, and sang in a quaint minor:

"Did you *ever* see the devil,
With his *pitchfork* and ladle,
And his *old* iron shovel,
And his old gourd head?

O, I *will* go to meetin',
And I *will* go to meetin',
Yes, I *will* go to meetin',
In an old tin pan."

Other songs followed, with utter irrelevance—mere snatches from "ballets" composed, mainly, by the mountaineers themselves, though some dated back to a long-forgotten age when the British ancestors of these Carolina woodsmen were battling with lance and long bow. It was one of modern and local origin that John was singing when there came a diversion from without—

La-a-ay down, boys,
Le's take a nap:
Thar's goin' to be trouble
In the Cumberland Gap—

Our ears were stunned by one sudden thundering crash. The roof rose visibly, as though pushed upward from within. In an instant we were blinded by moss and dried mud—the chinking blown from between the logs of our shabby cabin. Dred and Coaly cowered as though whipped, while "Doc's" little hound slunk away in the keen misery of fear. We men looked at each other with lowered eyelids and the grim smile that denotes readiness, though no special eagerness, for dissolution. Beyond the "gant-lot"* we could hear trees and limbs popping like pistol shots.

Then that tidal wave of air swept by. The roof settled again with only a few shingles missing. We went to "redding up." Squalls broke against the mountainside, hither and yon, like the hammer of Thor testing the foundations of the earth. But they were below us. Here, on top, there was only the steady drive of a great surge of wind; and speech was possible once more.

"Fellers, you want to mark whut you dream about, tonight: hit'll shore come true tomorrow."

"Yes: but you mustn't tell whut yer dream was till the hunt's over, or it'll spile the charm."

There ensued a grave discussion of dream lore, in which the illiterates of our party declared solemn faith. If one dreamt of blood, he would surely see blood the next day. Another lucky sign for a hunter was to dream of quarreling with a woman, for that meant a she-bear. It was favorable to dream of clear water, but muddy water meant trouble.

---

* *Gant-lot:* a fenced enclosure into which cattle are driven after cutting them out from those of other owners. So called cause the mountain cattle run wild, feeding only on grass and browse, and "they couldn't travel well to market when they were filled up on green stuff, so they're penned up to git *gant* and nimble."

The wind died away. When we went out for a last observation of the weather we found the air so clear that the lights of Knoxville were plainly visible, in the north-northwest, thirty-two miles in an air line. Not another light was to be seen on earth, although in some directions we could scan for nearly a hundred miles. The moon shone brightly. Things looked rather favorable for the morrow, after all.

"Brek-k-k-*fust!*"

I awoke to a knowledge that somebody had built a roaring fire and was stirring about. Between the cabin logs one looked out upon a starry sky and an almost pitch-dark world. What did that pottering vagabond mean by arousing us in the middle of the night? But I was hungry. Everybody half arose on elbows and blinked about. Then we got up, each after his fashion, except one scamp who resumed snoring.

"Whar's that brekfust you're yellin' about?"

"Hit's for you-uns to help *git!* I knowed I couldn't roust ye no other way. Here, you, go down to the spring and fetch water. Rustle out, boys; we've got to git a soon start if you want bear brains an' liver for supper."

The "soon start" tickled me into good humor.

Our dogs were curled together under the long bunk, having popped indoors as soon as the way was opened. Somebody trod on Coaly's tail. Coaly snapped Dred. Instantly there was action between the four. It is interesting to observe what two or three hundred pounds of dog can do to a ramshackle berth with a man on top of it. Poles and hay and ragged quilts flew in every direction. Sleepy Matt went down in the midst of the melee, swearing valiantly. I went out and hammered ice out of the washbasin while Granville and John quelled the riot. Presently our frying-pans sputtered and the huge coffeepot began to get up steam.

"Wal, who dreamt him a good dream?"

"I did," affirmed the writer. "I dreamt that I had an old colored woman by the throat and was choking dollars out of her mouth—"

"Good la!" exclaimed four men in chorus. "You hadn't orter a-told."

"Why? Wasn't that a lovely dream?"

"Hit means a she-bear, shore as a cap-shootin' gun, but you've spiled it all by tellin'. Mebbe somebody'll git her today, but *you* won't—your chanct is ruined."

So the reader will understand why, in this veracious narrative, I cannot relate any heroic exploits of my own in battling with Ursus Major.

There was still no sign of rose color in the eastern sky when we sallied forth. The ground, to use a mountaineer's expression, was "all spewed up with frost." Rime crackled underfoot and our mustaches soon stiffened in the icy wind.

It was settled that Little John Cable and the hunchback Cope should take the dogs far down into Bone Valley and start the drive, leaving Granville, Doc, Matt, and myself to picket the mountain. I was given a stand about half a mile east of the cabin, and had but a vague notion of where the others went.

By jinks, it was cold! I built a fire between the buttressing roots of a big mountain oak, but still my toes and fingers were numb. This was the 25th of November, and we were at an altitude where sometimes frost forms in July. The other men were more thinly clad than I, and with not a stitch of wool beyond their stocking; yet they seemed to revel in the keen air. I wasted some pity on Cope, who had no underwear worthy of the name; but afterwards I learned that he would not have worn more clothes if they had been given to him. This fellow never owned a coat until after his marriage. It is literal fact that some of these mountaineers (women and children, as well as men) think nothing of running around barefooted for hours in snow that is ankledeep. One of my neighbor's children went barefooted all one winter, when the thermometer several times went below zero Fahrenheit. Many a night my companions had slept out on the mountain without blanket or shelter, when the ground froze and every twig in the forest was coated with rime from the winter fog.

Away out yonder beyond the mighty bulk of Clingmans Dome, which, black with spruce and balsam, looked like a vast bear rising to contemplate the northern world, there streaked the first faint, nebulous hint of dawn. Presently the big bear's head was tipped with a golden crown flashing against the scarlet fires of the firmament, and the earth awoke.

A rustling some hundred yards below me gave signal that the gray squirrels were on their way to water. Out of a tree overhead popped a mountain "boomer" (red squirrel), and down he came, eyed me, and stopped.

Somewhere from the sky came a strange, half-human note, as of someone chiding: "*Wal*-lace, *Wal*-lace, *Wat!*" I could get no view for the trees. Then the thing sailed into sight—a raven—flexibly changing its voice to a deep-toned "Co-*logne*, Co-*logne*, Co-*logne*."

As the morning drew on, I let the fire die to ashes and basked lazily in the sun. Not a sound had I heard from the dogs. My hoodoo was working malignly. Well, let it work. I was comfortable now, and that old bear could go to any other doom she preferred. It was pleasant enough to lie here alone in the forest and be free! Aye, it was good to be alive, and to be far, far away from the broken bottles and old tin cans of civilization.

For many a league to the southward clouds covered all the valleys in billows of white, from which rose a hundred mountain tops, like islands in a tropic ocean. My fancy sailed among and beyond them, beyond the horizon's rim, even unto those far seas that I had sailed in my youth, to the old times and the old friends that I should never see again.

But a forenoon is long-drawn-out when one has breakfasted before dawn, and has nothing to do but sit motionless in the woods and watch and listen. I got to fingering my rifle trigger impatiently and wishing that a wild Thanksgiving gobbler might blunder into view. Squirrels made ceaseless chatter all around my stand. Large hawks shrilled by me within tempting range, whistling like spent bullets. A groundhog sat up on a log and whistled, too, after a manner of his own. He was so near that I could see his nose wiggle. A skunk waddled around for twenty minutes, and once came so close that I thought he would nibble my boot. I was among old mossy beeches, scaled with polyphori, and twisted into postures of torture by their battles with the storms. Below, among chestnuts and birches, I could hear the *t-wee*, *t-wee* of "joree-birds" (towhees), which winter in the valleys. Incessantly came the *chip-chip-chip* of ground squirrels, the saucy bark of the grays, and great chirruping among the "boomers."

Far off on my left a rifle cracked. I pricked up and listened intently, but there was never a yelp from a dog. Since it is a law of the chase to fire at nothing smaller than turkeys, lest big game be scared away, this shot might mean a gobbler. I knew that Matt Hyde, to save his soul, could not sit ten minutes on a stand without calling turkeys (and he *could* call them with his unassisted mouth better than anyone I ever heard perform with leaf or wing bone or any other contrivance).

Thus the slow hours dragged along. I yearned mightily to stretch my legs. Finally, being certain that no drive would approach my stand that day, I ambled back to the hut and did a turn at dinner-getting. Things were smoking, and smelt good, by the time four of our men turned up, all of them dog-tired and disappointed, but stoical.

"That pup Coaly chased off atter a wildcat," blurted John. "We held the old dogs together and let him rip. Then Dred started a deer. It was that old buck that everybody's shot at, and missed, this three year back. I'd believe he's a hant if 't wasn't for his tracks—they're the biggest I ever seen. He must weigh two hundred and fifty. But he's a foxy cuss. Tuk right down the bed o' Desolation, up the left prong of Roaring Fork, right through the Devil's Race-path (how a deer can git through thar *I* don't see!), crossed at the Meadow Gap, went down Eagle Creek, and by now he's in the Little Tennessee. That buck, shorely to God, has wings!"

We were at table in the Carolina room when Matt Hyde appeared. He was the worst tatterdemalion I had seen outside of a hobo camp, his lower extremities being almost naked. Sure enough, he bore a turkey hen.

"I was callin' a gobbler when this fool thing showed up. I fired a shoot as she riz in the air, but only bruk her wing. She made off on her legs like the devil whoppin' out fire. I run, an' she run. Guess I run her half a mile through all-fired thickets. She piped '*Quit—quit*,' but I said 'I'll see you in hell afore I quit!' and the chase resumed. Finally I knocked her over with a birch stob, and here we are."

Matt ruefully surveyed his legs. "Boys," said he, "I'm nigh breachless."

None but native-born mountaineers could have stood the strain of another drive that day, for the country that Cope and Cable had been through was fearful, especially the laurel up Roaring Fork and Killpeter Ridge. But the stamina of these withey little men was even more remarkable than their endurance of cold. After a slice of meat (about half what a Northern office man would eat), a chunk of half-baked johnny-cake, and a pint or so of coffee, they were as fresh as ever.

I had made the coffee strong, and it was good stuff that I had brought from home. After his first deep draught, Little John exclaimed: "Hah! boys, that coffee hits whar ye hold it!"

I thought that a neat compliment from a sharpshooter.

We took new stands; but the afternoon passed without incident to those of us on the mountain tops. I returned to camp about five o'clock, and was surprised to see three of our men lugging across the gant-lot a small female bear.

"Hyar's yer old black woman," shouted John.

"How's this? I didn't hear any drive."

"Thar wa'n't none."

"Then where did you get your bear?"

"In one of Steve Howard's traps, dum him! Boys, I wish we *hed* roasted the temper outen them trap springs, like we talked o' doin'."

"The bear was alive, wasn't it?"

"As live as a hot coal. See the pup's head!"

I examined Coaly, who looked sick. The flesh was torn from his lower jaw and hung down a couple of inches. Two holes in the top of his head showed where the bear's tusks had done their best to crack his skull.

"When the other dogs found her, he rushed right in. She hadn't been trapped more'n a few hours, and she larned Coaly somethin' about the bear business."

"Won't this spoil him for hunting hereafter?"

"Not if he has his daddy's and mammy's grit. We'll know by tomorrow whether he's a shore-enough bear dog; for I've larned now whar they're crossin'—seed sign a-plenty."

All of us were indignant at the setter of the trap. It had been hidden in a trail, with no sign to warn a man from stepping into it. In Tennessee, I was told, it is a penitentiary offense to set out a bear trap. We agreed that a similar law ought to be passed in North Carolina.

"It's only two years ago," said Granville, "that Jasper Millington, an old man living on the Tennessee side, started acrost the mountain to get work at the Everett mine. Not fur from where we are now he stepped into a bear trap that was hid in the leaves, like this one. It broke his leg, and he starved to death in it."

Despite our indignation meeting, it was decided to carry the trapped bear's hide to Howard, and for us to use only the meat as recompense for trouble, to say nothing of risk to life and limb. Such is the mountaineers' regard for property rights!

The animal we had ingloriously won was undersized, weighing a scant 175 pounds. The average weight of Smoky Mountain bears is not great, but occasionally a very large beast is killed. Matt Hyde told us that he killed one on the Welch Divide in 1901, the meat of which, dressed, without the hide, weighed 434 pounds, and the hide "squared eight feet" when stretched for drying.

We spent the evening in debate as to where the next drive should be made. Some favored moving six miles eastward to the old mining shack at Siler's Meadow and trying the head waters of Forney's Creek, around Rip Shin Thicket and the Gunstick Laurel, driving towards Clingmans Dome and over into the bleak gulf, southwest of the Sugarland Mountains, that I had named Godforsaken—a title that stuck. We knew there were bears in that region, though it was a desperately rough country to hunt in.

But John and the hunchback had found "sign" in the opposite direction. Bears were crossing from Little River in the neighborhood of Thunderhead and Briar Knob, coming up just west of the Devil's Court House and "using" around Block House, Woolly Ridge, Bear Pen, and thereabouts. The motion carried, and we adjourned to bed.

We breakfasted on bear meat, the remains of our Thanksgiving turkey and wheat bread shortened with bear's grease until it was light as a feather, and I made tea. It was the first time that Little John ever saw "store tea." He swallowed some of it as if it had been boneset, under the impression that it was some sort of "yerb" that would be good for his insides.

"Wal, people," exclaimed Matt, "I 'low I've done growed a bit, after that mess of meat. Le's be movin'."

It was a hard trip for me, climbing up the rock approach to Briar Knob. You may laugh as you please about a lowlander's lungs feeling rarefaction at 5,000 or 5,500 feet, but in the very moist air of the Southern mountains, with fog (cloud) in the bargain, most newcomers do feel it for a few days.

The boys were anxious for me to get a shot. I was paying them nothing; it was share-and-share alike; but their neighborly kindness moved them to do their best for the "furriner."

So they put on me what was probably the best stand for the day. It was above the Fire Scald, a *brûlé* or burnt-over space on the steep southern side of the ridge between Briar Knob and Laurel Top, overlooking the grisly slope of Killpeter. Here I could both see and hear an uncommonly long distance, and if the bear went either east or west I would have timely warning.

I had shivered on the mountain top for a couple of hours, hearing only an occasional bark from the dogs, which had been working in the thickets a mile or so below me, when suddenly there burst forth the devil of a racket. On came the chase, right in my direction. Presently I could even distinguish the different notes—the deep bellow of old Dred, the houndlike baying of

Rock and Coaly, and Little Towse's yelp. I thought that the bear might chance the comparatively open space of the Fire Scald, because there were still some ashes on the ground which would dust the dogs' nostrils and tend to throw them off the scent. And such, I do believe, was his intention. But the dogs caught up with him. They nipped him fore and aft. Time after time he shook them off; but they were true bear dogs, and knew no such word as *quit*.

I took a last squint at my rifle sights, made sure there was a cartridge in the chamber, and then felt my ears grow as I listened. Suddenly the chase swerved at a right angle and took straight up the side of Saddle-back. Either the bear would tree, or he would try to smash on through to the low rhododendron of the Devil's Court House, where dogs who followed might break their legs. I girded myself and ran, "wiggling and wingling" along the main divide, and then came the steep pull up Briar Knob. As I was grading around the summit with all the lope that was left in me, I heard a rifle crack, half a mile down Saddle-back. Old Doc was somewhere in that vicinity. I halted to listen. Creation, what a rumpus! Then another shot. Then the war whoop of the South that we read about.

By and by, up they came, John and Cope and Doc, carrying the bear on a trimmed sapling. Presently Hyde joined us, then came Granville, and we filed back to camp, where Doc told his story:

"Boys, them dogs' eyes shined like new money. Coaly fit again, all right, and got his tail bit. The bear div down into a sink-hole with the dogs atop o' him. Soon's I could shoot without hittin' a dog, I let him have it. Thought I'd shot him through the head, but he fit on. Then I jumped down into the sink an' kicked him loose from the dogs, or he'd a-killed Coaly. Wal, sir, he wa'n't hurt a bit—the ball just glanced off his head. He riz and knocked me down with his left paw, an' walked right over me, an' lit up the ridge. The dogs treed him in a minute. I went to shoot up at him, but my new hulls fit loose in this old chamber and the one drap out, so the gun stuck. Had to git my knife out and fit hit. Then the dad-burned gun wouldn't stand roostered (cocked); the feather-spring had jumped out o' place. But I held back with my thumb, and killed him anyhow."

"Bears," said John, "is all left-handed. Ever note that? Hit's the left paw you want to look out fer. He'd a-knocked somethin' out o' yer head if thar'd been much in it, Doc."

And so, laughing and chaffing, we finished dinner.

The mountaineers have a curious way of sharing the spoils of the chase. A bear's hide is sold and the proceeds divided equally among the hunters, but the meat is cut up into as many pieces as there are partners in the chase; then one man goes indoors or behind a tree, and somebody at the carcass, laying his hand on a portion, calls out: "Whose piece is this?"

"Granville Calhoun's," cries the hidden man, who cannot see it.

"Whose is this?"

"Bill Cope's."

And so on down the line. Everybody gets what chance determines for him, and there can be no charge of unfairness.

The next morning John announced that we were going to get another bear.

"Night afore last," he said, "Bill dremp that he saw a lot o' fat meat lyin' on the table; an' it done come true. Last night I dremp one that never was known to fail. Now you'll see it!"

It did not look like it by evening. We all worked hard and endured much—standers as well as drivers—but not a rifle had spoken up to the time when, from my far-off stand, I yearned for a hot supper.

Away down in the rear I heard the snort of a locomotive, one of those cog-wheel affairs that are specially built for mountain climbing. With a steam-loader and three camps of a hundred men each, it was despoiling the Tennessee forest. Slowly, but inexorably, a leviathan was crawling into the wilderness to consume it.

Wearily I plodded back to camp. No one had arrived but Doc. The old man had been thumped rather severely in yesterday's scrimmage, but complained only of "a touch o' rheumatiz." Just how the latter had left his clothes in tatters he did not explain.

It was late when Matt and Granville came in. The crimson and yellow of sunset had turned to a faultless turquoise, and this to a violet afterglow; then suddenly night rose from the valleys and enveloped us.

About nine o'clock I went out on the Little Chestnut Bald and fired signals, but there was no answer. The last we had known of the drivers was that they had been beyond Thunderhead, six miles of hard travel to the westward. There was fog on the mountain. Then Granville and Matt took the lantern and set out for Briar Knob. Doc was too stiff for travel, and I, being at that time a stranger in the Smokies, would be of no use hunting amid clouds and darkness. Doc and I passed a dreary three hours. Finally, at midnight, my shots were answered, and soon the dogs came limping in. Dred had been severely bitten in the shoulders and Rock in the head. Coaly was bloody about the mouth, where his first day's wound had reopened. Then came the four men, empty-handed, it seemed, until John slapped a bear's "melt" (spleen) upon the table. He limped from a bruised hip.

"That bear went 'way around all o' you-uns. We follered him clar over to the Spencer Place, and then he doubled and come back on the fur side o' the ridge. He crossed through the laurel on the Devil's Court House and tuk down an almighty steep place. It was plumb night by that time. I fell over a rock clift twenty feet down, and if't hadn't been for the laurel I'd a-bruk some bones. I landed right in the middle of them, bear and dogs, fightin' like gamecocks. The bear clim a tree. Bill sung out 'Is it fur down that?' and I said 'Pretty fur.' 'Wal, I'm a-comin',' says he; and with that he grabbed a laurel to swing hisself down by, but the stem bruk, and down he came suddent, to jine the music. Hit was so dark I couldn't see my gun barrel, and we wuz all tangled up in green briars as thick as plough-lines. I had to fire twicet afore he tumbled. Then Matt an' Granville come. The four of us tuk turn-about crawlin' up out o' thar with the bear on our back. Only one man could handle him at a time—and he'll go a good two hundred, that bear. We gutted him, and left him near the top, to fotch in the mornin'. Boys, this is the time I'd give nigh all I'm worth for half a gallon o' liquor—and I'd promise the rest!"

"You'd orter see what Coaly did to that varmint," said Bill. "He bit a hole under the fore leg, through hide and ha'r, clar into the holler, so that you can stick your hand in and seize the bear's heart."

"John, what was that dream?"

"I dremp I stole a feller's overcoat. Now d'ye see? That means a bear's hide."

Coaly, three days ago, had been an inconsequential pup; but now he looked up into my eyes with the calm dignity that no fool or braggart can assume. He had been knighted. As he licked his wounds he was proud of them. "Scars of battle, sir. You may have your swagger ribbons and prize collars in the New York dog show, but *this* for me!"

The American Wilderness; Wilderness Hunters and Wilderness Game

From **The Wilderness Hunter,** ***1893***

Theodore Roosevelt

Manifold are the shapes taken by the American wilderness. In the east, from the Atlantic Coast to the Mississippi Valley, lies a land of magnificent hardwood forest. In endless variety and beauty, the trees cover the ground, save only where they have been cleared away by man, or where toward the west the expanse of the forest is broken by fertile prairies. Toward the north, this region of hardwood trees merges insensibly into the southern extension of the great sub-arctic forest; here the silver stems of birches gleam against the sombre background of coniferous evergreens. In the southeast again, by the hot, oozy coasts of the South Atlantic and the Gulf, the forest becomes semi-tropical; palms wave their feathery fronds, and the tepid swamps teem with reptile life.

Some distance beyond the Mississippi, stretching from Texas to North Dakota, and westward to the Rocky Mountains, lies the plains country. This is a region of light rainfall, where the ground is clad with short grass, while cottonwood trees fringe the courses of the winding plains streams; streams that are alternately turbid torrents and mere dwindling threads of water. The great stretches of natural pasture are broken by gray sage-brush plains, and tracts of strangely shaped and colored Bad Lands; sun-scorched wastes in summer, and in winter arctic in their iron desolation. Beyond the plains rise the Rocky Mountains, their flanks covered with coniferous woods; but the trees are small, and do not ordinarily grow very closely together. Toward the north the forest becomes denser, and the peaks higher; and glaciers creep down toward the valleys from the fields of everlasting snow. The brooks are brawling, trout-filled torrents; the swift rivers foam over rapid and cataract, on their way to one or the other of the two great oceans.

Southwest of the Rockies evil and terrible deserts stretch for leagues and leagues, mere waterless wastes of sandy plain and barren mountain, broken here and there by narrow strips of fertile ground. Rain rarely falls, and there are no clouds to dim the brazen sun. The rivers run in deep canyons, or are swallowed by the burning sand; the smaller watercourses are dry throughout the greater part of the year.

Beyond this desert region rise the sunny Sierras of California, with their flower-clad slopes and groves of giant trees; and north of them, along the coast, the rain-shrouded mountain chains of Oregon and Washington, matted with the towering growth of the mighty evergreen forest.

The white hunters, who from time to time first penetrated the different parts of this wilderness, found themselves in such hunting grounds as those wherein, long ages before, their Old-World forefathers had dwelled; and the game they chased was much the same as that their lusty barbarian ancestors followed, with weapons of bronze and of iron, in the dim years before history dawned. As late as the end of the seventeenth century the turbulent village nobles of Lithuania and Livonia hunted the bear, the bison, the elk, the wolf, and the stag, and hung the spoils in their smoky wooden palaces; and so, two hundred years later, the free hunters of Montana, in the interludes between hazardous mining quests and bloody Indian campaigns, hunted game almost or quite the same in kind, through the cold mountain forests surrounding the Yellowstone and Flathead lakes, and decked their log cabins and ranch houses with the hides and horns of the slaughtered beasts.

Zoologically speaking, the north temperate zones of the Old and New Worlds are very similar, differing from one another much less than they do from the various regions south of them, or than these regions differ among themselves. The untrodden American wilderness resembles both in game and physical character the forests, the mountains, and the steppes of the Old World as it was at the beginning of our era. Great woods of pine and fir, birch and beech, oak and chestnut; streams where the chief game fish are spotted trout and silvery salmon; grouse of various kinds as the most common game birds; all these the hunter finds as characteristic of the New World as of the Old. So it is with most of the beasts of the chase, and so also with the furbearing animals that furnish to the trapper alike his life work and his means of livelihood. The bear, wolf, bison, moose, caribou, wapiti, deer, and bighorn, the lynx, fox, wolverine, sable, mink, ermine, beaver, badger, and otter of both worlds are either identical or more or less closely kin to one another. Sometimes of the two forms, that found in the Old World is the larger. Perhaps more often the reverse is true, the American beast being superior in size. This is markedly the case with the wapiti, which is merely a giant brother of the European stag, exactly as the fisher is merely a very large cousin of the European sable or marten. The extraordinary prong-buck, the only hollow-horned ruminant which sheds its horns annually, is a distant representative of the Old-World antelopes of the steppes; the queer white antelope-goat has for its nearest kinsfolk certain Himalayan species. Of the animals commonly known to our hunters and trappers, only a few, such as the cougar, peccary, raccoon, possum (and among birds the wild turkey), find their nearest representatives and type forms in tropical America.

Of course this general resemblance does not mean identity. The differences in plant life and animal life, no less than in the physical features of the land, are sufficiently marked to give the American wilderness a character distinctly its own. Some of the most characteristic of the woodland animals, some of those which have most vividly impressed themselves on the imagination of the hunters and pioneer settlers, are the very ones which have no Old-World representatives. The wild turkey is in every way the king of American game birds. Among the small beasts the coon and the possum are those which have left the deepest traces in the humbler lore of the frontier; exactly as the cougar—usually under the name of panther or mountain lion—is a favorite figure in the wilder hunting tales. Nowhere else is there anything to match the wealth of the eastern hardwood forests, in number, variety, and beauty of trees; nowhere else is it possible to find conifers approaching in size the giant redwoods and sequoias of the Pacific slope. Nature here is generally on a larger scale than in the Old-World home of our race. The lakes are like inland seas, the rivers, like arms of the sea. Among stupendous mountain chains there are valleys and canyons of fathomless depth and incredible beauty and majesty. There are tropical swamps, and sad, frozen marshes; deserts and Death Valleys, weird and evil, and the strange wonderland of the Wyoming geyser region. The waterfalls are rivers rushing over precipices; the prairies seem without limit, and the forest never ending.

At the time when we first became a nation, nine-tenths of the territory now included within the limits of the United States was wilderness. It was during the stirring and troubled years immediately preceding the outbreak of the Revolution that the most adventurous hunters, the vanguard of the hardy army of pioneer settlers, first crossed the Alleghanies, and roamed far and wide through the lonely, danger-haunted forests which filled the No-man's-land lying between the Tennessee and the Ohio. They waged ferocious warfare with Shawnee and Wyandot and wrought huge havoc among the herds of game with which the forest teemed. While the first Continental Congress was still sitting, Daniel Boone, the archetype of the American hunter, was leading his bands of tall backwoods riflemen to settle in the beautiful country of Kentucky, where the red and the white warriors strove with such obstinate rage that both races alike grew to know it as "the dark and bloody ground."

Boone and his fellow-hunters were the heralds of the oncoming civilization, the pioneers in that conquest of the wilderness which has at last been practically achieved in our own day. Where they pitched their camps and built their log huts or stockade hamlets, towns grew up, and men who were tillers of the soil, not mere wilderness wanderers, thronged in to take and hold the land. Then, ill-at-ease among the settlements for which they had themselves made ready the way, and fretted even by the slight restraints of the rude and uncouth semi-civilization of the border, the restless hunters moved onward into the yet unbroken wilds where the game dwelled and the red tribes marched forever to war and hunting. Their untamable souls ever found something congenial and beyond measure attractive in the lawless freedom of the lives of the very savages against whom they warred so bitterly.

Step by step, often leap by leap, the frontier of settlement was pushed westward; and ever from before its advance fled the warrior tribes of the red men and the scarcely less intractable array of white Indian fighters and game hunters. When the Revolutionary War was at its height, George Rogers Clark, himself a mighty hunter of the old backwoods type, led his handful of hunter-soldiers to the conquest of the French towns of the Illinois. This was but one of the many notable feats of arms performed by the wild soldiery of the backwoods. Clad in their fringed and tasseled hunting-shirt of buckskin or homespun, with coonskin caps and deer-hide leggings and moccasins, with tomahawk and scalping-knife thrust into their bead-worked belts, and long rifles in hand, they fought battle after battle of the most bloody character, both against the Indians, as at the Great Kanawha, at the Fallen Timbers, and at Tippecanoe, and against more civilized foes, as at King's Mountain, New Orleans, and the River Thames.

Soon after the beginning of the present century Louisiana fell into our hands, and the most daring hunters and explorers pushed through the forests of the Mississippi Valley to the great plains, steered across these vast seas of grass to the Rocky Mountains, and then through their rugged defiles onward to the Pacific Ocean. In every work of exploration, and in all the earlier battles with the original lords of the western and southwestern lands, whether Indian or Mexican, the adventurous hunters played the leading part; while close behind came the swarm of hard, dogged, border-farmers—a masterful race, good fighters and good breeders, as all masterful races must be.

Very characteristic in its way was the career of quaint, honest, fearless Davy Crockett, the Tennessee rifleman and Whig Congressman, perhaps the best shot in all our country, whose skill in the use of his favorite weapon passed into a proverb, and who ended his days by a hero's death in the ruins of the Alamo. An even more notable man was another mighty hunter, Houston, who when a boy ran away to the Indians; who while still a lad returned to his own people to serve under Andrew Jackson in the campaigns which that greatest of all the backwoods leaders waged against the Creeks, the Spaniards, and the British. He was wounded at the storming of one of the strongholds of Red

Eagle's doomed warriors, and returned to his Tennessee home to rise to high civil honor, and become the foremost man of his State. Then, while Governor of Tennessee, in a sudden fit of moody anger, and of mad longing for the unfettered life of the wilderness, he abandoned his office, his people, and his race, and fled to the Cherokees beyond the Mississippi. For years he lived as one of their chiefs; until one day, as he lay in ignoble ease and sloth, a rider from the south, from the rolling plains of the San Antonio and Brazos, brought word that the Texans were up, and in doubtful struggle striving to wrest their freedom from the lancers and carbineers of Santa Anna. Then his dark soul flamed again into burning life; riding by night and day he joined the risen Texans, was hailed by them as a heaven-sent leader, and at the San Jacinto led them on to the overthrow of the Mexican host. Thus the stark hunter, who had been alternately Indian fighter and Indian chief, became the President of the new Republic, and, after its admission into the United States, a Senator at Washington; and, to his high honor, he remained to the end of his days staunchly loyal to the flag of the Union.

By the time that Crockett fell, and Houston became the darling leader of the Texans, the typical hunter and Indian fighter had ceased to be a backwoodsman; he had become a plainsman, or mountain-man; for the frontier, east of which he never willingly went, had been pushed beyond the Mississippi. Restless, reckless, and hardy, he spent years of his life in lonely wanderings through the Rockies as a trapper; he guarded the slowly moving caravans, which for purposes of trade journeyed over the dangerous Santa Fe trail; he guided the large parties of frontier settlers who, driving before them their cattle, with all their household goods in their white-topped wagons, spent perilous months and seasons on their weary way to Oregon or California. Joining in bands, the stalwart, skin-clad riflemen waged ferocious war on the Indians, scarcely more savage than themselves, or made long raids for plunder and horses against the outlying Mexican settlements. The best, the bravest, the most modest of them all was the renowned Kit Carson. He was not only a mighty hunter, a daring fighter, a finder of trails, and maker of roads through the unknown, untrodden wilderness, but also a real leader of men. Again and again he crossed and recrossed the continent, from the Mississippi to the Pacific; he guided many of the earliest military and exploring expeditions of the United States Government; he himself led the troops in victorious campaigns against Apache and Navahoe; and in the Civil War he was made a colonel of the Federal Army.

After him came many other hunters. Most were pure-blooded Americans, but many were Creole Frenchmen, Mexicans, or even members of the so-called civilized Indian tribes, notably the Delawares. Wide were their wanderings, many their strange adventures in the chase, bitter their unending warfare with the red lords of the land. Hither and thither they roamed, from the desolate burning deserts of the Colorado to the grassy plains of the Upper Missouri; from the rolling Texas prairies, bright beneath their sunny skies, to the high snow peaks of the northern Rockies, or the giant pine forests, and soft rainy weather, of the coasts of Puget Sound. Their main business was trapping, furs being the only articles yielded by the wilderness, as they knew it, which were both valuable and portable. These early hunters were all trappers likewise, and, indeed, used their rifles only to procure meat or repel attacks. The chief of the fur-bearing animals they followed was the beaver, which abounded in the streams of the plains and mountains; in the far north they also trapped otter, mink, sable, and fisher. They married squaws from among the Indian tribes with which they happened for the moment to be at peace; they acted as scouts for the United States troops in their campaigns against the tribes with which they happened to be at war.

Soon after the Civil War the life of these hunters, taken as a class, entered on its final stage. The Pacific Coast was already fairly well settled, and there were few mining camps in the Rockies; but most of this Rocky Mountain region, and the entire stretch of plains country proper, the vast belt of level or rolling grass land lying between the Rio Grande and the Saskatchewan, still remained primeval wilderness, inhabited only by roving hunters and formidable tribes of Indian nomads, and by the huge herds of game on which they preyed. Beaver swarmed in the streams and yielded a rich harvest to the trapper; but trapping was no longer the mainstay of the adventurous plainsmen. Foremost among the beasts of the chase, on account of its numbers, its size, and its economic importance, was the bison or American buffalo; its innumerable multitudes darkened the limitless prairies. As the transcontinental railroads were pushed toward completion, and the tide of settlement rolled onward with ever-increasing rapidity, buffalo robes became of great value. The hunters forthwith turned their attention mainly to the chase of the great clumsy beasts, slaughtering them by hundreds of thousands for their hides; sometimes killing them on horseback, but more often on foot, by still-hunting, with the heavy long range Sharp's rifle. Throughout the fifteen years during which this slaughter lasted, a succession of desperate wars was waged with the banded tribes of the Horse Indians. All the time, in unending succession, long trains of big white-topped wagons crept slowly westward across the prairies, marking the steady oncoming of the frontier settlers.

By the close of 1883 the last buffalo herd was destroyed. The beaver were trapped out of all the streams, or their numbers so thinned that it no longer paid to follow them. The last formidable Indian war had been brought to a successful close. The flood of the incoming whites had risen over the land; tongues of settlement reached from the Mississippi to the Rocky Mountains, and from the Rocky Mountains to the Pacific. The frontier had come to an end; it had vanished. With it vanished also the old race of wilderness hunters, the men who spent all their days in the lonely wilds, and who killed game as their sole means of livelihood. Great stretches of wilderness still remained in the Rocky Mountains, and here and there in the plains country, exactly as much smaller tracts of wild land are to be found in the Alleghanies and northern New York and New England; and on these tracts occasional hunters and trappers still linger; but as a distinctive class, with a peculiar and important position in American life, they no longer exist.

There were other men besides the professional hunters, who lived on the borders of the wilderness, and followed hunting, not only as a pastime, but also as yielding an important portion of their subsistence. The frontier farmers were all hunters. In the Eastern backwoods, and in certain places in the West, as in Oregon, these adventurous tillers of the soil were the pioneers among the actual settlers; in the Rockies their places were taken by the miners, and on the great plains by the ranchmen and cowboys, the men who lived in the saddle, guarding their branded herds of horses and horned stock. Almost all of the miners and cowboys were obliged on occasions to turn hunters.

Moreover, the regular army which played so important a part in all the later stages of the winning of the West produced its full share of mighty hunters. The later Indian wars were fought principally by the regulars. The West Point officer and his little company of trained soldiers appeared abreast of the first hardy cattlemen and miners. The ordinary settlers rarely made their appearance until in campaign after campaign, always inconceivably wearing and harassing, and often very bloody in character, the scarred and tattered troops had broken and overthrown the most formidable among the Indian tribes. Faithful, uncomplaining, unflinching, the soldiers wearing the national uniform lived for many weary years at their lonely little posts, facing unending toil and danger with quiet endurance, surrounded by the desolation of vast solitudes, and menaced by the most merciless of foes. Hunting was followed not only as a sport, but also as the only means of keeping the posts and the expeditionary trains in meat. Many of the officers became equally proficient as marksmen and hunters. The three most famous Indian fighters since the Civil War, Generals Custer, Miles, and Crook, were all keen and successful followers of the chase.

Of American big game the bison, almost always known as the buffalo, was the largest and most important to man. When the first white settlers landed in Virginia the bison ranged east of the Alleghanies almost to the sea-coast, westward to the dry deserts lying beyond the Rocky Mountains, northward to the Great Slave Lake and southward to Chihuahua. It was a beast of the forests and mountains, in the Alleghanies no less than in the Rockies; but its true home was on the prairies and the high plains. Across these it roamed, hither and thither, in herds of enormous, of incredible magnitude; herds so large that they covered the waving grass land for hundreds of square leagues, and when on the march occupied days and days in passing a given point. But the seething myriads of shaggy-maned wild cattle vanished with remarkable and melancholy rapidity before the inroads of the white hunters, and the steady march of the oncoming settlers. Now they are on the point of extinction. Two or three hundred are left in that great national game preserve, the Yellowstone Park; and it is said that others still remain in the wintry desolation of Athabasca. Elsewhere only a few individuals exist—probably considerably less than half a hundred all told—scattered in small parties in the wildest and most remote and inaccessible portions of the Rocky Mountains. A bison bull is the largest American animal. His huge bulk, his short, curved black horns, the shaggy mane clothing his great neck and shoulders, give him a look of ferocity which his conduct belies. Yet he is truly a grand and noble beast, and his loss from our prairies and forest is as keenly regretted by the lover of nature and of wild life as by the hunter.

Next to the bison in size, and much superior in height to it and to all other American game—for it is taller than the tallest horse—comes the moose, or broad-horned elk. It is a strange, uncouth-looking beast, with very long legs, short thick neck, a big, ungainly head, a swollen nose, and huge shovel horns. Its home is in the cold, wet pine and spruce forests, which stretch from the sub-arctic region of Canada southward in certain places across our frontier. Two centuries ago it was found as far south as Massachusetts. It has now been exterminated from its former haunts in northern New York and Vermont, and is on the point of vanishing from northern Michigan. It is still found in northern Maine and northeastern Minnesota and in portions of northern Idaho and Washington; while along the Rockies it extends its range southward through western Montana to northwestern Wyoming, south of the Tetons. In 1884 I saw the fresh hide of one that was killed in the Bighorn Mountains.

The wapiti, or round-horned elk, like the bison, and unlike the moose, had its centre of abundance in the United States, though extending northward into Canada. Originally its range reached from ocean to ocean and it went in herds of thousands of individuals; but it has suffered more from the persecution of hunters than any other game except the bison. By the beginning of this century it had been exterminated in most localities east of the Mississippi; but a few lingered on for many years in the Alleghanies. Colonel Cecil Clay informs me that an Indian whom he knew killed one in Pennsylvania in 1869. A very few still exist here and there in northern Michigan and Minnesota, and in one or two spots on the western boundary of Nebraska and the Dakotas; but it is now properly a beast of the wooded Western mountains. It is still plentiful in western Colorado, Wyoming, and Montana, and in parts of Idaho, Washington, and Oregon. Though not as large as the moose it is the most beautiful and stately of all animals of the deer kind, and its antlers are marvels of symmetrical grandeur.

The woodland caribou is inferior to the wapiti both in size and symmetry. The tips of the many branches of its long irregular antlers are slightly palmated. Its range is the same as that of the moose, save that it does not go so far southward. Its hoofs are long and round; even larger than the long, oval hoofs of the moose, and much larger than those of the wapiti. The tracks of all three can be told apart at a glance, and can not be mistaken for the footprints of other game. Wapiti tracks, however, look much like those of yearling and two-year-old cattle, unless the ground is steep or muddy, in which case the marks of the false hoofs appear, the joints of wapiti being more flexible than those of domestic stock.

The whitetail deer is now, as it always has been, the best known and most abundant of American big game, and though its numbers have been greatly thinned it is still found in almost every State of the Union. The common blacktail or mule deer, which has likewise been sadly thinned in numbers, though once extraordinarily abundant, extends from the great plains to the Pacific; but it is supplanted on the Puget Sound coast by the Columbian blacktail. The delicate, heart-shaped footprints of all three are nearly indistinguishable; when the animal is running the hoof points are of course separated. The track of the antelope is more oval, growing squarer with age. Mountain sheep leave footmarks of a squarer shape, the points of the hoof making little indentations in the soil, well apart, even when the animal is only walking; and a yearling's track is not unlike that made by a big prong-buck when striding rapidly with the toes well apart. White-goat tracks are also square, and as large as those of the sheep; but there is less indentation of the hoof points, which come nearer together.

The antelope, or prong-buck, was once found in abundance from the eastern edge of the great plains to the Pacific, but it has everywhere diminished in numbers, and has been exterminated along the eastern and western borders of its former range. The bighorn, or mountain sheep, is found in the Rocky Mountains from northern Mexico to Alaska; and in the United States from the Coast and Cascade ranges to the Bad Lands of the western edges of the Dakotas, wherever there are mountain chains or tracts of rugged hills. It was never very abundant, and, though it has become less so, it has held its own better than most game. The white goat, however, alone among our game animals, has positively increased in numbers since the advent of settlers; because white hunters rarely follow it, and the Indians who once sought its skin for robes now use blankets instead. Its true home is in Alaska and Canada, but it crosses our borders along the lines of the Rockies and Cascades, and a few small isolated colonies are found here and there southward to California and New Mexico.

The cougar and wolf, once common throughout the United States, have now completely disappeared from all save the wildest regions. The black bear holds its own better; it was never found on the great plains. The huge grizzly ranges from the great plains to the Pacific. The little peccary or Mexican wild hog merely crosses our southern border.

The finest hunting ground in America was, and indeed is, the mountainous region of western Montana and northwestern Wyoming. In this high, cold land, of lofty mountains, deep forests, and open prairies, with its beautiful lakes and rapid rivers, all the species of big game mentioned above, except the peccary and Columbian blacktail, are to be found. Until 1880 they were very abundant, and they are still, with the exception of the bison, fairly plentiful. On most of the long hunting expeditions which I made away from my ranch, I went into this region.

The bulk of my hunting has been done in the cattle country, near my ranch on the Little Missouri, and in the adjoining lands round the lower Powder and Yellowstone. Until 1881 the valley of the Little Missouri was fairly thronged with game, and was absolutely unchanged in any respect from its original condition of primeval wildness. With the incoming of the stockmen all this changed, and the game was woefully slaughtered; but plenty of deer and antelope, a few sheep and bear, and an occasional elk are still left.

Since the professional hunters have vanished with the vast herds of game on which they preyed, the life of the ranchman is that which yields most chance of hunting. Life on a cattle ranch, on the great plains or among the foothills of the high mountains, has a peculiar attraction for those hardy, adventurous spirits who take most kindly to a vigorous out-of-door existence, and who are therefore most apt to care passionately for the chase of big game. The free ranchman lives in a wild, lonely country, and exactly as he breaks and tames his own horses, and guards and tends his own branded herds, so he takes the keenest enjoyment in the chase, which is to him not merely the pleasantest of sports, but also a means of adding materially to his comforts, and often his only method of providing himself with fresh meat.

Hunting in the wilderness is of all pastimes the most attractive, and it is doubly so when not carried on merely as a pastime. Shooting over a private game preserve is of course in no way to be compared to it. The wilderness hunter must not only show skill in the use of the rifle and address in finding and approaching game, but he must also show the qualities of hardihood, self-reliance, and resolution needed for effectively grappling with his wild surroundings. The fact that the hunter needs the game, both for its meat and for its hide, undoubtedly adds a zest to the pursuit. Among the hunts which I have most enjoyed were those made when I was engaged in getting in the winter's stock of meat for the ranch, or was keeping some party of cowboys supplied with game from day to day.

Tige's Lion

Zane Grey

Sportsmen who have hunted mountain lions are familiar with the details. The rock-ribbed ravines and spear-pointed pines, the patches of snow on the slopes, and the dry stone dust under the yellow cliffs with its pungent animal odor—these characterize the home of the big cat. The baying of the hounds, the cautious pursuit on foot or the long thrilling chase on horseback, ending before a dark cave or under a pine, and the "stand and deliver" with a heavy rifle—these are the features.

I have a story to tell of a hunt that was different.

The time was in May. With Buffalo Jones, the old plainsman, and his cowboys, I was camped on the northern rim of the Grand Canyon of Arizona, in what the Indians once named the Siwash. This heavily timbered plateau, bounded on three sides by the desert and on the fourth side by that strange delusive cleft called the canyon, is as wild and lonely, and as beautiful a place as was ever visited by man. Buckskin Mountain surmounts the plateau, and its innumerable breaks or ravines slope gently into the canyon. Here range thousands of deer and wild mustangs, and mountain lions live fat and unmolested.

On the morning of May 12, when Jones routed us out at five o'clock, as was his custom, a white frost, as deep as a light snow, clothed the forest. The air was nipping. An eager, crackling welcome came from the blazing campfire. Jim raked the hot coals over the lid of his oven. Frank and Lawson trooped in with the horses. Jones, as usual, had trouble with his hounds, particularly the ever-belligerent Tige.

Hounds in that remote section of Arizona retain a majority of their primitive instincts. Most of the time the meat they get they "rustle" for. So, taking the hard life into consideration, Jones' dogs were fairly well-behaved. Tige, a large-framed yellow bloodhound, was young, intractable, and as fierce as a tiger—whence his name. According to the cowboys, Tige was a cross between a locoed coyote and a maverick; in Jones' idea he had all the points of a great lion dog, only he needed his spirit curbed. Tige chased many a lion; he got tongue lashings and lashings of other kind, and even charge of fine shot; but his spirit remained untamed.

We had a captive lion in camp—one Jones had lassoed and brought in a few days before—and Tige had taken the matter as a direct insult to himself. Fight he would, and there was no use to club him. And on this morning when Jones slipped his chain he made for the lion again. After sundry knocks and scratches we dragged Tige to the campfire while we ate breakfast. Even then, with Jones' powerful grasp on his collar, he vented his displeasure and growled. The lion crouched close behind the pine and watched the hound with somber fiery eyes.

"Hurry, boys!" called Jones, in his sharp voice. "We'll tie up a lion this morning, sure as you're born. Jim, you and Lawson stick with us to-day. Yesterday, if we hadn't split, and lost each other, we'd have got one of those lions. If we get separated, keep yelling our signal."

Then he turned to me and shook his big finger: "Listen. I want you to hold in that black demon of a horse you're riding. He'll kill you if you are not careful. He hasn't been broke long. A year ago he was leading a band of wild mustangs over the mountain. Pull him in; hold him tight!"

"Which way?" asked Frank, as he swung into his saddle.

"I reckon it doesn't much matter," replied Jones, with his dry, grim chuckle. "We run across lion sign everywhere, don't we? Let's circle through the woods while the frost stays on."

We rode out under the stately silvered pines, down the long white aisles, with the rising sun tingeing the forest a delicate pink. The impatient hounds, sniffing and whining, trotted after Jones. They crossed fresh deer tracks with never a sign. Here and there deer, a species of mule deer almost as large as elk, bounded up the slopes. A mile or more from camp we ran over a lion trail headed for the mountain.

Sounder, the keenest hound we had, opened up first and was off like a shot. Tige gave tongue and leaped after him; then old Mose, with his short bark, led the rest of the pack. Our horses burst into action like a string of racers at the post. With Frank on his white mustang setting the pace, we drove through the forest glades swift as the wind.

"A hot trail, boys! Hi! Hi! Hi!" yelled Jones.

No need was there to inspire us. The music of the hounds did that. We split the cold air till it sang in our ears; we could scarcely get our breath, and no longer smelt the pine. The fresh and willing horses stretched lower and lower. The hounds passed out of sight into the forest, but their yelps and bays, now low, now clear, floated back to us. Either I forgot Jones' admonition or disregarded it, for I gave my horse, Satan, free rein and, without my realizing it at the time, he moved out ahead of the bunch. Compared to the riders in my rear I was a poor horseman, but as long as I could stick on, what did I care for that? Riding Satan was like sailing on a feather in a storm. Something wild in my blood leaped. My greatest danger lay in the snags and branches of the pines. Half the time I hugged Satan's neck to miss them. Many a knock and a brush I got. Looking backward once I saw I was leaving my companions, and grimly recalling former chases, in the finish of which I had not shown, I called to Satan.

"On! On! On, old fellow! This is our day!"

Then it seemed he had not been running at all. How he responded! His light, long powerful stride was a beautiful thing. The cold, sweet pine air, cutting between my teeth, left a taste in my mouth, and it had the exhilaration of old wine. I rejoiced in the wildness of movement and the indescribable blurred black and white around me; in sheer madness of sensorial perception I let out ringing yells. It was as if I were alone in the woods; it was all mine, and there was joy of chase, of action and of life.

The trail began to circle to the southwest, and in the next mile turned in the direction from which it had come. This meant the lion had probably been close at hand when we struck his trail, and hearing the hounds he had made for the canyon. Down the long, slightly swelling slope Satan thundered, and the pines resembled fence-pickets from a coasting sled. Often I saw gray, bounding flashes against the white background, and knew I had jumped deer. I wondered if any of the hounds were at fault, for sometimes they became confused at the crossing of a fresher scent. Satan kept a steady gait for five miles down the forest slope, and then raced out of the pines into a growth of scrubby oak. I knew I was not now far from the rim of the canyon, and despaired of coming up with the lion. Suddenly I realized I was not following a trail, as the frost had disappeared in the open. Neither did I hear the baying of the hounds. I hauled Satan up and, listening, heard no sound.

"Waa-hoo! Waa-hoo!" I yelled our signal cry. No answer came: only the haunting echo. While I was vainly trying to decide what to do, the dead silence was sharply broken by the deep bay of a hound. It was Tige's voice. In another second I had Satan plunging through the thicket of short oaks. Soon we were among the piñons near the rim of the canyon. Again I reined Satan to a standstill. From this point I could see out into the canyon, and as always, even under the most exciting circumstances, I drew a sharp breath at the wonder, the mystery, the sublimity of the scene. The tips of yellow crags and gray mesas and red turrets rose out of the blue haze of distance. The awful chasm, eighteen miles wide and more than a mile deep, stretched away clear and vividly outlined in the rare atmosphere for a hundred miles. The canyon seemed still wrapped in slumber, and a strange, vast silence that was the silence of ages, hung over the many-hued escarpments and sculptured domes.

Tige's bay, sounding close at hand, startled me and made Satan jump. I slid to the ground, and pulling my little Remington from the saddle, began hunting in the piñons for the hound.

Presently I sighted him, standing with his front paws against a big piñon. Tige saw me, wagged his tail, howled and looked up. Perhaps twenty feet from the ground a full-grown lion stood on branches that were swaying with his weight. He glared down at Tige and waved his long tail. He had a mean face, snarling, vicious. His fat sides heaved and I gathered he was not used to running, and had been driven to his limit.

"Tige, old boy, you're the real thing!" I yelled. "Keep him there!" For an instant I fingered the safety catch on my automatic. I did not much fancy being alone with that old fellow. I had already seen a grim, snarling face and outstretched claws in the air before my eyes—and once was enough! Still I did not want to kill him. Finally I walked cautiously to within fifty feet of him, and when he showed resentment in a slowly crouching movement I hastily snapped a picture of him. Hardly had I turned the film round when he leaped from the tree and bounded away. Knowing he would make for the rim and thus escape I dropped my camera and grabbed up the rifle. But I could not cut loose on him, because Tige kept nipping him, and I feared I might shoot the hound. Tige knew as well as I the intention of the lion and—brave fellow!—he ran between the beast and the canyon and turned him towards the woods. At this great work on the part of Tige I yelled frantically and dashed for my horse. Though the lion had passed close, Satan had not moved from his tracks.

"Hi! Hi! Hi! Take him, Tige!" I screamed, as the black launched out like an arrow.

On the open flat I spied Tige and his quarry, resembling yellow flashes in the scrub oak; and twice the hound jumped the lion. I swore in my teeth. The brave and crazy dog was going to his death. Satan fairly crashed through the thicket and we gained. I saw we were running along a cut-in from the main rim wall, and I thought the lion was making for a break where he could get down. Suddenly I saw him leap high into a pine on the edge of the forest. When I came up Tige was trying to climb the tree.

"Tige, old boy, I guess Jones had you sized up right," I cried, as I dismounted. "If that brute jumps again it will be his last."

At this moment I heard a yell, and I sent out three "Waahoos," which meant "come quickly!" In a few moments Sounder burst out of the forest, then Don, then Mose. How they did yelp! I heard the pounding of hoofs, more yells, and soon Frank dashed into the open, followed by the others. The big tawny lion was in plain sight, and as each hunter saw him a wild yell pealed out.

"Hi! Hi! There he is! Tige, you're the stuff!" cried Jones, whirling off his horse. "You didn't split on deer trails, like the rest of these blasted long-eared canines. You stuck to him, old dog! Well, he's your lion. Boys, spread out now and surround the tree. This is a good tree and I hope we can hold him here. If he jumps he'll get over the rim, sure. Make all the racket you can, and get ready for work when I rope him."

Sounder, Mose, Ranger and Don went wild while Jones began climbing the tree, and as for Tige, he went through antics never before seen in a dog. Jones climbed slowly, laboriously, with his lasso trailing behind him, his brawny arms bare. How grim and cool he looked! I felt sorry for the lion.

"Look out!" called Jim. "Shore thet lion means biz."

"Jones, he's an old cuss, an' won't stand no foolin'," said Frank.

The old buffalo hunter climbed just the same, calmly and deliberately, as if he were unaware of danger.

Lawson, who was afraid of nothing on earth except lions, edged farther and farther from under the pine. The lion walked back up the limb he had gone down, and he hissed and growled. When Jones reached the first fork, the lion spat. His eyes emitted flames; his sharp claws dug into the bark of the limb; he began to show restlessness and fear. All at once he made a quick start, apparently to descend and meet Jones. We yelled like a crew of demons, and he slipped back a bit.

"Far enough!" yelled Frank, and his voice rang.

"Cut me a pole," called Jones.

In a twinkling Frank procured a long sapling and handed it up. Jones hung the noose of his lasso on it, and slowly extended it toward the lion. I snapped a picture here, and was about to take another when Jim yelled to me.

"Here, you with the rifle! Be ready. Shore we'll have hell in a minute."

Hell there was, in less time. With the dexterity of a conjuror Jones slipped the noose over the head of the lion and tightened it. Spitting furiously the lion bit, tore and clawed at the rope.

"Pull him off, boys! Now! Hurry, while the rope is over that short limb. Then we'll hang him in the air for a minute while I come down and lasso his paws. Pull! Pull!"

The boys pulled with all their might but the lion never budged.

"Pull him off, dang it! Pull!" impatiently yelled Jones, punching the lion with the pole.

But the powerful beast would not be dislodged. His long body lengthened on the limb and his great muscles stood out in ridges. There was something grand in his defiance and his resistance. Suddenly Jones grasped the lasso and slid down it, hand over hand.

I groaned in my spirit. What a picture to miss! There I was with a rifle, the only one in the party, and I had to stand ready to protect life if possible—and I had to watch a rare opportunity, one in a lifetime, pass without even a try. It made me sick.

The men strained on the lasso, and shouted; the hounds whined, quivered and leaped into the air; the lion hugged the branch with his brawny paws.

"Throw your weight on the rope," ordered Jones.

For an instant the lion actually held the men off the ground; then with a scratching and tearing of bark he tumbled. But Jones had not calculated on the strength of the snag over which he expected to hang the lion. The snag was rotten; it broke. The lion whirled in the air. Crash! He had barely missed Lawson.

In a flash the scene changed from one of half-comic excitement to one of terrible danger and probably tragedy. There was a chorus of exclamation, and snarls and yelps, all coming from a cloud of dust. Then I saw a yellow revolving body in the midst of furry black whirling objects. I dared not shoot for fear of hitting my friends. Out of this snarling melee the lion sprang towards freedom. Jones pounced upon the whipping lasso, Frank and Jim were not an instant behind him, and the dogs kept at the heels of the lion. He turned on them like an exploding torpedo; then, giving a tremendous bound, straightened the lasso and threw the three men flat on their faces. But they held on.

Suddenly checked, the lion took a side jump bringing the tight lasso in connection with Lawson's flying feet. The frightened fellow had been trying to get out of the way. The lasso tripped him, giving him a hard fall. I tried to bring my rifle to bear just as the lion savagely turned on Lawson. But the brute was so quick, the action of the struggling men so confused and fast that it was impossible. I heard Jones bawl out some unintelligible command; I heard Lawson scream; I saw the flaming-eyed brute, all instinct with savage life, reach out with both huge paws.

It was at this critical instant that Tige bowled pell-mell into the very jaws of the lion. Then began a terrific wrestling combat. The lasso flew out of the hands of Frank and Jim, but the burly Jones, like his great dog, held on. Tige and the lion, fighting tooth and claw, began to roll down the incline. Jones was pulled to his feet, thrown flat again and dragged.

"Grab the rope!" he roared.

But no one could move. Jones rose to his knees, then fell, and lost the lasso.

Hound and lion in a savage clutch of death whirled down, nearer and nearer to the rim wall of the canyon. As they rolled I heard the rend and tear of hide. I knew Tige would never let go, even if he could, and I opened up with the automatic.

I heard the spats of the bullets, and saw fur, blood and gravel fly. On the very verge of the precipice the lion stretched out convulsively. Tige clung to his neck with a grim hold. Then they slipped over the wall.

Silence for a long second—then crash! There came up the rattle of stones, silence for a palpitating second—then crash! It was heavier, farther down and followed by a roar of sliding stones. Silence for a long, long moment. Finally a faint faraway sound which died instantly. The lion king lay at the foot of his throne and Tige lay with him.

Lobo: The King of Currumpaw

From Wild Animals I Have Known, *1899*

Ernest Thompson Seton

Currumpaw is a vast cattle range in northern New Mexico. It is a land of rich pastures and teeming flocks and herds, a land of rolling mesas and precious running waters that at length unite in the Currumpaw River, from which the whole region is named. And the king whose despotic power was felt over its entire extent was an old gray wolf.

Old Lobo, or the king, as the Mexicans called him, was the gigantic leader of a remarkable pack of gray wolves that had ravaged the Currumpaw Valley for a number of years. All the shepherds and ranchmen knew him well, and, wherever he appeared with his trusty band, terror reigned supreme among the cattle, and wrath and despair among their owners. Old Lobo was a giant among wolves, and was cunning and strong in proportion to his size. His voice at night was well-known and easily distinguished from that of any of his fellows. An ordinary wolf might howl half the night about the herdsman's bivouac without attracting more than a passing notice, but when the deep roar of the old king came booming down the cañon, the watcher bestirred himself and prepared to learn in the morning that fresh and serious inroads had been made among the herds.

Old Lobo's band was but a small one. This I never quite understood, for usually, when a wolf rises to the position and power that he had, he attracts a numerous following. It may be that he had as many as he desired, or perhaps his ferocious temper prevented the increase of his pack. Certain is it that Lobo had only five followers during the latter part of his reign. Each of these, however, was a wolf of renown, most of them were above the ordinary size, one in particular, the second in command, was a veritable giant, but even he was far below the leader in size and prowess. Several of the band, besides the two leaders, were especially noted. One of those was a beautiful white wolf that the Mexicans called Blanca; this was supposed to be a female, possibly Lobo's mate. Another was a yellow wolf of remarkable swiftness, which, according to current stories had, on several occasions, captured an antelope for the pack.

It will be seen, then, that these wolves were thoroughly well-known to the cowboys and shepherds. They were frequently seen and oftener heard, and their lives were intimately associated with those of the cattlemen, who would so gladly have destroyed them. There was not a stockman on the Currumpaw who would not readily have given the value of many steers for the scalp of any one of Lobo's band, but they seemed to possess charmed lives, and defied all manner of devices to kill them. They scorned all hunters, derided all poisons, and continued, for at least five years, to exact their tribute from the Currumpaw ranchers to the extent, many said, of a cow each day. According to this estimate, therefore, the band had killed more than two thousand of the finest stock, for, as was only too well-known, they selected the best in every instance.

The old idea that a wolf was constantly in a starving state, and therefore read to eat anything, was as far as possible from the truth in this case, for these freebooters were always sleek and well-conditioned, and were in fact most fastidious about what they ate. Any animal that had died from natural causes, or that was diseased or tainted, they would not touch, and they even rejected anything that had been killed by the stockmen. Their choice and daily food was the tenderer part of a freshly killed yearling heifer. An old bull or cow they disdained, and though they occasionally took a young calf or colt, it was quite clear that veal or horseflesh was not their favorite diet. It was also known that they were not fond of mutton, although they often amused themselves by killing sheep. One night in November, 1893, Blanca and the yellow wolf killed two hundred and fifty sheep, apparently for the fun of it, and did not eat an ounce of their flesh.

These examples of many stories which I might repeat, to show the ravages of this destructive band. Many new devices for their extinction were tried each year, but still they lived and throve in spite of all the efforts of their foes. A great price was set on Lobo's head, and in consequence poison in a score of subtle forms was put out for him, but he never failed to detect and avoid it. One thing only he feared—that was firearms, and knowing full well that all men in this region carried them, he never was known to attack or face a human being. Indeed, the set policy of his band was to take refuge in flight whenever, in the daytime, a man was descried, no matter at what distance. Lobo's habit of permitting the pack to eat only that which they themselves had killed, was in numerous cases their salvation, and the keenness of his scent to detect the taint of human hands or the poison itself, completed their immunity.

On one occasion, one of the cowboys heard the too familiar rallying-cry of Old Lobo, and stealthily approaching, he found the Currumpaw pack in a hollow, where they had 'rounded up' a small herd of cattle. Lobo sat apart on a knoll, while Blanca with the rest was endeavoring to 'cut out' a young cow, which they had selected; but the cattle were standing in a compact mass with their heads outward, and presented to the foe a line of horns, unbroken save when some cow, frightened by a fresh onset of the wolves, tried to retreat into the middle of the herd. It was only by taking advantage of these breaks that the wolves had succeeded at all in wounding the selected cow, but she was far from being disabled, and it seemed that Lobo at length lost patience with his followers, for he left his position on the hill, and, uttering a deep roar, dashed toward the herd. The terrified rank broke at his charge, and he sprang in among them. Then the cattle scattered like the pieces of a bursting bomb. Away went the chosen victim, but ere she had gone twenty-five yards Lobo was upon her. Seizing her by the neck he suddenly held back with all his force and so threw her heavily to the ground. The shock must have been tremendous, for the heifer was thrown heels over head. Lobo also turned a somersault, but immediately recovered himself, and his followers falling on the poor cow, killed her in a few seconds.

Lobo took no part in the killing—after having thrown the victim, he seemed to say, "Now, why could not some of you have done that at once without wasting so much time?"

The man now rode up shouting, the wolves as usual retired, and he, having a bottle of strychnine, quickly poisoned the carcass in three places, then went away, knowing they would return to feed, as they had killed the animal themselves. But next morning, on going to look for his expected victims, he found that, although the wolves had eaten the heifer, they had carefully cut out and thrown aside all those parts that had been poisoned.

The dread of this great wolf spread yearly among the ranchmen, and each year a larger price was set on his head, until at last it reached $1,000, an unparalleled wolf-bounty, surely; many a good man has been hunted down for less. Tempted by the promised reward, a Texan ranger named Tannerey came one day galloping up the cañon of the Currumpaw. He had a superb outfit for wolf-hunting—the best of guns and horses, and a pack of enormous wolf-hounds. Far out on the plains of the Panhandle, he and his dogs had killed many a wolf, and now he never doubted that, within a few days, Old Lobo's scalp would dangle at his saddle-bow.

Away they went bravely on their hunt in the gray dawn of a summer morning, and soon the great dogs gave joyous tongue to say that they were already on the track of their quarry. Within two miles, the grizzly band of Currumpaw leaped into view, and the chase grew fast and furious. The part of the wolf-hounds was merely to hold the wolves at bay till the hunter could ride up and shoot them, and this usually was easy on the open plains of Texas; but here a new feature of the country came into play, and showed how well Lobo had chosen his range; for the rocky cañons of the Currumpaw and its tributaries intersect the prairies in every direction. The old wolf at once made for the nearest of these and by crossing it got rid of the horsemen. His band then scattered and thereby scattered the dogs, and when they reunited at a distant point of course all of the dogs did not turn up, and the wolves no longer outnumbered, turned on their pursuers and killed or desperately wounded them all. That night when Tannerey mustered his dogs, only six of them returned, and of these, two were terribly lacerated. This hunter made two other attempts to capture the royal scalp, but neither of them was more successful than the first, and on the last occasion his best horse met its death by a fall; so he gave up the chase in disgust and went back to Texas, leaving Lobo more than ever the despot of the region.

Next year, two other hunters appeared, determined to win the promised bounty. Each believed he could destroy this noted wolf, the first by means of a newly devised poison, which was to be laid out in an entirely new manner; the other a French Canadian, by poison assisted with certain spells and charms, for he firmly believed that Lobo was a veritable "loup-garou," and could not be killed by ordinary means. But cunningly compounded poisons, charms, and incantations were all of no avail against this grizzly devastator. He made his weekly rounds and daily banquets as aforetime, and before many weeks had passed, Calone and Laloche gave up in despair and went elsewhere to hunt.

In the spring of 1893, after his unsuccessful attempt to capture Lobo, Joe Calone had a humiliating experience, which seems to show that the big wolf simply scorned his enemies, and had absolute confidence in himself. Calone's farm was on a small tributary of the Currumpaw, in a picturesque cañon, and among the rocks of this very cañon, within a thousand yards of the house, old Lobo and his mate selected their den and raised their family that season. There they lived all summer, and killed Joe's cattle, sheep, and dogs, but laughed at all his poisons and traps, and rested securely among the recesses of the cavernous cliffs, while Joe vainly racked his brain for some method of smoking them out, or of reaching them with dynamite. But they escaped entirely unscathed, and continued their ravages as before. "There's where he lived all last summer," said Joe, pointing to the face of the cliff, "and I couldn't do a thing with him. I was like a fool to him."

II

This history, gathered so far from the cowboys, I found hard to believe until in the fall of 1893, I made the acquaintance of the wily marauder, and at length came to know him more thoroughly than anyone else. Some years before, in the Bingo days, I had been a wolf-hunter, but my occupations since then had been of another sort, chaining me to stool and desk. I was much in need of a change, and when a friend, who was also a ranch-owner on the Currumpaw, asked me to come to New Mexico and try if I could do anything with this predatory pack, I accepted the invitation and, eager to make the acquaintance of its king, was as soon as possible among the mesas of that region. I spent some time riding about to learn the country, and at intervals, my guide would point to the skeleton of a cow to which the hide still adhered, and remark, "That's some of his work."

It became quite clear to me that, in this rough country, it was useless to think of pursuing Lobo with hounds and horses, so that poison or traps were the only available expedients. At present we had no traps large enough, so I set to work with poison.

I need not enter into the details of a hundred devices that I employed to circumvent this "loup-garou"; there was no combination of strychnine, arsenic, cyanide, or prussic acid that I did not essay; there was no manner of flesh that I did not try as bait; but morning after morning, as I rode forth to learn the result, I found that all my efforts had been useless. The old king was too cunning for me. A single instance will show his wonderful sagacity. Acting on the hint of an old trapper, I melted some cheese together with the kidney fat of a freshly killed heifer, stewing it in a china dish, and cutting it with a bone knife to avoid the taint of metal. When the mixture was cool, I cut it into lumps, and making a hole in one side of each lump, I inserted a large dose of strychnine and cyanide, contained in a capsule that was impermeable by any odor; finally I sealed the holes up with pieces of the cheese itself. During the whole process, I wore a pair of gloves steeped in the hot blood of the heifer, and even avoided breathing on the baits. When all was ready, I put them in a rawhide bag rubbed all over with blood, and rode forth dragging the liver and kidneys of the beef at the end of a rope. With this I made a ten-mile circuit, dropping a bait at each quarter of a mile, and taking the utmost care, always, not to touch any with my hands.

Lobo, generally, came into this part of the range in the early part of each week, and passed the latter part, it was supposed, around the base of Sierra Grande. This was Monday, and that same evening, as we were about to retire, I heard the deep bass howl of his majesty. On hearing it one of the boys briefly remarked, "There he is, we'll see."

The next morning I went forth, eager to know the result. I soon came on the fresh trail of the robbers, with Lobo in the lead—his track was always easily distinguished. An ordinary wolf's forefoot is 4½ inches long, that of a large wolf 4¾ inches, but Lobo's, as measured a number of times, was 5½ inches from claw to heel; I afterward found that his other proportions were commensurate, for he stood three feet high at the shoulder, and weighed 150 pounds. His trail, therefore, though obscured by those of his followers, was never difficult to trace. The pack had soon found the track of my drag, and as usual followed it. I could see that Lobo had come to the first bait, sniffed about it, and finally had picked it up.

Then I could not conceal my delight. "I've got him at last," I exclaimed; "I shall find him stark within a mile," and I galloped on with eager eyes fixed on the great broad track in the dust. It led me to the second bait and that also was gone. How I exulted—I surely have him now and perhaps several of his band. But there was the broad paw-mark still on the drag; and though I stood in the stirrup and scanned the plain I saw nothing that looked like a dead wolf. Again I followed—to find now that the third bait was gone—and the king-wolf's track led on to the fourth, there to learn that he had not really taken a bait at all, but had merely carried them in his mouth. Then having piled the three on the fourth, he scattered filth over them to express his utter contempt for my devices. After this he left my drag and went about his business with the pack he guarded so effectively.

This is only one of many similar experiences which convinced me that poison would never avail to destroy this robber, and though I continued to use it while awaiting the arrival of the traps, it was only because it was meanwhile a sure means of killing many prairie wolves and other destructive vermin.

About this time there came under my observation an incident that will illustrate Lobo's diabolic cunning. These wolves had at least one pursuit which was merely an amusement, it was stampeding and killing sheep, though they rarely ate them. The sheep are usually kept in flocks of from one thousand to three thousand under one or more shepherds. At night they are gathered in the most sheltered place available, and a herdsman sleeps on each side of the flock to give additional protection. Sheep are such senseless creatures that they are liable to be stampeded by the veriest trifle, but they have deeply ingrained in their nature one, and perhaps only one, strong weakness, namely, to follow their leader. And this the shepherds turn to good account by putting half a dozen goats in the flock of sheep. The latter recognize the superior intelligence of their bearded cousins, and when a night alarm occurs they crowd around them, and usually are thus saved from a stampede and are easily protected. But it was not always so. One night late in last November, two Perico shepherds were aroused by an onset of wolves. Their flocks huddled around the goats, which being neither fools nor cowards, stood their ground and were bravely defiant; but alas for them, no common wolf was heading this attack. Old Lobo, the were-wolf, knew as well as the shepherds that the goats were the moral force of the flock, so hastily running over the backs of the densely packed sheep, he fell on these leaders, slew them all in a few minutes, and soon had the luckless sheep stampeding in a thousand different directions. For weeks afterward I was almost daily accosted by some anxious shepherd, who asked, "Have you seen any stray OTO sheep lately?" and usually I was obliged to say I had; one day it was, "Yes, I came on some five or six carcasses by Diamond Springs;" or another, it was to the effect that I had seen a small "bunch" running on the Malpai Mesa; or again, "No, but Juan Meira saw about twenty, freshly killed, on the Cedra Monte two days ago."

At length the wolf traps arrived, and with two men I worked a whole week to get them properly set out. We spared no labor or pains, I adopted every device I could think of that might help to insure success. The second day after the traps arrived, I rode around to inspect, and soon came upon Lobo's trail running from trap to trap. In the dust I could read the whole story of his doings that night. He had trotted along in the darkness, and although the traps were so carefully concealed, he had instantly detected the first one. Stopping the onward march of the pack, he had cautiously scratched around it until he had disclosed the trap, the chain, and the log, then left them wholly exposed to view with the trap still unsprung, and passing on he treated over a dozen traps in the same fashion. Very soon I noticed that he stopped and turned aside as soon as he detected suspicious signs on the trail and a new plan to outwit him at once suggested itself. I set the traps in the form of an H; that is, with a row of traps on each side of the trail, and one on the trail for the cross-bar of the H. Before long, I had an opportunity to count another failure. Lobo came trotting along the trail, and was fairly between the parallel lines before he detected the single trap in the trail, but he stopped in time, and why or how he knew enough I cannot tell, the Angel of the wild things must have been with him, but without turning an inch to the right or left, he slowly and cautiously backed on his own tracks, putting each paw exactly in its old track until he was off the dangerous ground. Then returning at one side he scratched clods and stones with his hind feet till he had sprung every trap. This he did on many other occasions, and although I varied my methods and redoubled my precautions, he was never deceived, his sagacity seemed never at fault, and he might have been pursuing his career of rapine to-day, but for an unfortunate alliance that proved his ruin and added his name to the long list of heroes who, unassailable when alone, have fallen through the indiscretion of a trusted ally.

III

Once or twice, I had found indications that everything was not quite right in the Currumpaw pack. There were signs of irregularity, I thought; for instance there was clearly the trail of a smaller wolf running ahead of the leader, at times, and this I could not understand until a cowboy made a remark which explained the matter.

"I saw them to-day," he said, "and the wild one that breaks away is Blanca." Then the truth dawned upon me, and I added, "Now, I know that Blanca is a she-wolf, because were a he-wolf to act thus, Lobo would kill him at once."

This suggested a new plan. I killed a heifer, and set one or two rather obvious traps about the carcass. Then cutting off the head, which is considered useless offal, and quite beneath the notice of a wolf, I set it a little apart and around it placed six powerful steel traps properly deodorized and concealed with the utmost care. During my operations I kept my hands, boots, and implements smeared with fresh blood, and afterward sprinkled the ground with the same, as though it had flowed from the head; and when the traps were buried in the dust I brushed the place over with the skin of a coyote, and with a foot of the same animal made a number of tracks over the traps. The head was so placed that there was a narrow passage between it and some tussocks, and in this passage I buried two of my best traps, fastening them to the head itself.

Wolves have a habit of approaching every carcass they get the wind of, in order to examine it, even when they have no intention of eating of it, and I hoped that this habit would bring the Currumpaw pack within reach of my latest stratagem. I did not doubt that Lobo would detect my handiwork about the meat, and prevent the pack approaching it, but I did build some hopes on the head, for it looked as though it had been thrown aside as useless.

Next morning, I sallied forth to inspect the traps, and there, oh, joy! Were the tracks of the pack, and the place where the beef-head and its traps had been was empty. A hasty study of the trail showed that Lobo had kept the pack from approaching the meat, but one, a small wolf, had evidently gone on to examine the head as it lay apart and had walked right into one of the traps.

We set out on the trail, and within a mile discovered that the hapless wolf was Blanca. Away she went, however, at a gallop, and although encumbered by the beef-head, which weighed over fifty pounds, she speedily distanced my companion who was on foot. But we overtook her when she reached the rocks, for the horns of the cow's head became caught and held her fast. She was the handsomest wolf I had ever seen. Her coat was in perfect condition and nearly white.

She turned to fight, and raising her voice in the rallying cry of her race, sent a long howl rolling over the cañon. From far away upon the mesa came a deep response, the cry of Old Lobo. That was her last call, for now we had closed in on her, and all her energy and breath were devoted to combat.

Then followed the inevitable tragedy, the idea of which I shrank from afterward more than at the time. We each threw a lasso over the neck of the doomed wolf, and strained our horses in opposite directions until the blood burst from her mouth, her eyes glazed, her limbs stiffened and then fell limp. Homeward then we rode, carrying the dead wolf, and exulting over this, the first death-blow we had been able to inflict on the Currumpaw pack.

At intervals during the tragedy, and afterward as we rode homeward, we heard the roar of Lobo as he wandered about on the distant mesas, where he seemed to be searching for Blanca. He had never really deserted her, but knowing that he could not save her, his deep-rooted dread of firearms had been too much for him when he saw us approaching. All that day we heard him wailing as he roamed in his quest, and I remarked at length to one of the boys, "Now, indeed, I truly know that Blanca was his mate."

As evening fell he seemed to be coming toward the home cañon, for his voice sounded continually nearer. There was an unmistakable note of sorrow in it now. It was no longer the loud, defiant howl, but a long, plaintive wail; "Blanca! Blanca!" he seemed to call. And as night came down, I noticed that he was not far from the place where we had overtaken her. At length he seemed to find the trail, and when he came to the spot where we had killed her, his heart-broken wailing was piteous to hear. It was sadder than I could possibly have believed. Even the stolid cowboys noticed it, and said they had "never heard a wolf carry on like that before." He seemed to know exactly what had taken place, for her blood had stained the place of her death.

Then he took up the trail of the horses and followed it to the ranch-house. Whether in hopes of finding her there, or in quest of revenge, I know not, but the latter was what he found, for he surprised our unfortunate watchdog outside and tore him to little bits within fifty yards of the door. He evidently came alone this time, for I found but one trail next morning, and he had galloped about in a reckless manner that was very unusual with him. I had half expected this, and had set a number of additional traps about the pasture. Afterward I found that he had indeed fallen into one of these, but such was his strength, he had torn himself loose and cast it aside.

I believed that he would continue in the neighborhood until he found her body at least, so I concentrated all my energies on this one enterprise of catching him before he left the region, and while yet in this reckless mood. Then I realized what a mistake I had made in killing Blanca, for by using her as a decoy I might have secured him the next night.

I gathered in all the traps I could command, one hundred and thirty strong steel wolf-traps, and set them in fours in every trail that led into the cañon; each trap was separately fastened to a log, and each log was separately buried. In burying them, I carefully removed the sod and every particle of earth that was lifted we put in blankets, so that after the sod was replaced and all was finished the eye could detect no trace of human handiwork. When the traps were concealed I trailed the body of poor Blanca over each place, and made of it a drag that circled all about the ranch, and finally I took off one of her paws and made with it a line of tracks over each trap. Every precaution and device known to me I used, and retired at a late hour to await the result.

Once during the night I thought I heard Old Lobo, but was not sure of it. Next day I rode around, but darkness came on before I completed the circuit of the north cañon, and I had nothing to report. At supper one of the cowboys said, "There was a great row among the cattle in the north cañon this morning, maybe there is something in the traps there." It was afternoon of the next day before I got to the place referred to, and as I drew near a great grizzly form arose from the ground, vainly endeavoring to escape, and there revealed before me stood Lobo, King of the Currumpaw, firmly held in the traps. Poor old hero, he had never ceased to search for his darling, and when he found the trail her body had made he followed it recklessly, and so fell into the snare prepared for him. There he lay in the iron grasp of all four traps, perfectly helpless, and all around him were numerous tracks showing how the cattle had gathered about him to insult the fallen despot, without daring to approach within his reach. For two days and two nights he had lain there, and now was worn out with struggling. Yet, when I went near him, he rose up with bristling mane and raised his voice, and for the last time made the cañon reverberate with his deep bass roar, a call for help, the muster call of his band. But there was none to answer him, and, left alone in his extremity, he whirled about with all his strength and made a desperate effort to get at me. All in vain, each trap was a dead drag of over three hundred pounds, and in their relentless fourfold grasp, with great steel jaws on every foot, and the heavy logs and chains all entangled together, he was absolutely powerless. How his huge ivory tusks did grind on those cruel chains, and when I ventured to touch him with my rifle-barrel he left grooves on it which are there to this day. His eyes glared green with hate and fury, and his jaws snapped with a hollow "chop," as he vainly endeavored to reach me and my trembling horse. But he was worn out with hunger and struggling and loss of blood, and he soon sank exhausted to the ground.

Something like compunction came over me, as I prepared to deal out to him that which so many had suffered at his hands.

"Grand old outlaw, hero of a thousand lawless raids, in a few minutes you will be but a great load of carrion. It cannot be otherwise." Then I swung my lasso and sent it whistling over his head. But not so fast; he was yet far from being subdued, and, before the supple coils had fallen on his neck he seized the noose and, with one fierce chop, cut through its hard thick strands, and dropped it in two pieces at his feet.

Of course I had my rifle as a last resource, but I did not wish to spoil his royal hide, so I galloped back to the camp and returned with a cowboy and a fresh lasso. We threw to our victim a stick of wood which he seized in his teeth, and before he could relinquish it our lassoes whistled through the air and tightened on his neck.

Yet before the light had died from his fierce eyes, I cried, "Stay, we will not kill him; let us take him alive to the camp." He was so completely powerless now that it was easy to put a stout stick through his mouth, behind his tusks, and then lash his jaws with a heavy cord which was also fastened to the stick. The stick kept the cord in, and the cord kept the stick in so he was harmless. As soon as he felt his jaws were tied he made no further resistance, and uttered no sound, but looked calmly at us and seemed to say, "Well, you have got me at last, do as you please with me." And from that time he took no more notice of us.

We tied his feet securely, but he never groaned, nor growled, nor turned his head. Then with our united strength were just able to put him on my horse. His breath came evenly as though sleeping, and his eyes were bright and clear again, but did not rest on us. Afar on the great rolling mesas they were fixed, his passing kingdom, where his famous band was now scattered. And he gazed till the pony descended the pathway into the cañon, and the rocks cut off the view.

By travelling slowly we reached the ranch in safety, and after securing him with a collar and a strong chain, we staked him out in the pasture and removed the cords. Then for the first time I could examine him closely, and proved how unreliable is vulgar report when a living hero or tyrant is concerned. He had *not* a collar of gold about his neck, nor was there on his shoulders an inverted cross to denote that he had leagued himself with Satan. But I did find on one haunch a great broad scar, that tradition says was the fang-mark of Juno, the leader of Tannerey's wolf-hounds—a mark which she gave him the moment before he stretched her lifeless on the sand of the cañon.

I set meat and water beside him, but he paid no heed. He lay calmly on his breast, and gazed with those steadfast yellow eyes away past me down through the gateway of the cañon, over the open plains—his plains—nor moved a muscle when I touched him. When the sun went down he was still gazing fixedly across the prairie. I expected he would call up his band when night came, and prepared for them, but he had called once in his extremity, and none had come; he would never call again.

A lion shorn of his strength, an eagle robbed of his freedom, or a dove bereft of his mate, all die, it is said, of a broken heart; and who will aver that this grim bandit could bear the threefold brunt, heart-whole? This only I know; that when the morning dawned, he was lying there still in his position of calm repose, but his spirit was gone—the old king-wolf was dead.

I took the chain from his neck, a cowboy helped me to carry him to the shed where lay the remains of Blanca, and as we laid him beside her, the cattle-man exclaimed: "There, you *would* come to her, now you are together again."

My Antelope

From A Woman Tenderfoot, *1900*

Grace Gallatin Thompson Seton

It was a week later when I did something which those old guides could understand and appreciate—I made a dead shot. I committed a murder, and from that time, the brotherhood of pards was open to us, had we cared to join. It was all because I killed an antelope.

Nimrod and I started out that morning with the understanding that, if we saw an antelope, I was to have a chance.

In about six miles, Nimrod spied two white specks moving along the rocky ridge to the east of us, which rose abruptly from the plain where we were. I was soon able to make out that they were antelope. But the antelope had also seen us, and there was as much chance of getting near to them, by direct pursuit, as of a snail catching a hare. So we rode on calmly northward for half a mile, making believe we had not seen them, until we passed out of sight behind a long hill. Then we began an elaborate detour up the mountain, keeping well out of sight, until we judged that the animals, providing they had not moved, were below us, under the rocky ledge nearly a mile back.

We tied up the horses on that dizzy height, and stole, Nimrod with a carbine, I with the rifle, along a treacherous, shaly bank which ended, twenty feet below, in the steep rocky bluffs that formed the face of the cliff. Every step was an agony of uncertainty as to how far one would slide, and how much loose shale one would dislodge to rattle down over the cliff and startle the antelope we hoped were there. To move about on a squeaking floor without disturbing a light sleeper is child's play compared with our progress. A misstep would have sent us flying over the cliff, but I did not think of that—my only care was not to startle the shy fleet-footed creatures we were pursuing. I hardly dared to breathe; every muscle and nerve was tense with the long suspense.

Suddenly I clutched Nimrod's arm and pointed at an oblong tan coloured bulk fifty yards above us on the mountain.

"Antelope! Lying down!" I whispered in his ear. He nodded and motioned me to go ahead. I crawled nearer, inch by inch, my gaze riveted on that object. It did not move. I grew more elated the nearer it allowed me to approach. It was not so very hard to get at an antelope, after all. I felt astonishingly pleased with my performance. Then—rattle, crash—and a stone went bounding down. What a pity, after all my painful contortions not to do it! I instantly raised the rifle to get a shot before the swift animal went flying away.

But it was strangely quiet. I stole a little nearer—and then turned and went gently back to Nimrod. He was convulsed with silent and unnecessary laughter. My elaborate stalk had been made on—a nice buff stone.

We continued our precarious journey for another quarter of a mile, when I motioned that I was going to try to get a sight of the antelope, which, according to my notion, were under the rock some hundred feet below, and signed to Nimrod to stay behind.

Surely my guardian angel attended that descent. I slid down a crack in the rock three feet wide, which gave me a purchase on the sides with my elbows and left hand. The right hand grasped the rifle, to my notion an abominably heavy awkward thing. One of these drops was eight feet, another twelve. A slip would probably have cost me my life. Then I crawled along a narrow ledge for about the width of a town-house front, and, making another perilous slide, landed on a ledge so close to the creatures I was hunting that I was as much startled as they.

Away those two beautiful animals bounded, their necks proudly arched and their tiny feet hitting the only safe places with unerring aim. They were far out of range before I thought to get my rifle in position, and my random shot only sent them farther out on the plain, like drifting leaves on autumn wind.

It was impossible to return the way I had come; so I rolled and jumped and generally tumbled to the grassy hill below, and waited for Nimrod to go back along the shaly stretch, and bring down the horses the way they had gone up.

Then we took some lunch from the saddle bags and sat down in the waving, yellow grass of the foot hill with a sweep of miles before us, miles of grassy tableland shimmering in the clear air like cloth of gold in the sun, where cattle grow fat and the wild things still are at home.

During lunch Nimrod tried to convince me that he knew all the time that the antelope I stalked on the mountainside was a stone. Of course wives should believe their husbands. The economy of State and Church would collapse otherwise. However, the appearance of a large band of antelope, a sight now very rare even in the Rockies, caused the profitless discussion to be engulfed in the pursuit of the real thing.

The antelope were two miles away, mere specks of white. We could not tell them from the twinkling plain until they moved. We mounted immediately and went after those antelope—by pretending to go away from them. For three hours, we drew nearer to the quietly browsing animals. We hid behind low hills, and crawled down a water-course, and finally dismounted behind the very mound of prairie on the other side of which they were resting, a happy, peaceful family. There were twenty does, and proudly in their midst moved the king of the harem, a powerful buck with royal horns.

The crowning point of my long day's hunt was before me. That I should have my chance to get one of the finest bucks ever hunted was clear. What should I do, should I hit or miss? Fail! What a thought—never!

Just then a drumming of hoofs which rapidly faded away showed that the wind had betrayed us and the whole band was off like a flight of arrows.

"Shoot! Shoot!" cried Nimrod, but my gun was already up and levelled on the flying buck—now nearly a hundred yards away.

Bang! The deadly thing went forth to do its work. Sliding another cartridge into the chamber, I held ready for another shot.

There was no need. The fleet-footed monarch's reign was over, and already he had gone to his happy hunting ground. The bullet had gone straight to his heart, and he had not suffered. But the does, the twenty beating hearts of his harem! There they were, not one hundred yards away, huddled together with ears erect, tiny feet alert for the next bound—yet waiting for their lord and master, the proud tyrant, so strangely still on the ground. Why did he not come? And those two creatures whose smell they feared—why did he stay so near?

They took a few steps nearer and again waited, eyes and ears and uplifted hoofs asking the question, "Why doesn't he come? Why does he let those dreadful creatures go so close?" Then, as we bent over their fallen hero, they knew he was forever lost to them, and fear sent them speeding out of sight.

The Woman Afield

From **Game Bird Shooting,** *1931*

Capt. Charles Askins

I DOUBT IF MANY WOMEN REALLY BECOME FOND OF DUCK shooting. Blinds are cramped, messy, sometimes muddy, and the weather is liable to be bad. Perhaps the most attractive shooting is quail hunting in the South, horseback. The wide fields of cotton and corn, the winding paths through the pine woods, the half hidden, clapboard covered cabin, with its brood of scurrying small blacks, the wide ranging dogs, the stand, the brisk canter to reach a point are all romance, lived again as in days of old. Then the winter evenings in the old mansion house with a great hickory-wood fire going in the open fireplace, the men collecting in that room for a mint julep—maybe the girls too—as all watch the table being loaded by smiling blacks, with the good things that a man or a woman would like to eat after a hard day in the saddle, bring out the idealism, and the poetry and the romance that never seems to be deeply hidden in the souls of women.

Chicken shooting was in high favor with women, in the days not very long gone by. The outfit was a good prairie team, hitched to a buckboard, with a crate of dogs on the back. Two saddle horses were included, now to be ridden and now tied on behind. Shells, lunch, blankets and wraps were under the seat. The air was clear, the dying grass had a sweet smell, and the yellowing Nebraska prairies stretched far away on every hand. Roads were no more than trails, rarely followed for fences were few.

The chickens and the sharp-tailed grouse would break cover presently, or maybe mallards from the cane-bordered lake. The coyotes barked saucily at danger, the chickens cackled derisively as the sun flashed on whirring wings, and the mallards swam out into the middle of the lake, unafraid.

Presently horses were mounted, guns in scabbard, and the dogs cast off. They whipped the waving grass, and passed over a ridge, there to be found standing. Dismounting, the girl killed her first chicken with the first shot. Noon came and the lunch was spread under the shade of the cottonwoods that grew in the yard of a deserted sod-house, with a lone bevy of quail chirping from the weed-grown garden.

I remember a likable and companionable woman who shot in those days—a capital shot she was. I was chicken shooting in Nebraska, along the Big Piney River when they came out. The Baron and Baroness Cederstrom, and Count von Meltendorff were from Washington, attached to foreign legations. I was asked to look after them for a week or two, so established them in a double log cabin on the Piney, twenty miles out. The Baron and Count spoke excellent English, better than I did, and the Madame should have, for she was a Virginia girl.

Once the Baron learned that there were brook trout in the Piney, no chicken shooting could I get out of him. He whipped that stream all day, fried his trout, and ate quantities of them. The Count shot chickens when Madame gave him a chance. The Count was a good staunch walker, but couldn't ride a horse after the first half day, and anyway, Madame told him to drive the wagon and take care of the red dog which belonged to her and couldn't be put in the crate with other dogs. All of us did precisely what the lady told us, except the Baron. The Madame rode like a Western girl and shot like a Southern girl and looked like a million dollars.

There you have us, then. Above the bluffs of the Piney the level prairie rolled away to the north far into the Dakotas. Patches of wild rosebuds gleamed in the morning sun. Now a great flock of chickens climbed out of a deeper swale where the grass grew rank, and now a flow of sharptails broke from a thicket of choke-cherries. The black and white setter ranged far and wide, going a slashing gait, but the lemon colored pointer investigated scent and drew straight to his points. Back of them rode the Baroness and I, sometimes slowly, again at a sharp canter as the dogs disappeared over a ridge and didn't come back. Yet back of us came the Count, holding the red setter on chain, gun between his knees, driving a pair of stout Western broncs. Now and then we would find the dogs on stand, and motion to the Count to come on, which he would do at a gallop. Just before he got there the Madame's eyes would begin to shine, and she would cluck to the yellow pointer—all the signal he needed to draw in and flush. The big, brown birds jumped and cackled all about, and we killed and missed, not missing often.

The Count drove up in time to see it all, holding to the red dog, trying to load is gun, watching the pointer creeping in and knowing just what would happen. It was all so evidently the fault of the pointer, Tim, and he didn't dare to swear, even in German, even at Tim. The Madame was smiling and there was mischief in her eyes, as she expressed demure regret at the shooting the Count had missed. Then we mounted and rode on, while Count von Meltendorff drove slowly after us. What he thought, nobody ever knew. He paid a certain penalty for hunting with a beautiful woman, as one time and another all of us have.

Is shooting good for women? I do not know. Why not? I have always looked upon it from the standpoint of a man. A woman brings into the sport a fresh enthusiasm, an abandonment of sheer enjoyment that the man may have lost with the days of his early youth.

And so if the Madame thinks she would like to shoot by all means buy her a gun, teach her how to handle it, and take her along. Or if it is a daughter or a cousin or a sweetheart, buy her a gun and take her along. A woman never was so safe from sentiment as she is when whole heartedly engaged in shooting, with a man whose time is fully occupied with his own end of the game.

The Mountain Goat at Home

William T. Hornaday, Sc.D.

John Phillips and I were scrambling along the steep and rough eastern face of Bald Mountain, a few yards below timberline, half-way up 'twixt creek and summit. He was light of weight, well-seasoned and nimble-footed; I was heavy, ill-conditioned, and hungry for more air. Between the sliderock, down timber and brush, the going had been undeniably bad, and in spite of numerous rests I was almost fagged.

Far below us, at the bottom of the V-shaped valley, the horse-bell faintly tinkled, and as Mack and Charlie whacked out the trail, the packtrain crept forward. We were thankful that the camping-place, on Goat Pass, was only a mile beyond.

Presently we heard a voice faintly shouting to us from below.

"Look above you—at the *goats!*"

Hastily we moved out of a brush-patch, and looked aloft. At the top of the precipice that rose above our slope, a long, irregular line of living forms perched absurdly on the sky-line, and looked over the edge, at us. Quickly we brought our glasses to bear, and counted fourteen living and wild Rocky Mountain goats.

"All nannies, young billies, and kids," said Mr. Phillips. "They are trying to guess what kind of wild animals we are." I noticed that he was quite calm; but I felt various things which seemed to sum themselves up in the formula—"the Rocky Mountain goat—*at last!*"

For fully ten minutes, the entire fourteen white ones steadfastly gazed down upon us, with but few changes of position, and few remarks. Finally, one by one they drew back from the edge of the precipice, and quietly drifted away over the bald crest of the mountain.

For twenty years I had been reading the scanty scraps of mountain-goat literature that at long intervals have appeared in print. I had seen seven specimens alive in captivity, and helped to care for four of them. With a firm belief that the game was worth it, I had traveled twenty-five hundred miles or more in order to meet this strange animal in its own home, and cultivate a close acquaintance with half a dozen wild flocks.

At three o'clock we camped at timberline, on a high and difficult pass between the Elk River and the Bull. That night we christened the ridge Goat Pass. While the guides and the cook unpacked the outfit and pitched the tents, Mr. Phillips hurried down the western side of the divide. Fifteen minutes later he and Kaiser—in my opinion the wisest hunting-dog in British Columbia—had twenty-eight nanny goats and kids at bay on the top of a precipice, and were photographing them at the risk of their lives.

Rifle and glass in hand, I sat down on a little knoll a few yards above the tents, to watch a *lame* billy goat who was quietly grazing and limping along the side of a lofty ridge that came down east of us from Phillips Peak. A lame wild animal in a country wherein a shot had not been fired for five years, was, to all of us, a real novelty; and with my glasses I watched the goat long and well. It was his left foreleg that was lame, and it was the opinion of the party that the old fellow was suffering from an accident received on the rocks. Possibly a stone had been rolled down upon him, by another goat.

Suddenly sharp cries of surprise came up from the camp, and I sprang up to look about. *Three goats were running past the tents* at top speed—a big billy, and two smaller goats.

"Hi, there! Goats! Goats!" cried Smith and Norboe.

The cook was stooping over the fire, and looking under his right arm he saw the bunch charging straight toward him, at a gallop. A second later, the big billy was almost upon him.

"*Hey! You son-of-a-gun!*" yelled Huddleston, and as the big snow-white animal dashed past him he struck it across the neck with a stick of firewood. The goat's tracks were within six feet of the campfire.

The billy ran straight through the camp, then swung sharply to the left, and the last I saw of him was his humpy hindquarters wildly bobbing up and down among the dead jack pines, as he ran for Bald Mountain.

The two smaller goats held their course, and one promptly disappeared. The other leaped across our water-hole, and as it scrambled out of the gully near my position, and paused for a few seconds to look backward, instinctively I covered it with my rifle. But only for an instant. "Come as they may," thought I, "my first goat shall *not* be a small one!" And as the goat turned and raced on up, my .303 Savage came down.

We laughed long at the utter absurdity of three wild goats actually breaking into the privacy of our camp, on our first afternoon in Goatland. In the Elk Valley, Charlie Smith had promised me that we would camp "right among the goats," and he had royally kept his word.

At evening, when we gathered round the campfire, and counted up, we found that on our first day in Goatland, we had seen a total of fifty-three goats; and no one had fired a shot. As for myself, I felt quite set up over my presence of mind in *not* firing at the goat which I had "dead to rights" after it had invaded our camp, and which might have been killed as a measure of self-defence.

Our camp was pitched in a most commanding and awe-inspiring spot. We were precisely at timberline, in a grassy hollow on the lowest summit between Bald and Bird Mountains, on the north, and Phillips Peak, on the south. From our tents the ground rose for several hundred feet, like the cables of the Brooklyn Bridge, until it stopped against a rock wall which went on up several hundred feet more. In a notch quite near us was a big bank of eternal ice. In that country, such things are called glaciers; and its melting foot was the starting-point of Goat Creek. Fifty paces taken eastward from our tents brought us to a projecting point from which we looked down a hundred feet to a rope of white water, and on down Goat Creek as it drops five hundred feet to the mile, to the point where it turns a sharp corner to the right, and disappears.

Westward of camp, after climbing up a hundred feet or so, through dead standing timber, the ridge slopes steeply down for a mile and a half to the bottom of a great basin half filled with green timber, that opens toward Bull River. It was on this slope, at a point where a wall of rock cropped out, that Mr. Phillips cornered his flock of goats and photographed them.

At our camp, water and wood were abundant; there was plenty of fine grass for our horses, spruce boughs for our beds, scenery for millions, and what more could we ask?

The day following our arrival on Goat Pass was dull and rainy, with a little snow, and we all remained in camp. At intervals, someone would stroll out to our lookout point above Goat Creek, and eye-search the valley below "to see if an old silver-tip could come a-moochin' up, by accident," as Guide Smith quaintly phrased it.

That gray day taught me something of color values in those mountains. As seen from our lookout point, the long, even stretch of house-roof mountain-slope on the farther side of Goat Creek was a revelation. In the full sunlight of a clear day, its tints were nothing to command particular attention. Strong light seemed to take the colors out of everything. But a cloudy day, with a little rain on the face of nature, was like new varnish on an old oil-painting.

During the forenoon, fleecy white clouds chased each other over the pass and through our camp, and for much of the time the Goat Creek gorge was cloud-filled. At last, however, about noon, they rose and drifted away, and then the mountain opposite revealed a color pattern that was exquisitely beautiful.

For a distance of a thousand yards the ridge-side stretched away down the valley, straight and even; and in that distance it was furrowed from top to bottom by ten or twelve gullies, and ribbed by an equal number of ridges. At the bottom of the gorge was a dense green fringe of tall, obelisk spruces, very much alive. In many places, ghostly processions of dead spruces, limbless and gray, forlornly climbed the ridges, until half-way up the highest stragglers stopped. Intermixed with these tall poles were patches of trailing juniper of a dark olive-green color, growing tightly to the steep slope.

The apex of each timbered ridge was covered with a solid mass of great willow-herb or "fireweed" (*Chamaenerion anguistifolium*), then in its brightest autumn tints of purple and red. The brilliant patches of color which they painted on the mountainside would have rejoiced the heart of an artist. This glorious plant colored nearly every mountainside in that region during our September there.

Below the fireweed, the ridges were dotted with small, cone-shaped spruces, and trailing junipers (*Juniperus prostrata*), of the densest and richest green. The grassy sides of the gullies were all pale yellow—green, softly blended at the edges with the darker colors that framed them in. At the bottom of each washout was a mass of light-gray sliderock, and above all this rare pattern of soft colors loomed a lofty wall of naked carboniferous limestone rock, gray, grim and forbidding.

It seemed to me that I never elsewhere had seen mountains so rich in colors as the ranges between the Elk and the Bull in that particular September.

The rain and the drifting clouds were with us for one day only. Very early on the second morning, while Mr. Phillips and I lay in our sleeping-bags considering the grave question of getting or not getting up, Mack Norboe's voice was heard outside, speaking low but to the point:

"Director, there's an old billy goat, lying right above our camp!"

It was like twelve hundred volts. We tumbled out of our bags, slipped on our shoes, and ran out. Sure enough, a full-grown male goat was lying on the crest of the divide that led up to the summit of Bald Mountain, seventy-five feet above us, and not more than two hundred and fifty yards away. The shooting of him was left to me.

I think I could have bagged that animal as he lay; but what would there have been in that of any interest to a sportsman? I had not asked any goats to come down to our camp, and lie down to be shot!

Not caring greatly whether I got that goat or not, I attempted a stalk along the western side of the ridge, through the dead timber, and well below him. But the old fellow was not half so sleepy as he looked. When finally I came up to a point that was supposed to command his works, I found that he had winded me. He had vanished from his resting-place, and was already far up the side of Bald Mountain, conducting a masterly retreat.

After a hurried breakfast, we made ready for a day with the goats on the northern mountains. Although there are many things in favor of small parties—the best consisting of one guide and one hunter—we all went together—Mr. Phillips, Mack, Charlie and I. Our leader declared a determination to "see the Director shoot his first goat," and I assured the others that the services of all would be needed in carrying home my spoils.

As we turned back toward camp, and took time to look "at the sceneries," the view westward, toward Bull River, disclosed a cloud effect so beautiful that Mr. Phillips insisted upon photographing it, then and there. To give the "touch of life" which he always demanded, I sat in, as usual.

By Mr. Phillips' advice, I put on suspenders and loosened my cartridge-belt, in order to breathe with perfect freedom. We wore no leggings. Our shoes were heavily hobnailed, and while I had thought mine as light as one dared use in that region of ragged rocks, I found that for cliff-climbing they were too heavy, and too stiff in the soles. Of course knee-breeches are the thing, but they should be so well cut that in steep climbing they will not drag on the knees, and waste the climber's horsepower; and there should be a generous opening at the knee.

In those mountains, four things, and only four, are positively indispensable to every party: rifles, axes, fieldglasses and blankets. Each member of our hunting party carried a good glass, and never stirred from camp without it. For myself, I tried an experiment. Two months previously Mrs. Hornaday selected for me, in Paris, a very good opera-glass, made by Lemaire, with a field that was delightfully large and clear. While not quite so powerful a magnifier as the strongest binoculars now on the market, its field was so much clearer that

I thought I would prefer it. It was much smaller than any regulation fieldglass, and I carried it either in a pocket of my trousers, or loose inside my hunting-shirt, quite forgetful of its weight.

It proved a great success. We found much interest in testing it with binoculars five times as costly, and the universal verdict was that it would reveal an animal as far as a hunter could go to it, and find it. I mention this because in climbing I found it well worthwhile to be free from a dangling leather case that is always in the way, and often is too large for comfort.

From our camp we went north, along the top of the eastern wall of Bald Mountain. Two miles from home we topped a sharp rise, and there directly ahead, and only a quarter of a mile away on an eastern slope lay a band of eleven goats, basking in the welcome sunshine. The flock was composed of nannies, yearling billies and kids, with not even one old billy among those present. Two old chaperons lay with their heads well up, on the lookout, but all the others lay full length upon the grass, with their backs uphill. Three of the small kids lay close against their mothers.

They were on the northerly point of a fine mountain meadow, with safety rocks on three sides. Just beyond them lay a ragged hogback of rock, both sides of which were so precipitous that no man save an experienced mountaineer would venture far upon it. It was to this rugged fortress that the goats promptly retreated for safety when we left off watching them, and rose from our concealment. Their sunning-ground looked like a sheep-yard, and we saw that goats had many times lain upon that spot.

Nearby, behind a living windbreak, was a goat-bed, that looked as if goats had lain in it five hundred times. By some curious circumstance, a dozen stunted spruces had woven themselves together, as if for mutual support, until they formed a tight evergreen wall ten feet long and eight feet high. It ranged north and south, forming an excellent hedge-like shield from easterly winds, while the steep mountain partially cut off the winds from the west. On the upper side of that natural windbreak, the turf had been worn into dust, and the droppings were several inches deep. Apparently it was liked because it was a good shelter, in the center of a fine sky-pasture, and within a few jumps of ideal safety rocks.

From the spot where the goats had lain, looking ahead and to our left, we beheld a new mountain. Later on we christened it Bird Mountain, because of the flocks of ptarmigan we found upon its summit. Near its summit we saw five more goats, all females and kids. At our feet lay a deep, rich-looking basin, then a low ridge, another basin with a lakelet in it, and beyond that another ridge, much higher than the first. Ridge No. 2 had dead timber upon it, but it was very scattering, for it was timberline; and its upper end snugged up against the eastern wall of Bird Mountain. Later on we found that the northern side of that ridge ended in a wall of rock that was scalable by man in one place only.

"Yonder are two big old billies!" said someone with a glass in action.

"Yes sir; there they are; all alone, and heading this way, too. Those are your goats this time, Director, sure enough."

"Now boys," said I, "if we can stalk those two goats successfully, and bag them both, neatly and in quick time, we can call it genuine goat-hunting!"

They were distant about a mile and a half, jogging along down a rocky hill, through a perfect maze of gullies, ridges, grassplots and rocks, one of them keeping from forty to fifty feet behind the other.

Even at that distance they looked big, and very, very white. Clearly, they were heading for Bird Mountain. We planned to meet them wherever they struck the precipitous side of the mountain ahead of us, and at once began our stalk.

From the basin which contained the little two-acre tarn, the rocky wall of Bird Mountain rose almost perpendicularly for about eight hundred feet. As we were passing between the lake and the cliff, we heard bits of loose rock clattering down.

"Just look yonder!" said Mr. Phillips, with much fervor.

Close at hand, and well within fair rifle-shot, were four goats climbing the wall; and two more were at the top, looking down as if deeply interested. The climbers had been caught napping, and being afraid to retreat either to right or left, they had elected to seek safety by climbing straight up! It was a glorious opportunity to see goats climb in a difficult place, and forthwith we halted and watched as long as the event lasted, utterly oblivious of our two big billies. Our binoculars brought them down to us wonderfully well, and we saw them as much in detail as if we had been looking a hundred feet with the unaided eye.

The wall was a little rough, but the angle of it seemed not more than 10 degrees from perpendicular. The footholds were merely narrow edges of rock, and knobs the size of a man's fist. Each goat went up in a generally straight course, climbing slowly and carefully all the while. Each one chose its own course, and paid no attention to those that had gone before. The eyes looked ahead to select the route, and the front hoofs skillfully sought for footholds. It seemed as if the powerful front legs performed three-fourths of the work, reaching up until a good foothold was secured, then lifting the heavy body by main strength, while the hindlegs "also ran." It seemed that the chief function of the hind limbs was to keep what the forelegs won. As an exhibition of strength of limb, combined with surefootedness and nerve, it was marvelous, no less.

Often a goat would reach toward one side for a new foothold, find none, then rear up and pivot on its hindfeet, with its neck and stomach pressed against the wall, over to the other side. Occasionally a goat would be obliged to edge off five or ten feet to one side in order to scramble on up. From first to last, no goat slipped and no rocks gave way under their feet, although numerous bits of loose sliderock were disturbed and sent rattling down.

It was a most inspiring sight, and we watched it with breathless interest. In about ten minutes the four goats had by sheer strength and skill climbed about two hundred feet of the most precipitous portion of the cliff, and reached easy going. After that they went on up twice as rapidly as before, and soon passed over the summit, out of our sight. Then we compared notes.

Mr. Phillips and I are of the opinion that nothing could have induced mountain sheep to have made that appalling climb, either in the presence of danger or otherwise. Since that day we have found that there are many mountain hunters who believe that as a straightaway cliff-climber, the goat does things that are impossible for sheep.

As soon as the goat-climbing exhibition had ended, we hurried on across the basin, and up the side of Ridge No. 2. This ridge bore a thin sprinkling of low spruces, a little fallen timber, much purple fireweed and some good grass. As seen at a little distance, it was a purple ridge. The western end of it snugged up against the mountain, and it was there that we met our two big billy goats. They had climbed nearly to the top of our ridge, close up to the mountain, and when we first sighted them they were beginning to feed upon a lace-leaved anemone (*Pulsatilla occidentalis*), at the edge of their newly found pasture. We worked toward them, behind a small clump of half-dead spruces, and finally halted to wait for them to come within range.

After years of waiting, Rocky Mountain goats, *at last!* How amazingly white and soft they look; and how big they are! The high shoulder hump, the big, round barrel of the body, and the knee-breeches on the legs make the bulk of the animal seem enormous. The whiteness of "the driven snow," of cotton and of paper seem by no means to surpass the incomparable white of those soft, fluffy-coated animals as they appear in a setting of hard, gray limestone, rugged sliderock and dark-green vegetation. They impressed me as being the whitest living objects I ever beheld, and far larger than I had expected to find them. In reality, their color had the effect of magnifying their size; for they looked as big as two-year-old buffaloes.

Of course only Mr. Phillips and I carried rifles; and we agreed that the left man should take the left animal.

"It's a hundred and fifty yards!" said Mack Norboe, in a hoarse whisper.

My goat was grazing behind the trunk of a fallen tree, which shielded his entire body. I waited, and waited; and there he stood, with his head down, and calmly cropped until I became wildly impatient. I think he stood in one spot for five minutes, feeding upon *Pulsatilla*.

"Why don't you shoot?" queried Phillips, in wonder.

"I can't! My goat's hiding behind a tree."

"Well, fire when you're ready, Gridley, and I'll shoot when you do!"

It must have been five minutes, but it seemed like twenty-five, before that goat began to feel a thrill of life along his keel, and move forward. The annoying suspense had actually made me unsteady; besides which, my Savage was a new one, and unchristened. Later on I found that the sights were not right for me, and that my first shooting was very poor.

At last my goat stood forth, in full view—white, immaculate, high of hump, low of head, big and bulky. I fired for the vitals behind the shoulder.

"You've overshot!" exclaimed Norboe, and

"Bang!" said Mr. Phillips' Winchester.

Neither of us brought down our goat at the first fire!

I fired again, holding much lower, and the goat reared up a foot. Mr. Phillips fired again, whereupon his goat fell over like a sack of oats, and went rolling down the hill. My goat turned to run, and as he did so I sent two more shots after him. Then he disappeared behind some rocks. Mack, John and I ran forward, to keep him in sight, and fire more shots if necessary. But no goat was to be seen.

"He can't get away!" said Norboe, reassuringly.

"He's *dead!*" said I, by way of an outrageous bluff. "You'll find him down on the sliderock!" But inwardly I was torn by doubts.

We hurried down the steep incline, and presently came to the top of a naked wall of rock. Below that was a wide expanse of sliderock.

"Thar he is!" cried Norboe. "Away down yonder, out on the sliderock, dead as a wedge."

From where he stood when I fired, the goat had run back about two hundred feet, where he fell dead, and then began to roll. We traced him by a copious stream of blood on the rocks. He fell down the rock wall, for a hundred feet, in a slanting direction, and then—to my great astonishment—he rolled two hundred feet farther (by measurement) on that ragged, jagged slide rock before he fetched up against a particularly large chunk of stone, and stopped. We expected to find his horns broken, but they were quite uninjured. The most damage had been inflicted upon his nose, which was badly cut and bruised. The bullet that ended his life (my second shot) went squarely through the valves of his heart; but I regret to add that one thigh-bone had been broken by another shot, as he ran from me.

Mr. Phillips' goat behaved better than mine. It rolled down the grassy slope, and lodged on a treacherous little shelf of earth that overhung the very brink of the precipice. One step into that innocent-looking fringe of green juniper bushes meant death on the sliderock below; and it made me nervous to see Mack and Charlie stand there while they skinned the animal.

As soon as possible we found the only practicable route down the rock wall, and scrambled down. The others say that I slid down the last twenty feet; but that is quite immaterial. I reached the goat a few paces in advance of the others, and thought to divert my followers by reciting a celebrated quotation beginning, "To a hunter, the moment of triumph," etc. As I laid my hand upon the goat's hairy side and said my little piece, I heard a deadly "click."

"Got him!" cried Mr. Phillips; and then three men and a dog laughed loud and derisively. Since seeing the picture I have altered that quotation, to this: "To a hunter, the moment of humiliation is when the first sees his idiotic smile on a surreptitious plate." It is inserted solely to oblige Mr. Phillips, as evidence of the occasion when he got ahead of me.

The others declared that the goat was "a big one, though not the very biggest they ever grow." Forthwith we measured him; and in taking his height we shoved his foreleg up until the elbow came to the position it occupies under the standing, living animal. The measurements were as follows:

Rocky Mountain Goat *Oreamnos montanus*	
Male, six years old. Killed September 8, 1905, near the Bull River, British Columbia.	
	Inches
Standing height at shoulder	38
Length, nose to root of tail	59.25
Length of tail vertebrae	3.50
Girth behind foreleg	55
Girth around abdomen	58
Girth of neck behind ears (unskinned)	18
Circumference of forearm, skinned	11.25
Width of chest	14
Length of horn on curve	9.75
Spread of horns at tips	5
Circumference of horn at base	5.60
Circumference of front hoof	10.50
Circumference of rear hoof	7.75
Base of ear to end of nostrils	10.50
Front corner of eye to rear corner	9
nostril opening	7
Widest spread of ears, tip to tip	15
Total weight of animal by scales, allowing 8 lbs. for blood lost	258 lbs.

The black and naked glands in the skin behind the horn were on that date small, and inconspicuous; but they stood on edge, with the naked face of each closely pressed against the base of the horn in front of it.

On another occasion I shot a thin old goat that stood forty-two inches high at the shoulders, and Mr. Phillips shot another that weighed two hundred and seventy-six pounds. After we had thoroughly dissected my goat, weighed it, examined the contents of its stomach, and saved a good sample of its food for close examination at camp, we tied up the hindquarters, head and pelt, and set out for camp.

And thus ended our first day in the actual hunting of mountain goats, in the course of which we saw a total of forty-two animals. The stalking, killing and dissecting of our two goats was very interesting, but the greatest event of the day was our opportunity to watch those five goats climb an almost perpendicular cliff.

This day, also, was the eleventh of September . . .

Mr. Phillips, Charlie Smith and I descended the steep side of Goat Pass, crossed the basin and slowly climbed the grassy divide that separates it from the source of Avalanche Creek. When half way down the southern side of that divide, we looked far up the side of Phillips Peak and saw two big old billy goats of shootable size. They were well above timberline, lying where a cloud-land meadow was suddenly chopped off at a ragged precipice. The way up to them was long, and very steep.

"That's a long climb, Director," said Mr. Phillips; "but there are no bad rocks."

I said that I could make it, in time—as compared with eternity—if the goats would wait for me.

"Oh, they'll wait! We'll find 'em there, all right," said Charlie, confidently. So we started.

As nearly as I can estimate, we climbed more than a mile, at an angle that for the upper half of the distance was about 30 degrees—a very steep ascent. At first our way up led through green timber, over smooth ground that was carpeted with needles of spruce and pine. That was comparatively easy, no more difficult, in fact, than climbing the stairs of four Washington monuments set one upon another.

At climbing steep mountains, Mr. Phillips, Charlie Smith and the two Norboes are perfect friends. They are thin, tough and long-winded, and being each of them fully forty pounds under my weight, I made no pretence at trying to keep up with them. As it is in an English workshop, the slowest workman set the pace.

In hard climbing, almost every Atlantic-coast man perspires freely, and is very extravagant in the use of air. It frequently happened that when half way up a high mountain, my lungs consumed the air so rapidly that a vacuum was created around me, and I would have to stop and wait for a new supply of oxygen to blow along. My legs behaved much better than my lungs, and to their credit be it said that they never stopped work until my lungs ran out of steam.

As I toiled up that long slope, I thought of a funny little engine that I saw in Borneo, pulling cars over an absurd wooden railway that ran from the bank of the Sadong River to the coalmines. It would run about a mile at a very good clip, then suddenly cease pulling, and stop. Old Walters, the superintendent, said:

"There's only one thing ails that engine. The bloomin' little thing can't make steam fast enough!"

I was like that engine. I couldn't "keep steam"; and whenever my lungs became a perfect vacuum, I had to stop and rest, and collect air. Considering the fact that there was game above us, I thought my comrades were very considerate in permitting me to set the pace. Now had someone glared at me with the look of a hungry cannibal, and hissed between his teeth, "*Step lively!*" it would have made me feel quite at home.

In due time we left the green timber behind us, and started up the last quarter of the climb. There we found stunted spruces growing like scraggy brush, three feet high, gnarled and twisted by the elements, and enfeebled by the stony soil on which they bravely tried to grow. Only the bravest of trees could even rear their heads on that appalling steep, scorched by the sun, rasped by the wind, drenched by the rains and frozen by the snow. But after a hundred yards or so, even the dwarf spruces gave up the struggle. Beyond them, up to our chosen point, the mountain-roof was smooth and bare, except for a sprinkle of fine, flat sliderock that was very treacherous stuff to climb over.

"Let me take your rifle, Director!" said Charlie, kindly.

"No, thank you. I'll carry it up, or stay down. But you may keep behind me if you will, and catch me if I start to roll!"

On steep slopes, such as that was, my companions had solemnly warned me not to fall backward and start rolling; for a rolling man gathers no moss. A man bowling helplessly down a mountainside at an angle of 30 degrees quickly acquires a momentum which spells death. Often have I looked down a horribly steep stretch, and tried to imagine what I would feel, and *think,* were I to overbalance backward, and go bounding down. A few hours later we saw a goat carcass take a frightful roll down a slope not nearly so steep as where we climbed up, and several times it leaped six feet into the air.

To keep out of the sight of the goats it was necessary for us to bear well toward our left; and this brought us close to the edge of the precipice, where the mountainside was chopped off. In view of the loose stones underfoot, I felt like edging more to the right; for the twin chances of a roll down and a fall over began to abrade my nerves. Mr. Phillips and Charlie climbed along so close to the drop that I found myself wondering which of them would be the first to slip and go over.

"Keep well over this way, Director, or the goats may wind you!" said Charlie, anxiously.

"That's all right, Charlie; he's winded now!" said John.

I said we would rest on that; and before I knew the danger, Mr. Phillips had taken a picture of me, resting, and smiling a most idiotic smile.

At last we reached the pinnacle which we had selected when we first sighted our game. As nearly as we could estimate, afterward, by figuring up known elevations, we were at a height of about nine thousand feet, and though not the highest, it was the dizziest point I ever trod. Except when we looked ahead, we seemed to be fairly suspended in mid-air! To look down under one's elbow was to look into miles of dizzy, bottomless space.

The steep slope had led us up to the sharp point of a crag that stuck up like the end of a man's thumb and terminated in a crest as sharp as the comb of a houseroof. Directly in front, and also on the left, was a sheer drop. From the right, the ragged edge of the wall ran on up, to the base of Phillips Peak. Beyond our perch, twelve feet away, there yawned a great basin-abyss, and on beyond that rocky gulf rose a five-hundred-foot wall at the base of the Peak. A little to the right of our position another ragged pinnacle thrust its sharp apex a few feet higher than ours, and eventually caused me much trouble in securing my first shot.

We reached the top of our crag, and peered over its highest rocks just in time to see our two goats quietly walk behind a ragged point of rock farther up the wall, and disappear. They were only a hundred and fifty yards distant; but they had not learned of our existence, and were not in the least alarmed. Naturally, we expected them to saunter back into view, for we felt quite sure they did not mean to climb down that wall to the bottom of the basin. So we lay flat upon the slope, rifles in hand, and waited, momentarily expecting the finish. They were due to cross a grassy slope between two crags, not more than forty feet wide, and if not fired at within about *ten seconds* of their reappearance, they would be lost behind the rocks! The chance was not nearly so good as it looked.

But minutes passed, and no goats returned. It became evident that the dawdling pair had lain down behind the sheltering crag, for a siesta in the sun. We composed ourselves to await their pleasure, and in our first breath of opportunity, looked off southeasterly, over the meadow whereon the two goats had been feeding. And then we saw a sight of sights.

Rising into view out of a little depression on the farther side of the meadow, lazily sauntering along, there came ten big, snow-white billy goats! They were heading straight toward us, and there was not a nanny, nor a kid, nor even a young billy in the bunch. The air was clear; the sun was shining brightly, the meadow was like dark olive-brown plush, and how grandly those big, pure-white creatures did loom up! When first seen they were about four hundred yards away, but our glasses made the distance seem only one-third of that.

For more than an hour we lay flat on our pinnacle, and watched those goats. No one thought of time. It was a chance of a lifetime. My companions were profoundly surprised by the size of the collection; for previous to that moment, no member of our party ever had seen more than four big male goats in one bunch.

The band before us was at the very top of a sky-meadow of unusual luxuriance, which climbed up out of the valley on our right, and ran on up to the comb of rock that came down from Phillips Peak. In area the meadow was five hundred yards wide, and half a mile long. Afterward, when we walked over it, we found it was free from stones, but full of broad steps, and covered with a dense, greenish-purple matting of ground verdure that was as soft to the foot as the thickest pile carpet. The main body of this verdure is a moss-like plant called mountain avens, closely related to cinquefoil, and known botanically as *Dryas octopetala*. It has a very pretty leaf measuring about 7/16 by 3/16 inches, with finely serrated edges. In September a mass of it contains a mixture of harmonious colors: olive-green, brown, gray and purple. On this the goats were feeding. This plant is very common in those mountains above timberline, especially on southern slopes; but it demands a bit of ground almost exclusively for itself, and thrives best when alone.

Along with this there grew a moss-like saxifrage (*Saxifraga austromontana*), which to any one not a botanist seems to be straight moss. It grows in cheerful little clumps of bright green, and whenever it is found on a mountain-pasture, one is pleased to meet it.

I record these notes here, because our ten goats had been in no hurry. They were more than deliberate; they were almost stagnant. In an hour, the farthest that any one of them moved was about one hundred yards, and most of them accomplished even less than that. They were already so well fed that they merely minced at the green things around them. Evidently they had fed to satiety in the morning hours, before we reached them.

As they straggled forward, they covered about two acres of ground. Each one seemed steeped and sodden in laziness. When out grazing, our giant tortoises move faster than they did on that lazy afternoon. When the leader of this band of weary Willies reached the geographical center of the sky-meadow, about two hundred yards from us, he decided to take a sunbath on the most luxurious basin possible to him. Slowly he focused his mind upon a level bench of earth, about four feet wide. It contained an old goat-bed of loose earth, and upon this he lay down, with his back uphill.

At this point, however, he took a sudden resolution. After about a minute of reflection, he decided that the head of his bed was too high and too humpy; so, bracing himself back with his right foreleg, like an ancient Roman senator at a feast, he set his left leg in motion and flung out from under his breast a quantity of earth. The loose soil rose in a black shower, two feet high, and the big hoof flung it several feet down the hill. After about a dozen rakes, he settled down to bask in the warm sunshine, and blink at the scenery of Avalanche Valley.

Five minutes later, a little higher up the slope, another goat did the same thing; and eventually two or three others laid down. One, however, deliberately sat down on his haunches, dog-fashion, with his back uphill. For fully a quarter of an hour he sat there in profile, slowly turning his head from side to side, and gazing at the scenery while the wind blew through his whiskers.

So far as I could determine, no sentinel was posted. There was no leader, and no individual seemed particularly on the alert for enemies. One and all, they felt perfectly secure.

In observing those goats one fact became very noticeable. At a little distance, their legs looked very straight and stick-like, devoid of all semblance of gracefulness and of leaping power. The animals were very white and immaculate—as were all the goats that we saw—and they stood out with the sharpness of clean snow-patches on dark rock. Nature may have known about the much overworked principle of "protective coloration" when she fashioned the mountain goat, but if so, she was guilty of cruelty to goats in clothing this creature with pelage which, in the most comfortable season for hunting, renders it visible for three miles or more. Even the helpless kidling is as white as cotton, and a grand mark for eagles.

That those goats should look so stiff and genuinely ungraceful on their legs, gave me a distinct feeling of disappointment. From that moment I gave up all hope of ever seeing a goat perform any feats requiring either speed or leaping powers; for we saw that of those short, thick legs—nearly as straight as four Indian clubs—nothing is to be expected save power in lifting and sliding, and rocklike steadfastness. In all the two hundred and thirty-nine goats that we saw, we observed nothing to disprove the conclusive evidence of that day regarding the physical powers of the mountain goat.

While we watched the band of mountain loafers, still another old billy goat, making No. 13, appeared across the rock basin far to our left. From the top of the northern ridge, he set out to walk across the wide rock wall that formed the western face of Phillips Peak. From where we were the wall seemed almost smooth, but to the goat it must have looked otherwise. Choosing a narrow, light-gray line of stratification that extended across the entire width of the wall, the solitary animal set out on its promenade. The distance to be traversed to reach the uppermost point of our sky-pasture was about fifteen hundred feet, and the contour line chosen was about four hundred feet above our position. The incident was like a curtain-raiser to a tragic play.

That goat's walk was a very tame performance. The animal plodded steadily along, never faster, never slower, but still with a purposeful air, like a postman delivering mail. For a mountain goat, not pursued or frightened, it was a rapid walk, probably three miles an hour. Its legs swung to and fro with the regularity and steadiness of four pendulums, and I think they never once paused. The animal held to that one line of stratification, until near the end of its promenade. There a great mass of rock had broken away from the face of the cliff, and the goat was forced to climb down about fifty feet, then up again, to regain its chosen route. A few minutes later its ledge ran out upon the apex of the sky-meadow. There Billy paused for a moment, to look about him; then he picked out a soft spot, precisely where the steep slope of the meadow ended against the rocky peak, and lay down to rest.

Up to that time, Mr. Phillips and I had killed only one goat each, and as we lay there we had time to decide upon the future. He resolved to kill one fine goat as a gift to the Carnegie Museum, and I wished two more for my own purposes. We decided that at a total of three goats each—two less than our lawful right—we would draw the line, and kill no more.

The first shot at the pair of invisible goats was to be mine; and as already suggested, the circumstances were like those surrounding a brief moving target in a shooting-gallery. Before us were two rocky crag-points, and behind the one on the left, the animals lay hidden for full an hour. Between the two crags the V-shaped spot of the meadow, across which I knew my goat would walk or run, looked very small. If he moved a yard too far, the right-hand crag would hide him from me until he would be three hundred yards away. I was compelled to keep my rifle constantly ready, and one eye to the front, in order to see my goat in time to get a shot at him while he crossed that forty feet of ground.

And after all, I came ever so near to making a failure of my vigil. I was so absorbed in watching that unprecedented band of billies that before I knew it, the two goats were in the center of the V-shaped stage, and moving at a good gait across it. Horrors!

Hurriedly I exclaimed to Mr. Phillips, "There they are!" took a hurried aim at the tallest goat, and just as his head was going out of sight, let go. He flinched upward at the shoulders, started forward at a trot, and instantly disappeared from my view.

The instant my rifle cracked, Mr. Phillips said, imperatively,

"Don't move! Don't make a sound, and those goats will stay right where they are."

Instantly we "froze." All the goats sprang up, and stood at attention. All looked fixedly in our direction, but the distant eleven were like ourselves, frozen into statues. In that band not a muscle moved for fully three minutes.

Finally the goats decided that the noise they had heard was nothing at which to be alarmed. One by one their heads began to move, and in five minutes their fright was over. Some went on feeding, but three or four of the band decided that they would saunter down our way and investigate that noise.

But what of my goat?

John slid over to my left, to look as far as possible behind the intercepting crag. Finally he said,

"He's done for! He's lying out there, dead."

As soon as possible I looked at him; and sure enough, he lay stretched upon the grass, back uphill, and apparently very dead. The other goat had gone on and joined the ten.

The investigating committee came walking down toward us with a briskness which soon brought them within rifle-shot; and then Mr. Phillips picked out his Carnegie Museum goat and opened fire, at a range of about three hundred yards. The first shot went high, but at the next the goat came down, hit behind the shoulder. This greatly alarmed all the other goats, but they were so confused that three of them came down toward us at a fast trot. At two hundred yards I picked out one, and fired. At my third shot, it fell, but presently scrambled up, ran for the edge of the precipice and dropped over out of sight. It landed, mortally wounded, on some ragged rocks about fifty feet down, and to end its troubles a shot from the edge quickly finished it.

Mr. Phillips killed his first goat, and before the bunch got away, broke the leg of another. This also got over the edge of the precipice, and had to be finished up from the edge.

But a strange thing remains to be told.

By the time Mr. Phillips and I had each fired about two shots of the last round, in the course of which we ran well over to the right in order to command the field, to our blank amazement my first goat—*the dead one!*—staggered to his feet, and started off toward the edge of the precipice. It was most uncanny to see a dead animal thus come to life!

"Look, Director," cried Charlie Smith, "your first goat's come to life! Kill him again! Kill him again, quick!"

I did so; and after the second killing he remained dead. I regret to say that in my haste to get those goats measured, skinned and weighed before night, I was so absorbed that I forgot to observe closely where my first shot struck the goat that had to be killed twice. I think however, that it went through his liver and other organs without touching the vital portions of the lungs.

My first goat was the tallest one of the six we killed on that trip, but not the heaviest. He was a real patriarch, and decidedly on the downhill side of life. He was so old that he had but two incisor teeth remaining, and they were so loose they were almost useless. He was thin in flesh, and his pelage was not up to the mark in length. But in height he was tall, for he stood forty-two inches at the shoulders, with the foreleg pushed up where it belongs in a standing animal.

Mr. Phillips' Carnegie Museum goat was the heaviest one shot on that trip, its gross weight being two hundred and seventy-six pounds.

Charlie decided to roll the skinned carcass of my goat down the mountain, if possible within rifle-shot of the highest point of green timber, in the hope that a grizzly might find it, and thereby furnish a shot. He cut off the legs at the knees, and started the body rolling on the sky-pasture, end over end. It went like a wheel, whirling down at a terrific rate, sometimes jumping fifty feet. It went fully a quarter of a mile before it reached a small basin, and stopped. The other carcass, also, was rolled down. It went sidewise, like a bag of grain, and did not roll quite as far as the other.

By the time we had finished our work on the goats—no trifling task—night was fast approaching, and leaving all the heads, skins and meat for the morrow, we started for our new camp, five miles away.

We went down the meadow (thank goodness!), and soon struck the green timber; and then we went on down, down, and still farther down, always at thirty degrees, until it seemed to me we never would stop going down, never reach the bottom and the trail. But everything earthly has an end. At the end of a very long stretch of plunging and sliding, we reached Avalanche Creek, and drank deeply of the icy-cold water for which we had so long been athirst.

After three miles of travel down the creek, over sliderock, through green timber, yellow willows, more green timber and some down timber, we heard the cheerful whack of Huddleston's axe, and saw on tree-trunk and bough the ruddy glow of the new campfire.

The new camp was pitched in one of the most fascinating spots I ever camped within. The three tents stood at the southern edge of a fine, open grove of giant spruces that gave us good shelter on rainy days. Underneath the trees there was no underbrush, and the ground was deeply carpeted with dry needles. Grand mountains rose on either hand, practically from our campfire, and for our front view a fine valley opened southward for six miles, until its lower end was closed by the splendid mass of Roth Mountain and Glacier. Close at hand was a glorious pool of icewater, and firewood "to burn." Yes, there was one other feature, of great moment, abundant grass for our horses, in the open meadow in front of the tents.

To crown all these luxuries, Mr. Phillips announced that, according to mountain customs already established, and precedents fully set, that camp would then and there be named in my honor—"Camp Hornaday." What more could any sportsman possibly desire?

Red Letter Days in British Columbia

Lt. Townsend Whelen

IN THE MONTH OF JULY, 1901, MY PARTNER, BILL ANDREWS, and I were at a small Hudson Bay post in the northern part of British Columbia, outfitting for a long hunting and exploring trip in the wild country to the North. The official map showed this country as "unexplored," with one or two rivers shown by dotted lines. This map was the drawing card which had brought us thousands of miles by rail, stage and pack train to this out-of-the-way spot. By the big stove in the living room of the factor's house we listened to weird tales of this north country, of its enormous mountains and glaciers, its rivers and lakes and of the quantities of game and fish. The factor told us of three men who had tried to get through there in the Klondike rush several years before and had not been heard from yet. The trappers and Siwashes could tell us of trails which ran up either side of the Scumscum, the river on which the post stood, but no one knew what lay between that and the Yukon to the north.

We spent two days here outfitting and on the morning of the third said goodbye to the assembled population and started with our pack train up the east bank of the Scumscum. We were starting out to live and travel in an unknown wilderness for over six months, and our outfit may perhaps interest my readers: We had two saddle horses, four pack horses and a dog. A small tent formed one pack cover. We had ten heavy army blankets, which we used for saddle blankets while traveling, they being kept clean by using canvas sweat pads under them. We were able to pack 150 pounds of grub on each horse, divided up as nearly as I can remember as follows: One hundred and fifty pounds flour, 50 pounds sugar, 30 pounds beans, 10 pounds rice, 10 pounds dried apples, 20 pounds prunes, 30 pounds corn meal, 20 pounds oatmeal, 30 pounds potatoes, 10 pounds onions, 50 pounds bacon, 25 pounds salt, 1 pound pepper, 6 cans baking powder, 10 pounds soap, 10 pounds tobacco, 10 pounds tea, and a few little incidentals weighing probably 10 pounds. We took two extra sets of shoes for each horse, with tools for shoeing, 2 axes, 25 boxes of wax matches, a large can of gun oil, canton flannel for gun rags, 2 cleaning rods, a change of underclothes, 6 pairs of socks and 6 moccasins each, with buckskin for resoling, toilet articles, 100 yards of fishing line, 2 dozen fish hooks, an oil stove, awl, file, screw-driver, needles and thread, etc.

For cooking utensils we had 2 frying pans, 3 kettles to nest, 2 tin cups, 3 tin plates and a gold pan. We took 300 cartridges for each of our rifles. Bill carried a .38–55 Winchester, model '94, and I had my old .40–72 Winchester, model '95, which had proved too reliable to relinquish for a high-power small bore. Both rifles were equipped with Lyman sights and carefully sighted. As a precaution we each took along extra front sights, firing pins and main-springs, but did not have a chance to use them. I loaded the ammunition for both rifles myself, with black powder, smokeless priming, and lead bullets. Both rifles proved equal to every emergency.

Where the post stood the mountains were low and covered for the most part with sage brush, with here and there a grove of pines or quaking aspen. As our pack train wound its way up the narrow trail above the river bank we saw many Siwashes spearing salmon, a very familiar sight in that country. These gradually became fewer and fewer, then we passed a miner's cabin and a Siwash village with its little log huts and its hay fields, from which grass is cut for the winter consumption of the horses. Gradually all signs of civilization disappeared, the mountains rose higher and higher, the valley became a cañon, and the roar of the river increased, until finally the narrowing trail wound around an outrageous corner with the river a thousand feet below, and looming up in front of us appeared a range of snow-capped mountains, and thus at last we were in the haven where we would be.

That night we camped on one of the little pine-covered benches above the cañon. My, but it was good to get the smell of that everlasting sage out of our nostrils, and to take long whiffs of the balsam-ladened air! Sunset comes very late at this latitude in July, and it was an easy matter to wander up a little draw at nine in the evening and shoot the heads of three grouse. After supper it was mighty good to lie and smoke and listen to the tinkle of the horse bells as they fed on the luscious mountain grass. We were old campmates, Bill and I, and it took us back to many trips we had had before, which were, however, to be surpassed many times by this one. I can well remember how as a boy, when

I first took to woods loafing, I used to brood over a little work which we all know so well, entitled, "Woodcraft," by that grand old man, "Nessmuk," and particularly that part where he relates about his eight-day tramp through the then virgin wilderness of Michigan. But here we were, starting out on a trip which was to take over half a year, during which time we were destined to cover over 1,500 miles of unexplored mountains, without the sight of a human face or an axe mark other than our own.

The next day after about an hour's travel, we passed the winter cabin of an old trapper, now deserted, but with the frames for stretching bear skins and boards for marten pelts lying around—betokening the owner's occupation. The dirt roof was entirely covered with the horns of deer and mountain sheep, and we longed to close our jaws on some good red venison. Here the man-made trails came to an end, and henceforth we used the game trails entirely. These intersect the country in every direction, being made by the deer, sheep and caribou in their migrations between the high and low altitudes. In some places they were hardly discernible, while in others we followed them for days, when they were as plainly marked as the bridle paths in a city park. A little further on we saw a whole family of goats sunning themselves on a high bluff across the river, and that night we dined on the ribs of a fat little spike buck which I shot in the park where we pitched our tent.

To chronicle all the events which occurred on that glorious trip would, I fear, tire my readers, so I will choose from the rich store certain ones which have made red-letter days in our lives. I can recollect but four days when we were unable to kill enough game or catch enough fish to keep the table well supplied, and as luck would have it, those four days came together, and we nearly starved. We had been camped for about a week in a broad wooded valley, having a glorious loaf after a hard struggle across a mountain pass, and were living on trout from a little stream alongside camp, and grouse which were in the pine woods by the thousands. Tiring of this diet we decided to take a little side trip and get a deer or two, taking only our three fattest horses and leaving the others behind to fatten up on the long grass in the valley, for they had become very poor owing to a week's work high up above timber line. The big game here was all high up in the mountains to escape the heat of the valley. So we started one morning, taking only a little tea, rice, three bannocks, our bedding and rifles, thinking that we would enjoy living on meat straight for a couple of days. We had along with us a black mongrel hound named Lion, belonging to Bill. He was a fine dog on grouse but prone to chase a deer once in a while.

About eight miles up the valley could be seen a high mountain of green serpentine rock and for many days we had been speculating on the many fine bucks which certainly lay in the little ravines around the base, so we chose this for our goal. We made the top of the mountain about three in the afternoon, and gazing down on the opposite side we saw a little lake with good horse feed around it and determined to camp there. About half way down we jumped a doe and as it stood on a little hummock Bill blazed away at it and undershot. This was too much for Lion, the hound, and he broke after the deer, making the mountainside ring with his baying for half an hour. Well, we hunted all the next day, and the next, and never saw a hair. That dog had chased the deer all out of the country with his barking.

By this time our little grub-stake of rice, bannocks and tea was exhausted, and, to make things worse, on the third night we had a terrific hail storm, the stones covering the ground three inches deep. Breakfast the next morning consisted of tea alone and we felt pretty glum as we started out, determining that if we did not find game that day we would pull up stakes for our big camp in the valley. About one o'clock I struck a fresh deer trail and had not followed it long before three or four others joined it, all traveling on a game trail which led up a valley. This valley headed up about six miles from our camp in three little ravines, each about four miles long. When I got to the junction of these ravines it was getting dark and I had to make for camp. Bill was there before me and had the fire going and some tea brewing, but nothing else. He had traveled about twenty miles that day and had not seen a thing. I can still see the disgusted look on his face when he found I had killed nothing. We drank our tea in silence, drew our belts tighter and went to bed.

The next morning we saddled up our horses and pulled out. We had not tasted food for about sixty hours and were feeling very faint and weak. I can remember what an effort it was to get into the saddle and how sick and weak I felt when old Baldy, my saddle horse, broke into a trot. Our way back led near the spot where I had left the deer trail the night before, and we determined to ride that way hoping that perhaps we might get a shot at them. Bill came first, then Loco, the pack horse, and I brought up the rear. As we were crossing one of the little ravines at the head of the main valley Loco bolted and Bill took after him to drive him back into the trail. I sat on my horse idly watching the race, when suddenly I saw a mouse-colored flash and then another and heard the thump, thump of cloven feet. Almost instantly the whole ravine seemed to be alive with deer. They were running in every direction. I leaped from my horse and cut loose at the nearest, which happened to be a doe. She fell over a log and I could see her tail waving in little circles and knew I had her. Then I turned on a big buck on the other side of the ravine and at the second shot he stumbled and rolled into the little stream. I heard Bill shooting off to the left and yelled to him that we had enough, and he soon joined me, saying he had a spike buck down. It was the work of but a few minutes to dress the deer and soon we had a little fire going and the three livers hanging in little strips around it. Right here we three, that is, Bill, the dog and myself, disposed of a liver apiece, and my! how easily and quickly it went—the first meat in over a week. Late that night we made our horse camp in the lower valley, having to walk all the way as our horses packed the meat. The next day was consumed entirely with jerking meat, cooking and eating. We consumed half the spike buck that day. When men do work such as we were doing their appetites are enormous, even without a fast of four days to sharpen them up.

One night I well remember after a particularly hard day with the pack train through a succession of wind-falls. We killed a porcupine just before camping and made it into a stew with rice, dough balls, onions and thick gravy, seasoned with curry. It filled the kettle to within an inch of the top and we ate the whole without stopping, whereat Bill remarked that it was enough for a whole boarding-house. According to the catalogue of Abercrombie and Fitch that kettle held eight quarts.

We made it the rule while our horses were in condition, to travel four days in the week, hunt two and rest one. Let me chronicle a day of traveling; it may interest some of you who have never traveled with a pack train. Arising at the first streak of dawn, one man cooked the breakfast while the other drove in the horses. These were allowed to graze free at every camping place, each horse having a cow bell around its neck, only Loco being hobbled, for he had a fashion of wandering off on an exploring expedition of his own and leading all the other horses with him. The horses were liable to be anywhere within two miles of camp, and it was necessary to get behind them to drive them in. Four miles over these mountains would be considered a pretty good day's work in the East. Out here it merely gave one an appetite for his breakfast. If you get behind a pack of well-trained horses they will usually walk right straight to camp, but on occasions I have walked, thrown stones and cussed from seven until twelve before I managed to get them in. Sometimes a bear will run off a pack of horses. This happened to us once and it took two days to track them to the head of a canon, fifteen miles off, and then we had to break Loco all over again.

Breakfast and packing together would take an hour, so we seldom got started before seven o'clock. One of us rode first to pick out the trail, then followed the four pack horses and the man in the rear, whose duty it was to keep them in the trail and going along. Some days the trail was fine, running along the grassy south hillsides with fine views of the snow-capped ranges, rivers, lakes and glaciers; and on others it was one continual struggle over fallen logs, boulders, through ice-cold rivers, swifter than the Niagara rapids, and around bluffs so high that we could scarcely distinguish the outlines of the trees below. Suppose for a minute that you have the job of keeping the horses in the trail. You ride behind the last horse, lazily watching the train. You do not hurry them as they stop for an instant to catch at a whiff of bunch grass beside the trail. Two miles an hour is all the speed you can hope to make. Suddenly one horse will leave the trail enticed by some particularly green grass a little to one side, and leaning over in your saddle you pick up a stone and hurl it at the delinquent, and he falls into line again. Then everything goes well until suddenly one of the pack horses breaks off on a faint side trail going for all he is worth. You dig in your spurs and follow him down the mountain side over rocks and down timber until he comes to a stop half a mile below in a thicket of quaking aspen. You extricate him and drive him back. The next thing you know one of the horses starts to buck and you notice that his pack is turning; then everything starts at once. The pack slides between the horse's legs, he bucks all the harder, the frying pan comes loose, a side pack comes off and the other horses fly in every direction. Perhaps in an hour you have corralled the horses, repacked the cause of your troubles and are hitting the trail again. In another day's travel the trail may lead over down timber and big boulders and for eight solid hours you are whipping the horses to make them jump the obstructions, while your companion is pulling at the halters.

Rustling with a pack train is a soul-trying occupation. Where possible we always aimed to go into camp about three in the afternoon. Then the horses got a good feed before dark—they will not feed well at night—and we had plenty of time to make a comfortable camp and get a good supper. We seldom pitched our tent on these one-night camps unless the weather looked doubtful, preferring to make a bed of pine boughs near the fire. The blankets were laid on top of a couple of pack sheets and the tent over all.

For several days we had been traveling thus, looking for a pass across a long snow-capped mountain range which barred our way to the north. Finally we found a pass between two large peaks where we thought we could get through, so we started up. When we got up to timber line the wind was blowing so hard that we could not sit on our horses. It would take up large stones the size of one's fist and hurl them down the mountain side. It swept by us cracking and roaring like a battery of rapid-fire guns. To cross was impossible, so we back-tracked a mile to a spot where a little creek crossed the trail, made camp and waited. It was three days before the wind went down enough to allow us to cross.

The mountain sheep had made a broad trail through the pass and it was easy to follow, being mostly over shale rock. That afternoon, descending the other side of the range, we camped just below timber line by a little lake of the most perfect emerald hue I have ever seen. The lake was about a mile long. At its head a large glacier extended way up towards the peaks. On the east was a wall of bright red rock, a thousand feet high, while to the west the hillside was covered with dwarf pine trees, some of them being not over a foot high and full-grown at that. Below our camp the little stream, the outlet of the lake, bounded down the hillside in a succession of waterfalls. A more beautiful picture I have yet to see. We stayed up late that night watching it in the light of the full moon and thanked our lucky stars that we were alive. It was very cold; we put on all the clothes we owned and turned in under seven blankets. The heavens seemed mighty near, indeed, and the stars crackled and almost exploded with the still silver mountains sparkling all around. We could hear the roar of the waterfalls below us and the bells of the horses on the hillside above. Our noses were very cold. Far off a coyote howled and so we went to sleep—and instantly it was morning.

I arose and washed in the lake. It was my turn to cook, but first of all I got my telescope and looked around for signs of game. Turning the glass to the top of the wooded hillside, I saw something white moving, and getting a steady position, I made it out to be the rump of a mountain sheep. Looking carefully I picked out four others. Then I called Bill. The sheep were mine by right of discovery, so we traded the cook detail and I took my rifle and belt, stripped to trousers, moccasins and shirt, and started out, going swiftly at first to warm up in the keen mountain air. I kept straight up the hillside until I got to the top and then started along the ridge toward the sheep. As I crossed a little rise I caught sight of them five hundred yards ahead, the band numbering about fifty. Some were feeding, others were bedded down in some shale. From here on it was all stalking, mostly crawling through the small trees and bushes which were hardly knee-high. Finally, getting within one hundred and fifty yards, I got a good, steady prone position between the bushes, and picking out the largest ram, I got the white Lyman sight nicely centered behind his shoulder and very carefully and gradually I pressed the trigger. The instant the gun went off I knew he was mine, for I could call the shot exactly. Instantly the sheep were on the move. They seemed to double up, bunch and then vanish. It was done so quickly that I doubt if I could have gotten in another shot even if I had wished it. The ram I had fired at was knocked completely off its feet, but picked himself up instantly and started off with the others; but after he had run about a hundred yards I saw his head drop and turning half a dozen somersaults, he rolled down the hill and I knew I had made a heart shot. His horns measured 16½ inches at the base, and the nose contained an enormous bump, probably caused in one of his fights for the supremacy of the herd.

I dressed the ram and then went for the horses. Bill, by this time, had everything packed up, so after going up the hill and loading the sheep on my saddle horse, we started down the range for a region where it was warmer and less strenuous and where the horse feed was better. That night we had mountain sheep ribs—the best meat that ever passed a human's mouth—and I had a head worth bringing home. A 16½-inch head is very rare in these days. I believe the record head measured about 19 inches. I remember distinctly, however, on another hunt in the Lillooet district of British Columbia, finding in the long grass of a valley the half-decayed head of an enormous ram. I measured the pith of the skull where the horn had been and it recorded

18 inches. The horn itself must have been at least 21 inches. The ram probably died of old age or was unable to get out of the high altitude when the snow came.

We journeyed on and on, having a glorious time in the freedom of the mountains. We were traveling in a circle, the diameter of which was about three hundred miles. One day we struck an enormous glacier and had to bend way off to the right to avoid it. For days as we travelled that glacier kept us company. It had its origin way up in a mass of peaks and perpetual snow, being fed from a dozen valleys. At least six moraines could be distinctly seen on its surface, and the air in its vicinity was decidedly cool. Where we first struck it it was probably six miles wide and I believe it was not a bit less than fifty miles long. We named it Chilco glacier, because it undoubtedly drained into a large lake of that name near the coast. At this point we were not over two hundred miles from the Pacific Ocean.

As the leaves on the aspen trees started to turn we gradually edged around and headed toward our starting point, going by another route, however, trusting to luck and the careful map we had been making to bring us out somewhere on the Scumscum river above the post. The days were getting short now and the nights very cold. We had to travel during almost all the daylight and our horses started to get poor. The shoes we had taken for them were used up by this time and we had to avoid as much as possible the rocky country. We travelled fast for a month until we struck the headwaters of the Scumscum; then knowing that we were practically safe from being snowed up in the mountain we made a permanent camp on a hillside where the horsefeed was good and started to hunt and tramp to our hearts' delight, while our horses filled up on the grass. We never killed any more game than we could use, which was about one animal every ten days. In this climate meat will keep for a month if protected from flies in the daytime and exposed to the night air after dark.

We were very proud of our permanent camp. The tent was pitched under a large pine tree in a thicket of willows and quaking aspen. All around it was built a windbreak of logs and pine boughs, leaving in front a yard, in the center of which was our camp fire. The windbreak went up six feet high and when a fire was going in front of the tent we were as warm as though in a cabin, no matter how hard the wind blew. Close beside the tent was a little spring, and a half a mile away was a lake full of trout from fifteen pounds down. We spent three days laying in a supply of firewood. Altogether it was the best camp I ever slept in. The hunting within tramping distance was splendid. We rarely hunted together, each preferring to go his own way. When we did not need meat we hunted varmints, and I brought in quite a number of prime coyote pelts and one wolf. One evening Bill staggered into camp with a big mountain lion over his shoulders. He just happened to run across it in a little pine thicket. That was the only one we saw on the whole trip, although their tracks were everywhere and we frequently heard their mutterings in the still evenings. The porcupines at this camp were unusually numerous. They would frequently get inside our windbreak and had a great propensity for eating our soap. Lion, the hound, would not bother them; he had learned his lesson well. When they came around he would get an expression on his face as much as to say, "You give me a pain."

The nights were now very cold. It froze every night and we bedded ourselves down with lots of skins and used enormous logs on the fire so that it would keep going all night. We shot some marmots and made ourselves fur caps and gloves and patched up our outer garments with buckskin. And still the snow did not come.

One day while out hunting I saw a big goat on a bluff off to my right and determined to try to get him for his head, which appeared through my telescope to be an unusually good one. He was about half a mile off when I first spied him and the bluff extended several miles to the southwest like a great wall shutting off the view in that direction. I worked up to the foot of the bluffs and then along; climbing up several hundred feet I struck a shelf which appeared to run along the face at about the height I had seen the goat. It was ticklish work, for the shelf was covered with slide rock which I had to avoid disturbing, and then, too, in places it dwindled to a ledge barely three feet wide with about five hundred feet of nothing underneath. After about four hundred yards of this work I heard a rock fall above me and looking up saw the billy leaning over an outrageous corner looking at me. Aiming as nearly as I could straight up I let drive at the middle of the white mass. There was a grunt, a scramble and a lot of rocks, and then down came the goat, striking in between the cliff and a big boulder and not two feet from me. I fairly shivered for fear he would jump up and butt me off the ledge, but he only gave one quiver and lay still. The 330-grain bullet entering the stomach, had broken the spine and killed instantly. He was an old grandfather and had a splendid head, which I now treasure very highly. I took the head, skin, fat and some of the meat back to camp that night, having to pack it off the bluff in sections. The fat rendered out into three gold-pans full of lard. Goat-fat is excellent for frying and all through the trip it was a great saving on our bacon.

Then one night the snow came. We heard it gently tapping on the tent, and by morning there was three inches in our yard. The time had come only too soon to pull out, which we did about ten o'clock, bidding good-bye to our permanent camp with its comfortable windbreak, its fireplace, table and chairs. Below us the river ran through a canon and we had to cross quite a high mountain range to get through. As we ascended the snow got deeper and deeper. It was almost two feet deep on a level on top of the range. We had to go down a very steep hog-back, and here had trouble in plenty. The horses' feet balled up with snow and they were continually sliding. A pack horse slid down on top of my saddle horse and started him. I was on foot in front and they knocked me down and the three of us slid until stopped by a fallen tree. Such a mess I never saw. One horse was on top of another. The pack was loose and frozen ropes tangled up with everything. It took us half an hour to straighten up the mess and the frozen lash ropes cut our hands frightfully. My ankle had become slightly strained in the mix-up and for several days I suffered agonies with it. There was no stopping—we had to hit the trail hard or get snowed in. One day we stopped to hunt. Bill went out while I nursed my leg. He brought in a fine seven-point buck.

Speaking of the hunt he said: "I jumped the buck in a flat of down timber. He was going like mad about a hundred yards off when I first spied him. I threw up the old rifle and blazed away five times before he tumbled. Each time I pulled I was conscious that the sights looked just like that trademark of the Lyman sight showing the running deer and the sight. When I went over to look at the buck I had a nice little bunch of five shots right behind the shoulder. Those Lyman sights are surely the sights for a hunting rifle." Bill was one of the best shots on game I ever saw. One day I saw him cut the heads off of three grouse in trees while he sat in the saddle with his horse walking up hill. Both our rifles did mighty good work. The more I use a rifle the more I become convinced of the truth of the saying, "Beware of the man with one gun." Get a good rifle to suit you exactly. Fix the trigger pull and sights exactly as you wish them and then stick to that gun as long as it will shoot accurately and you will make few misses in the field.

Only too soon we drove our pack-train into the post. As we rode up two men were building a shack. One of them dropped a board and we nearly jumped out of our skins at the terrific noise. My! how loud everything sounded to our ears, accustomed only to the stillness of those grand mountains. We stayed at the post three days, disposing of our horses and boxing up our heads and skins, and then pulled out for civilization. Never again will such experiences come to us. The day of the wilderness hunter has gone for good. And so the hunt of our lives came to an end.

The Alaskan Grizzly

Harold McCracken

THE GREAT ALASKAN GRIZZLY—THE KODIAK BROWN BEAR (*Ursus middendorffi*) and its even larger Alaska Peninsula brother (*Ursus gyas*)—is probably as far famed as either the African lion or the Bengal tiger. And yet, probably less is known of its life history than of any of the other larger mammals. He is, nevertheless, a sort of fictitious by-word at the hearths of all those hunter-sportsmen who enjoy the savor of genuine hazard in their quest for sport and trophies. A beast whom most prefer to "talk" about hunting, rather than face in mortal combat. And his 1,000 to 2,000 pounds of brawn and power is unquestionably the embodiment of all that even the most adventurous care to seek. He is supreme in size, in brute power, as well as in physical dexterity, sagacity, and pernicious damnableness in the animal kingdom. And this, not in the mere belief of a casual observer, but weighed and tried on the scales of science. To go into details regarding the life history, the "whys" and "whens" and "hows" of his life career, would entail a goodly volume, which, though immensely interesting in every detail, would be far too cumbersome in such a place as this.

His home is that long, slightly curved arm that reaches out from the southwestern corner of Alaska, separating the North Pacific Ocean from the Bering Sea, and dabbling off in the spattered Aleutian Islands. The Alaska Peninsula is today one of the most wild, least visited and less known of all the districts on this continent.

But in reality, the Alaska Peninsula is, for the most part, a terribly wild Garden of Eden. Its waterways boast more fine fish than any other similar sized section of the globe; on its rounded undulating hills and tundra lands are great herds of caribou, the finest of edible flesh; it is carpeted with berry bushes; there are fine furred animals in abundance; millions of wildfowl, duck, geese, eiders, seals, sea lions; big bears—everything necessary for the welfare and happiness of primitive man. It is a truly primitive land.

While the great Alaska Peninsula bear is a carnivore, or flesh eater—and what applies to this bear also applies in many respects to his brothers, the sub- and sub-sub-species of other districts of Alaska—yet he has frequently and correctly been called "the great grass-eating bear" and also "the great fish-eating bear." All animals subsist in the manner and on the foods that demand the least efforts, hazard and inconvenience to their life and comforts. Thus the bears of the Alaska Peninsula have chosen fish and grass and berries as their main diet of food, varied with an occasional caribou, a seal, or meal from the carcass of a dead whale or walrus washed up on the beach. During most of the months of the year, the streams are choked with salmon, affording him an inexhaustible supply until well into the middle of the winter.

And as hibernation is for the most part only an alternative for existing under winter conditions, when it is hard or sometimes impossible to get food, and as the Alaska Peninsula is in winter moderated by the warming Japan Current, making it a quite mild and livable heath for old Gyas, he is forced to spend but a relatively short period in the "long sleep." This increased activity, together with the abundance of fine food, accounts for the unusual size to which the bears of that district grow.

And he is very much aware of his size and strength; and the fact that he has had no outside natural enemy through the line of his ancestors has made him aggressive, haughty and overbearing, fearing nothing and crushing all that impedes his way.

Thus the Alaska Peninsula grizzly is to be found a most unscrupulous fighter, and his acquaintance with man and his high-powered rifles is as yet too short and limited to have impressed upon his brute mind that here is a most powerful mortal enemy. He usually charges when wounded, more than frequently when a female with very young cubs is suddenly surprised or attacked, and occasionally when watching a fresh "kill" or "cache," and surprised. And, if old Gyas decides to fight, woe betide our bold Nimrod unless he is a good shot and nonexcitable, or accompanied by someone who possesses these valuable faculties. For a wounded grizzly will not stop for one to reload his gun, nor pause to be shot at until the vital spot is struck. He means blood! Fifty bullets that are not placed in the proper spot will not stop him; and you can't back out once he accepts your challenge. Not that one is certain of being charged by every Alaskan grizzly that he fells; I have had even females retreat until knocked down. But these cases are really the exception, and the experiences of practically all the old bear hunters of that district—I have known most of them—will bear me out in the statement that these Alaskan grizzlies almost invariably charge under the three circumstances I have cited. The natives of Alaska do not often go to look for these big bears. They have a great deal of respect for them—as all others who know them have.

We are at King Cove, a native village near the site of the once famous village of Belkovski, center of the sea otter hunting grounds of old. We are about 600 miles southwest of Kodiak, the nearest town of over fifteen white inhabitants; and very near the extreme western end of the Alaska Peninsula, and almost due north of Honolulu by location. And here, where the traveler is almost never seen, we will start out to hunt for the biggest of carnivora—start it by incidentally being shipwrecked, almost drowned and getting a foot severely frozen.

It was on the morning of Wednesday, November 1, 1916, that I left King Cove in a 28-foot covered-over powerboat with Captain Charlie Madsen. We headed for the Isanotski Straits, at the end of the peninsula, and the Bering Sea country, where I intended hunting Grant's Barren Ground caribou and the big grizzlies at several desirable localities near the end of the peninsula.

It was cloudy; looked like another snowstorm; but the wind being from the north, rave it might and the low hills of the mainland would protect us until we reached the end of the peninsula, where we could hunt bear and wait for more favorable winds. But the winds of the North are most fickle!

It was a most magnetic sight as we plied out towards the cape at the entrance of the bay, sending flock after flock of salt-water ducks flopping off over the swelling surface of the blue-green sea. An occasional seal could be seen plunging headlong into the water from the jut of a reef or an outcrop of the rocky shoreline. The hills were gray, dappled with the first settling snows of winter, and the clouds were heavy and leaden looking.

As we rounded the cape the swells became more pronounced, carrying a deep, rolling, green-sided trough. But our boat plied steadily on, plunging its nose fearlessly into the rising waves.

Breasting some five miles of rocky coastline, we rounded the second cape at the entrance to Cold (Morofski) Bay, which protrudes some twenty-five miles back into the peninsula, almost making what is to the west an island and what is to the east the end of the peninsula. As we had expected, the wind was raging out of the bay to seaward. But heading the boat's nose towards Thin Point, about ten miles distant, we started fighting our way to the protection of the opposite cape.

Madsen had been watching the sky with misgiving and shortly announced that the wind was changing to the southwest.

I naturally inquired what would be the best course to pursue, knowing that it undoubtedly meant more storm and that we would soon be in the thick of it.

"Cap" decided we would take a chance on reaching Thin Point before the wind had swung to the southwest and thrown the storm in our faces. Once behind the cape we would be safe.

But we were not halfway across when the wind, swinging out past the protection of the peninsula and clashing against the tide, was soon lashing the sea into a stormy havoc. Diving into one great swell, the wind toppled its crest over the boat, washing overboard the hatch-cover and pouring a volume of water into the hold upon our supplies and outfit. I got on deck and endeavored to get a piece of canvas nailed over the open hatchway before another big one should pour its volume into the boat, at the same time clinging as best I could to the pitching vessel.

In the midst of all this, and as if to impress more forcibly upon us our insignificance in this big affair, our engine stopped. Gas engines are hellish things anyhow, and always buck in just the wrong place. But one must act quickly in a case such as this, and almost before I knew it the boat's sail was up and we were racing back before the wind, toward the entrance to the bay we had not long left.

I took the rope and wheel, while Madsen endeavored to get the engine running again, though vainly.

But the wind was now coming in such gusts that each one nigh turned our boat onto its nose. It was also snowing and sleeting, almost hiding the outline of the coast.

A gust hit our sail, turning the boat clear on its side, taking water over the rail, and we narrowly escaped finding ourselves in the arms of Neptune himself. Madsen left the engine and decided we would run before the wind and tack into King Cove Bay.

We crossed the entrance to the bay, driven at top speed towards the opposite cape and line of rocky reefs.

Going as close to as safe, the sail was drawn in with an endeavor to throw it to the opposite side, thus turning the boat.

But the wind was too strong and the sea too rough, and try as we might, we would only be driven helplessly on towards the reef where the waves were dashing their foam and spray high in the air. Then a big wave took the flopping sail, pulling the boat over onto its side until the canvas was torn from end to end. As a last resort the anchor was thrown out; this failed to catch sufficiently to hold us and was regained at great difficulty when we saw that hitting the reef was inevitable.

The first rock of the reef that the boat hit jammed its head through the bottom of the hull and we clambered out into the big dory we were towing and started for shore through the narrow, raging channels in the reef. But this being an open boat, it soon swamped in the breakers and we were forced to take to the water and make shore as best we could. Swimming was impossible, but keeping our heads above the water as best we could, and riding the waves, we were soon washed up on the rocky shore, like half-drowned rats.

To build a fire was impossible for lack of material; we must wait until the boat washed over the reef and was driven ashore. So, wet and cold, and facing a biting snow and sleet and rain-pelleted wind, we walked back and forth over the rocks and waited.

Through all this, while we had been battling with the elements for our very lives, I had noticed with no small interest how very little the storming and havoc had inconvenienced the little creatures that made their homes in or on the sea. The ducks swam about, quacking, and apparently thoroughly enjoying their buoyant existence. So even storms at sea, it seemed, were a mere matter of relativity and part of the everyday life of those that made their home thereon.

Eventually the boat came ashore—it was fortunately high tide—and getting aboard we got out block and tackle, sunk our anchor as a deadman, and pulled the boat up as best we could. Supplies and everything were drenched and several planks in the hull were smashed.

When we had done all that we could we started for the village—a hard hike. It was well after dark when we reached the squatty barrabaras, or native dirt huts, of King Cove, and we were wet and tired and miserable—ready for a meal and the blankets.

As I began to thaw out, however, I found that part of my right foot had frozen—the leather boots I had been wearing having shrunk and stopped the circulation of blood, causing the freezing. I was laid up for over a week with my foot, though it took Madsen, with the assistance of several natives, somewhat longer to get the boat repaired and back to the village.

Such are but a bit of the "pleasures" that often come with hunting big bear at the western end of the Alaskan Peninsula.

I was especially fortunate in making a one-day bag of four of these Alaska Peninsula bears, a big female and her three yearling cubs, the latter being as large as quite mature Southern brown bears I have gotten.

Deciding to spend a day alone in the hills after caribou, I took the .30–40 Winchester—in consideration of the bear—and followed the beach of a lagoon or bay to its head about two and half miles from the village. From the head of the lagoon a valley rose at an easy pitch for about two miles to a low divide on the opposite side of which was a large valley extending out onto the Pacific. This was a very good place for caribou.

At the head of the lagoon I stopped to shoot some salt-water ducks with a .22 Colt revolver, but had fired but a few shots when I was attracted by the bawling of a bear. Glancing in the direction of the sound, I saw a brown bear making a speedy, somewhat noisy, getaway up through the alders from where he had been no doubt eating salmon in the creek a few hundred yards up-valley from me. He was then a good five hundred yards distant and in the alders. I fired, hoping at least to turn him back down the hillside, but he made the top of the ridge and went over it out of sight. I started a speedy climb up through the alders towards the top, not far from where he went over. By the time I reached this, Mr. Ursus had gone down the other side and was making a "hiyu clattewa" along the opposite side of the valley. I started up the ridge toward an open space in the alders with the intent of hurrying down to the creek and descending it with hopes of heading the bear off or getting a shot at him while crossing a wide rock slide a few hundred yards below. But I had not gone a dozen steps when I saw three other bears coming along at a good pace on quite the same course that Number One had taken. This was somewhat more of a "bear party" than I had really anticipated inviting myself to!

I felt quite certain that they would cross a small saddle through which the previous one had passed, and I decided to wait until they had come out of this and were somewhat below me before chancing a shot. I was alone, I remembered.

Squatting down in the alders, I waited with gun ready and, I must say, nerves tense. The first one to come through the saddle was the old female, a big, high-shouldered brute that strode in a manner indicating it was looking for me every bit as much as I was waiting for it. She was followed by her other two yearlings—big fellows almost as tall and as broad as they were long. Being alone, and feeling that the female would undoubtedly fight, I deemed it most wise to play doubly safe. Conditions were fortunately in my favor. The wind was from seaward, and the alders were heavy enough to conceal me from her none too good eyesight, and it would be difficult for her to determine from just which direction the report of my rifle came. The dispatching of the old one was of course my first move. The rest would be comparatively easy. I did not have an opportunity of a good shot, however, until the three had reached the creek bed and crossed and started up along the other side. I slipped into a heavy clump of alders and waited. She was not then, I was quite sure, aware of my whereabouts at least. She lumbered slowly along, yet ever watchful, I could see. Coming out in a little open space she stopped and made an apparent survey of the surrounding vicinity. I took a coarse bead and let drive at her shoulder. I could fairly hear the bullet slap into her. With a nasal bellow she wheeled and made a vicious swipe at the nearest yearling. I fired again, at which she wheeled and charged madly along the hillside opposite me. She went into a small ravine and in a moment came up into sight on one side and stopped, snout swaying high in the air to catch a scent of the danger. I steadied my aim and at the report she went down in a heap and rolled out of sight. "A bull's-eye!" I thought, and breathed a sigh of relief.

The two cubs had made off in the opposite direction, stopping occasionally to look about. I knocked down one of these at the second shot, breaking his back, though he raised on his forelegs and bawled for all he was worth. I was about to let him have another, when out of the ravine came Mrs. Ursus, mad and apparently as much alive as ever, although dragging her right foreleg. She scrambled through the alders straight to the bawling cub. Greatly surprised, and a little uneasy, I again let drive at her. She threw her head to one side, at the same time letting forth another nasal cry. At my next shot she wheeled completely around and charged along the mountainside for a short distance with head held high and every nerve strained to its utmost to locate the cause of her molestation—snarling and bawling in a manner that made me perspire uncomfortably. She was desperate and no doubt calling upon the souls of all her past ancestors to assist her in locating the peculiar new enemy. Then she charged back to the cub. Finally she made a dash almost straight in my direction.

One does not fully appreciate the thrills of real bear hunting until he has experienced just such circumstances as this. To be alone in such a case is a quite different matter from being in company—poor though it may be.

She at last came to a standstill, standing half sidelong to me, and I clamped the gold bead square on her neck and let drive. She went down, got up, and tearing a few alders up by the roots, unwillingly sank in a heap. She had finished her career as a big brown bear on the Alaska Peninsula.

The rest was quite easy and uneventful.

With the assistance of three natives I skinned the four, took the necessary measurements for mounting, and brought the pelts in by boat. The natives, however, made a second trip, bringing in every bit of the meat of all four, salting it down for winter use. The pelts were in fine condition and beautiful specimens, the large one measuring a full ten feet. They are now in the Ohio State Museum.

It was on Sunday, November 19, 1916, that I bagged the original "bearcat"—one of the largest bears ever killed on the continent.

We were hunting around the eastern side of Frosty Peak, a high volcanic mountain towering between Morzhovi and Morofski Bays and about ten miles from the Pacific. This is about twenty miles from King Cove, near the end of the peninsula, and a very good place for big bears. It was a *big* one that I wanted now; and though numerous tracks and one medium-sized bear were seen, none were bothered until the original "bearcat" was found. That took two days under Old Frosty.

I had previously been hunting Grant's Barren Ground caribou on the Bering Sea side of the peninsula and before we landed at the foot of Frosty Peak on our return there was a good twelve inches of snow on the ground. In places it had already drifted to a depth of five feet. Bear hunting was quite an easy matter—though a little unpleasant on account of the snow and cold—as it was a small matter to track the animals. As the streams were still open and full of salmon, but a small percentage of the bruins had sought their winter quarters, the pads of their big clawed feet having beaten paths along the iced shores of the stream where they came periodically to gorge themselves.

It was late afternoon of the second day under Frosty Peak that we found the fresh trail of our longed-for quarry. We had been investigating the broad alder-patched table of one of the valleys that cut up toward the pinnacle of Old Frosty. There were numerous tracks along the creek where the brownies had been feasting on the silver salmon, though no fresh ones of a really large bear. But as we came well up to the head of the valley we saw the well-distinguished trail of an unquestionably large bear where it had made its way up through the snow on the mountainside into a heavy growth of alders. This was at the very foot of the peak and in the highest growth of alders. Upon reaching the tracks we were well satisfied that they could have been made only by the paw and claw of just the bear that we were seeking. Although it was evident that he had been in no special hurry in making the climb, yet it was all that a six-foot man could possibly do to step from one track to the next.

To the left of the alder patch was a comparatively open track of rocky ground with only a spare patch of brush here and there. It was certain that he could not, if still in the thicket, escape in that direction without being noticed. But on the right there was a low ridge, the opposite side of which dipped down into a deep wide ravine. The alders extended to within a few yards of this ridge, and to see the other side it was necessary to mount to the top of it. Also, it was quite probable that the bear had already gone over this ridge and might then be high up in the canyon near to its hibernation quarters.

Being unable to locate the bear with my glasses, I decided to make a complete detour around the patch, to be assured whether or not he was still in there.

So leaving Charlie on the flat below, I took the two natives and started up through the alders on the trail of old Ursus. As soon as possible we mounted the ridge at the right and went along the extent of it to assure ourselves that the bear had not crossed. This he had not. But to make doubly sure that he was still in the alder patch, we went above and around it to complete the circle about the place. He was without question lying somewhere in that thicket.

Upon reaching the flat, and as a last resource, we fired several volleys up through the alders. Then one of the natives spotted him standing in a thick growth of the alders, where he had gotten up and was looking inquiringly down at us. We moved down opposite to him and I fired from the shoulder. He started off along the mountainside, like an animal that had just broken from its cage. Then I fired again. Mounting a little knoll in the open he peered dubiously down at us—in unmistakable defiance. I held on him full in the chest for my next shot, at which he let out a bellow and came for us. My shots had hit, though he had not so much as bit or clawed at the wound on either occasion—merely jumped slightly. He was then about 200 yards distant, though I was well aware of the short time that it would take him to cover that distance. And he was a big fellow—looked literally more like a load of hay than a bear, coming down the mountainside.

I had previously told the others not to shoot until I called for help, as I was anxious to fell this big brute single-handed. But on he came, and though try as I might, I could not stop him. My shots seemed to be taking no effect whatever. And then, when he had come about half the distance, I yelled "Shoot!" And I'd have liked to have done so long before. The four guns spoke simultaneously, but old Gyas still kept coming.

I squatted down in the snow, and resting my elbows on my knees, decided to take the long chance—a shot for the head. I was confident that Madsen could stop him before he reached us, and determined to take a chance shot of dropping him in a heap. The two natives, however, were not so confident and began to move backward, shooting as they went.

He turned an angle to cross a small ravine, and while he was mounting the opposite side at a decreased pace I held just forward of the snout. The first shot missed, as I saw a small flit of snow where it hit just in front of him. But at the second shot he dropped in a heap, falling on his belly with his nose run into the snow. After waiting for some moments to make certain he was beyond the trouble point, we climbed up through the alders to where he lay. The others stood by with guns ready while I went up and poked him with the end of my own gun. He was dead.

This had all taken but a few moments, though relatively it seemed a great deal longer.

He was indeed a big fellow—a genuine bearcat. We gutted him, and as it was then getting late, hit for camp. The next morning we went back to skin the animal—and no small task it was!

He had been hit twelve times, we found. Nine of the shots had entered the neck and shoulder and two in the head and one in the abdomen. One bullet had hit him squarely in the mouth, shattering the tops of his lower teeth on one side, piercing the tongue and lodging in the back of his throat. Four of the .30 caliber leads were retrieved from the shoulder, where they had not so much as reached the bone. The shot that stopped him struck well up on the brain box, but squarely enough to break the casing of the bone and penetrate the skull, though only a part of the lead entered the brain, the most of it spattering off in the fleshy part of the head. It was a lucky shot on an even more lucky day!

We estimated his live weight at from 1,600 to 1,800 pounds, and the skin at twelve feet in length. The actual measurements of the tanned skin, however, as made by Chas. A. Ziege, noted taxidermist of Spokane, Wash., are: eleven feet four inches maximum length, by ten feet six inches spread of fore legs. The skull, measured one year after killing, eighteen and one-quarter inches, or one-half inch under the world record, according to Washington, D.C., authorities.

The Hunt for the Man-Eaters of Tsavo

Lt. Col. J. M. Patterson, D.S.O.

Editor's note: *When assigned to help supervise the building of a Uganda Railroad bridge over the Tsavo River in east Africa in March, 1898, Lt. Col. J. H. Patterson, D.S.O., had little idea of the magnitude of the adventure upon which he was embarking. The site of the bridge, which is today a part of Kenya, became the scene of savage attacks by man-eating lions preying on the workers. Colonel Patterson's stirring book,* The Man-Eaters of Tsavo, *remains in print to this day. The drama was also captured quite well in the film* The Ghost and the Darkness, *starring Val Kilmer and Michael Douglas.*

Unfortunately this happy state of affairs did not continue for long, and our work was soon interrupted in a rude and startling manner. Two most voracious and insatiable man-eating lions appeared upon the scene, and for over nine months waged an intermittent warfare against the railway and all those connected with it in the vicinity of Tsavo. This culminated in a perfect reign of terror in December, 1898, when they actually succeeded in bringing the railway works to a complete standstill for about three weeks. At first they were not always successful in their efforts to carry off a victim, but as time went on they stopped at nothing and indeed braved any danger in order to obtain their favourite food. Their methods then became so uncanny, and their man-stalking so well-timed and so certain of success, that the workmen firmly believed that they were not real animals at all, but devils in lions' shape. Many a time the coolies solemnly assured me that it was absolutely useless to attempt to shoot them. They were quite convinced that the angry spirits of two departed native chiefs had taken this form in order to protect against a railway being made through their country, and by stopping its progress to avenge the insult thus shown to them.

I had only been a few days at Tsavo when I first heard that these brutes had been seen in the neighbourhood. Shortly afterwards one or two coolies mysteriously disappeared, and I was told that they had been carried off by night from their tents and devoured by lions. At the time I did not credit this story, and was more inclined to believe that the unfortunate men had been the victims of foul play at the hands of some of their comrades. They were, as it happened, very good workmen, and had each saved a fair number of rupees, so I thought it quite likely that some scoundrels from the gangs had murdered them for the sake of their money. This suspicion, however, was very soon dispelled. About three weeks after my arrival, I was roused one morning about daybreak and told that one of my *jemadars,* a fine powerful Sikh named Ungan Singh, had been seized in his tent during the night, and dragged off and eaten.

Naturally I lost no time in making an examination of the place, and was soon convinced that the man had indeed been carried off by a lion, and its "pug" marks were plainly visible in the sand, while the furrows made by the heels of the victim showed the direction in which he had been dragged away. Moreover, the *jemadar* shared his tent with half a dozen other workmen, and one of his bedfellows had actually witnessed the occurrence. He graphically described how, at about midnight, the lion suddenly put its head in at the open tent door and seized Ungan Singh—who happened to be nearest the opening—by the throat. The unfortunate fellow cried out "*Choro*" ("Let go"), and threw his arms up round the lion's neck. The next moment he was gone, and his panic-stricken companions lay helpless, forced to listen to the terrible struggle which took place outside. Poor Ungan Singh must have died hard; but what chance had he? As a coolie gravely remarked, "Was he not fighting with a lion?"

On hearing this dreadful story I at once set out to try to track the animal, and was accompanied by Captain Haslem, who happened to be staying at Tsavo at the time, and who, poor fellow, himself met with a tragic fate very shortly afterwards. We found it an easy matter to follow the route taken by the lion, as he appeared to have stopped several times before beginning his meal. Pools of blood marked these halting-places, where he doubtless indulged in the man-eaters' habit of licking the skin off so as to get at the fresh blood. (I have been led to believe that this is their custom from the appearance of two half-eaten bodies which I subsequently rescued: the skin was gone in places, and the flesh looked dry, as if it had been sucked.) On reaching the spot where the body had been devoured, a dreadful spectacle presented itself. The ground all round was covered with blood and morsels of flesh and bones, but the unfortunate *jemadar*'s head had been left intact, save for the holes made by the lion's tusks on seizing him, and lay a short distance away from the other remains, the eyes staring wide open with a startled, horrified look in them. The place was considerably cut up, and on closer examination we found that two lions had been there and had probably struggled for possession of the body. It was the most gruesome sight I had ever seen. We collected the remains as well as we could and heaped stones on them, the head with its fixed, terrified stare seeming to watch us all the time, for it we did not bury, but took back to camp for identification before the Medical Officer.

Thus occurred my first experience of man-eating lions, and I vowed there and then that I would spare no pains to rid the neighbourhood of the brutes. I little knew the trouble that was in store for me, or how narrow were to be my own escapes from sharing poor Ungan Singh's fate.

That same night I sat up in a tree close to the late *jemadar*'s tent, hoping that the lions would return to it for another victim. I was followed to my perch by a few of the more terrified coolies, who begged to be allowed to sit up in the tree with me; all the other workmen remained in their tents, but no more doors were left open. I had with me my .303 and 12-bore shot gun, one barrel loaded with ball and the other with slug. Shortly after settling down to my vigil, my hopes of bagging one of the brutes were raised by the sound of their ominous roaring coming closer and closer. Presently this ceased, and quiet reigned for an hour or two, as lions always stalk their prey in complete silence. All at once, however, we heard a great uproar and frenzied cries coming from another camp about half a mile away; we knew then that the lions had seized a victim there, and that we should see or hear nothing further of them that night.

Next morning I found that one of the brutes had broken into a tent at Railhead Camp—whence we had heard the commotion during the night—and had made off with a poor wretch who was lying there asleep. After a night's rest, therefore, I took up my position in a suitable tree near this tent. I did not at all like the idea of walking the half-mile to the place after dark, but all the same I felt fairly safe, as one of my men carried a bright lamp close behind me. He in his turn was followed by another leading a goat, which I tied under my tree in the hope that the lion might be tempted to seize it instead of a coolie. A steady drizzle commenced shortly after I had settled down to my night of watching, and I was soon thoroughly chilled and wet. I stuck to my uncomfortable post, however, hoping to get a shot, but I well remember the feeling of impotent disappointment I experienced when about midnight I heard screams and cries and a heartrending shriek, which told me that the man-eaters had again eluded me and had claimed another victim elsewhere.

At this time the various camps for the workmen were very scattered, so that the lions had a range of some eight miles on either side of Tsavo to work upon; and as their tactics seemed to be to break into a different camp each night, it was most difficult to forestall them. They almost appeared, too, to have an extraordinary and uncanny faculty of finding out our plans beforehand, so that no matter in how likely or how tempting a spot we lay in wait for them, they invariably avoided that particular place and seized their victim for the night from some other camp. Hunting them by day moreover, in such a dense wilderness as surrounded us, was an exceedingly tiring and really foolhardy undertaking. In a thick jungle of the kind round Tsavo the hunted animal has every chance against the hunter, as however careful the latter may be, a dead twig or something of the sort is sure to crackle just at the critical moment and so give the alarm. Still I never gave up hope of some day finding their lair, and accordingly continued to devote all my spare time to crawling about through the undergrowth. Many a time when attempting to force my way through this bewildering tangle I had to be released by my gun-bearer from the fast clutches of the "wait-a-bit"; and often with immense pains I succeeded in tracing the lions to the river after they had seized a victim, only to lose the trail from there onwards, owing to the rocky nature of the ground which they seemed to be careful to choose in retreating to their den.

At this early stage of the struggle, I am glad to say, the lions were not always successful in their efforts to capture a human being for their nightly meal, and one or two amusing incidents occurred to relieve the tension from which our nerves were beginning to suffer. On one occasion an enterprising *bunniah* (Indian trader) was riding along on his donkey late one night, when suddenly a lion sprang out on him knocking over both man and beast. The donkey was badly wounded, and the lion was just about to seize the trader, when in some way or other his claws became entangled in a rope by which two empty oil tins were strung across the donkey's neck. The rattle and clatter made by these as he dragged them after him gave him such a fright that he turned tail and bolted off into the jungle, to the intense relief of the terrified *bunniah,* who quickly made his way up the nearest tree and remained there, shivering with fear, for the rest of the night.

Shortly after this episode, a Greek contractor named Themistocles Pappadimitrini had an equally marvellous escape. He was sleeping peacefully in his tent one night, when a lion broke in, and seized and made off with the mattress on which he was lying. Though rudely awakened, the Greek was quite unhurt and suffered from nothing worse than a bad fright. This same man, however, met with a melancholy fate not long afterwards. He had been to the Kilima N'jaro district to buy cattle, and on the return journey attempted to take a short cut across country to the railway, but perished miserably of thirst on the way.

On another occasion fourteen coolies who slept together in a large tent were one night awakened by a lion suddenly jumping on to the tent and breaking through it. The brute landed with one claw on a coolie's shoulder, which was badly torn; but instead of seizing the man himself, in his hurry he grabbed a large bag of rice which happened to be lying in the tent, and made off with it, dropping it in disgust some little distance away when he realised his mistake.

These, however, were only the earlier efforts of the man-eaters. Later on, as will be seen, nothing flurried or frightened them in the least, and except as food they showed a complete contempt for human beings. Having once marked down a victim, they would allow nothing to deter them from securing him, whether he were protected by a thick fence, or inside a closed tent, or sitting round a brightly burning fire. Shots, shouting and firebrands they alike held in derision.

The Attack on the Goods-Wagon

All this time my own tent was pitched in an open clearing, unprotected by a fence of any kind round it. One night when the medical officer, Dr. Rose, was staying with me, we were awakened about midnight by hearing something tumbling about among the tent ropes, but on going out with a lantern we could discover nothing. Daylight, however, plainly revealed the "pug" marks of a lion, so that on that occasion I fancy one or other of us had a narrow escape. Warned by this experience, I at once arranged to move my quarters, and went to join forces with Dr. Brock, who had just arrived at Tsavo to take medical charge of the district. We shared a hut of palm leaves and boughs, which we had constructed on the eastern side of the river, close to the old caravan route leading to Uganda; and we had it surrounded by a circular *boma,* or thorn fence, about seventy yards in diameter, well made and thick and high. Our personal servants also lived within the enclosure, and a bright fire was always kept up throughout the night. For the sake of coolness, Brock and I used to sit out under the verandah of this hut in the evenings; but it was rather trying to our nerves to attempt to read or write there, as we never knew when a lion might spring over the *boma,* and be on us before we were aware. We therefore kept our rifles within easy reach, and cast many an anxious glance out into the inky darkness beyond the circle of the firelight. On one or two occasions, we found in the morning that the lions had come quite close to the fence; but fortunately they never succeeded in getting through.

By this time, too, the camps of the workmen had also been surrounded by thorn fences; nevertheless the lions managed to jump over or to break through some one or other of these, and regularly every few nights a man was carried off, the reports of the disappearance of this or that workman coming in to me with painful frequency. So long, however, as Railhead Camp—with its two or three thousand men, scattered over a wide area—remained at Tsavo, the coolies appeared not to take much notice of the dreadful deaths of their comrades. Each man felt, I suppose, that as the man-eaters had such a large number of victims to choose from, the chances of their selecting him in particular were very small. But when the large camp moved ahead with the railway, matters altered considerably. I was then left with only some few hundred men to complete the permanent works; and as all the remaining workmen were naturally camped together the attentions of the lions became more apparent and made a deeper impression. A regular panic consequently ensued, and it required all my powers of persuasion to induce the men to stay on. In fact, I succeeded in doing so only by allowing them to knock off all regular work until they had built exceptionally thick and high *bomas* round each camp. Within these enclosures fires were kept burning all night, and it was also the duty of the night-watchman to keep clattering half a dozen empty oil tins suspended from a convenient tree. These he manipulated by means of a long rope, while sitting in the hopes of terrifying away the man-eaters. In spite of all these precautions, however, the lions would not be denied, and men continued to disappear.

When the railhead workmen moved on, their hospital camp was left behind. It stood rather apart from the other camps, in a clearing about three-quarters of a mile from my hut, but was protected by a good thick fence and to all appearance was quite secure. It seemed, however, as if barriers were of no avail against the "demons," for before very long one of them found a weak spot in the *boma* and broke through. On this occasion the Hospital Assistant had a marvellous escape. Hearing a noise outside, he opened the door of his tent and was horrified to see a great lion standing a few yards away looking at him. The beast made a spring towards him, which gave the Assistant such a fright that he jumped backwards, and in doing so luckily upset a box containing medical stores. This crashed down with such a loud clatter of breaking glass that the lion was startled for the moment and made off to another part of the enclosure. Here, unfortunately, he was more successful, as he jumped on to and broke through a tent in which eight patients were lying. Two of them were badly wounded by his spring, while a third poor wretch was seized and dragged off bodily through the thorn fence. The two wounded coolies were left where they lay; a piece of torn tent having fallen over them; and in this position the doctor and I found them on our arrival soon after dawn next morning. We at once decided to move the hospital closer to the main camp; a fresh site was prepared, a stout hedge built round the enclosure, and all the patients were moved in before nightfall.

As I had heard that lions generally visit recently deserted camps, I decided to sit up all night in the vacated *boma* in the hope of getting an opportunity of bagging one of them; but in the middle of my lonely vigil I had the mortification of hearing shrieks and cries coming from the direction of the new hospital, telling me only too plainly that our dreaded foes had once more eluded me. Hurrying to the place at daylight I found that one of the lions had jumped over the newly erected fence and had carried off the hospital *bhisti* (water-carrier), and that several other coolies had been unwilling witnesses of the terrible scene which took place within the circle of light given by the big camp fire. The *bhisti,* it appears, had been lying on the floor, with his head towards the centre of the tent and his feet nearly touching the side. The lion managed to get its head in below the canvas, seized him by the foot and pulled him out. In desperation the unfortunate water-carrier clutched hold of a heavy box in a vain attempt to prevent himself being carried off, and dragged it with him until he was forced to let go by its being stopped by the side of the tent. He then caught hold of a tent rope, and clung tightly to it until it broke. As soon as the lion managed to get him clear of the tent, he sprang at his throat and after a few vicious shakes the poor *bhisti*'s agonising cries were silenced for ever. The brute then seized him in his mouth, like a huge cat with a mouse, and ran up and down the *boma* looking for a weak spot to break through. This he presently found and plunged into, dragging his victim with him and leaving shreds of torn cloth and flesh as ghastly evidences of his passage through the thorns. Dr. Brock and I were easily able to follow his track, and soon found the remains about four hundred yards away in the bush. There was the usual horrible sight. Very little was left of the unfortunate *bhisti*—only the skull, the jaws, a few of the larger bones and a portion of the palm with one or two fingers attached. On one of these was a silver ring, and this, with the teeth (a relic much prized by certain castes), was sent to the man's widow in India.

Again it was decided to move the hospital; and again, before nightfall, the work was completed, including a still stronger and thicker *boma.* When the patients had been moved, I had a covered goods-wagon placed in a favourable position on a siding which ran close to the site which had just been abandoned, and in this Brock and I arranged to sit up that night. We left a couple of tents still standing within the enclosure, and also tied up a few cattle in it as bait for the lions, who had been seen in no less than three different places in the neighbourhood during the afternoon (April 23). Four miles from Tsavo they had attempted to seize a coolie who was walking along the line. Fortunately, however, he had just time to escape up a tree, where he remained, more dead than alive, until he was rescued by the Traffic Manager, who caught sight of him from a passing train. They next appeared close to Tsavo Station, and a couple of hours later some workmen saw one of the lions stalking Dr. Brock as he was returning about dusk from the hospital.

In accordance with our plan, the doctor and I set out after dinner for the goods-wagon, which was about a mile away from our hut. In the light of subsequent events, we did a very foolish thing in taking up our position so late; nevertheless, we reached our destination in safety, and settled down to our watch about ten o'clock. We had the lower half of the door of the wagon closed, while the upper half was left wide open for observation: and we faced, of course, in the direction of the abandoned *boma*, which, however, we were unable to see in the inky darkness. For an hour or two everything was quiet, and the deadly silence was becoming very monotonous and oppressive, when suddenly, to our right, a dry twig snapped, and we knew that an animal of some sort was about. Soon afterwards we heard a dull thud, as if some heavy body had jumped over the *boma*. The cattle, too, became very uneasy, and we could hear them moving about restlessly. Then again came dead silence. At this juncture I proposed to my companion that I should get out of the wagon and lie on the ground close to it, as I could see better in that position should the lion come in our direction with his prey. Brock, however, persuaded me to remain where I was; and a few seconds afterwards I was heartily glad that I had taken his advice, for at that very moment one of the man-eaters—although we did not know it—was quietly stalking us, and was even then almost within springing distance. Orders had been given for the entrance to the *boma* to be blocked up, and accordingly we were listening in the expectation of hearing the lion force his way out through the bushes with his prey. As a matter of fact, however, the doorway had not been properly closed, and while we were wondering what the lion could be doing inside the *boma* for so long, he was outside all the time, silently reconnoitring our position.

Presently I fancied I saw something coming very stealthily towards us. I feared, however, to trust to my eyes, which by that time were strained by prolonged staring through the darkness, so under my breath I asked Brock whether he saw anything, at the same time covering the dark object as well as I could with my rifle. Brock did not answer; he told me afterwards that he, too, thought he had seen something move, but was afraid to say so lest I should fire and it turn out to be nothing after all. After this there was intense silence again for a second or two, then with a sudden bound a huge body sprang at us. "The lion!" I shouted, and we both fired almost simultaneously—not a moment too soon, for in another second the brute would assuredly have landed inside the wagon. As it was, he must have swerved off in his spring, probably blinded by the flash and frightened by the noise of the double report which was increased a hundredfold by the reverberation of the hollow iron roof of the truck. Had we not been very much on the alert, he would undoubtedly have got one of us, and we realised that we had had a very lucky and very narrow escape. The next morning we found Brock's bullet embedded in the sand close to a footprint; it could not have missed the lion by more than an inch or two. Mine was nowhere to be found.

Thus ended my first direct encounter with one of the man-eaters.

The Reign of Terror

The lions seemed to have got a bad fright the night Brock and I sat up in wait for them in the goods-wagon, for they kept away from Tsavo and did not molest us in any way for some considerable time—not, in fact, until long after Brock had left me and gone on *safari* (a caravan journey) to Uganda. In this breathing space which they vouchsafed us, it occurred to me that should they renew their attacks, a trap would perhaps offer the best chance of getting at them, and that if I could construct one in which a couple of coolies might be used as bait without being subjected to any danger, the lions would be quite daring enough to enter it in search of them and thus be caught. I accordingly set to work at once, and in a short time managed to make a sufficiently strong trap out of wooden sleepers, tram-rails, pieces of telegraph wire, and a length of heavy chain. It was divided into two compartments—one for the men and one for the lion. A sliding door at one end admitted the former, and once inside this compartment they were perfectly safe, as between them and the lion, if he entered the other, ran a cross wall of iron rails only three inches apart, and embedded both top and bottom in heavy wooden sleepers. The door which was to admit the lion was, of course, at the opposite end of the structure, but otherwise the whole thing was very much on the principle of the ordinary rat-trap, except that it was not necessary for the lion to seize the bait in order to send the door clattering down. This part of the contrivance was arranged in the following manner. A heavy chain was secured along the top part of the lion's doorway, the ends hanging down to the ground on either side of the opening; and to these were fastened, strongly secured by stout wire, short lengths of rails placed about six inches apart. This made a sort of flexible door which could be packed into a small space when not in use, and which abutted against the top of the doorway when lifted up. The door was held in this position by a lever made of a piece of rail, which in turn was kept in its place by a wire fastened to one end and passing down to a spring concealed in the ground inside the cage. As soon as the lion entered sufficiently far into the trap, he would be bound to tread on the spring; his weight on this would release the wire, and in an instant down would come the door behind him; and he could not push it out in any way, as it fell into a groove between two rails firmly embedded in the ground.

In making this trap, which cost us a lot of work, we were rather at a loss for want of tools to bore holes in the rails for the doorway, so as to enable them to be fastened by the wire to the chain. It occurred to me, however, that a hard-nosed bullet from my .303 would penetrate the iron, and on making the experiment I was glad to find that a hole was made as cleanly as if it had been punched out.

When the trap was ready I pitched a tent over it in order further to deceive the lions, and built an exceedingly strong *boma* round it. One small entrance was made at the back of the enclosure for the men, which they were to close on going in by pulling a bush after them; and another entrance just in front of the door of the cage was left open for the lions. The wiseacres to whom I showed my invention were generally of the opinion that the man-eaters would be too cunning to walk into my parlour; but, as will be seen later, their predictions proved false. For the first few nights I baited the trap myself, but nothing happened except that I had a very sleepless and uncomfortable time, and was badly bitten by mosquitoes.

As a matter of fact, it was some months before the lions attacked us again, though from time to time we heard of their depredations in other quarters. Not long after our night in the goods-wagon, two men were carried off from the railhead, while another was taken from a place called Engomani, about ten miles away. Within a very short time, this latter place was again visited by the brutes, two more men being seized, one of whom was killed and eaten, and the other so badly mauled that he died within a few days. As I have said, however, we at Tsavo enjoyed complete immunity from attack, and the coolies, believing that their dreaded foes had permanently deserted the district, resumed all their usual habits and occupations, and life in the camps returned to its normal routine.

At last we were suddenly startled out of this feeling of security. One dark night the familiar terror-stricken cries and screams awoke the camps, and we knew that the "demons" had returned and had commenced a new list of victims. On this occasion a number of men had been sleeping outside their tents for the sake of coolness, thinking, of course, that the lions had gone for good, when suddenly in the middle of the night one of the brutes was discovered forcing its way through the *boma*. The alarm was at once given, and sticks, stones and firebrands were hurled in the direction of the intruder. All was of no avail, however, for the lion burst into the midst of the terrified group, seized an unfortunate wretch amid the cries and shrieks of his companions, and dragged him off through the thick thorn fence. He was joined outside by the second lion, and so daring had the two brutes become that they did not trouble to carry their victim any further away, but devoured him within thirty yards of the tent where he had been seized. Although several shots were fired in their direction by the *jemadar* of the gang to which the coolie belonged, they took no notice of these and did not attempt to move until their horrible meal was finished. The few scattered fragments that remained of the body I would not allow to be buried at once, hoping that the lions would return to the spot the following night; and on the chance of this I took up my station at nightfall in a convenient tree. Nothing occurred to break the monotony of my watch, however, except that I had a visit from a hyena, and the next morning I learned that the lions had attacked another camp about two miles from Tsavo—for by this time the camps were again scattered, as I had works in progress all up and down the line. There the man-eaters had been successful in obtaining a victim, whom, as in the previous instance, they devoured quite close to the camp. How they forced their way through the *bomas* without making a noise was, and still is, a mystery to me; I should have thought that it was next to impossible for an animal to get through at all. Yet they continually did so, and without a sound being heard.

After this occurrence, I sat up every night for over a week near likely camps, but all in vain. Either the lions saw me and then went elsewhere, or else I was unlucky, for they took man after man from different places without ever once giving me a chance of a shot at them. This constant night watching was most dreary and fatiguing work, but I felt that it was a duty that had to be undertaken, as the men naturally looked to me for protection. In the whole of my life I have never experienced anything more nerve-shaking than to hear the deep roars of these dreadful monsters growing gradually nearer and nearer, and to know that some one or other of us was doomed to be their victim before morning dawned. Once they reached the vicinity of the camps, the roars completely ceased, and we knew that they were stalking for their prey. Shouts would then pass from camp to camp, "*Khabar dar, bhaieon, shaitan ata*" ("Beware, brothers, the devil is coming"), but the warning cries would prove of no avail, and sooner or later agonising shrieks would break the silence and another man would be missing from roll-call next morning.

I was naturally very disheartened at being foiled in this way night after night, and was soon at my wits' end to know what to do; it seemed as if the lions were really "devils" after all and bore a charmed life. As I have said before, tracking them through the jungle was a hopeless task; but as something had to be done to keep up the men's spirits, I spent many a wry day crawling on my hands and knees through the dense undergrowth of the exasperating wilderness around us. As a matter of fact, if I had come up with the lions on any of these expeditions, it was much more likely that they would have added me to their list of victims than that I should have succeeded in killing either of them, as everything would have been in their favour. About this time, too, I had many helpers, and several officers—civil, naval and military—came to Tsavo from the coast and sat up night after night in order to get a shot at our daring foes. All of us, however, met with the same lack of success, and the lions always seemed capable of avoiding the watchers, while succeeding at the same time in obtaining a victim.

I have a very vivid recollection of one particular night when the brutes seized a man from the railway station and brought him close to my camp to devour. I could plainly hear them crunching the bones, and the sound of their dreadful purring filled the air and rang in my ears for days afterwards. The terrible thing was to feel so helpless; it was useless to attempt to go out, as of course the poor fellow was dead, and in addition it was so pitch dark as to make it impossible to see anything. Some half a dozen workmen, who lived in a small enclosure close to mine, became so terrified on hearing the lions at their meal that they shouted and implored me to allow them to come inside my *boma.* This I willingly did, but soon afterwards I remembered that one man had been lying ill in their camp, and on making enquiry I found that they had callously left him behind alone. I immediately took some men with me to bring him to my *boma,* but on entering his tent I saw by the light of the lantern that the poor fellow was beyond need of safety. He had died of shock at being deserted by his companions.

From this time matters gradually became worse and worse. Hitherto, as a rule, only one of the man-eaters had made the attack and had done the foraging, while the other waited outside in the bush; but now they began to change their tactics, entering the *bomas* together and each seizing a victim. In this way two Swahili porters were killed during the last week of November, one being immediately carried off and devoured. The other was heard moaning for a long time, and when his terrified companions at last summoned up sufficient courage to go to his assistance, they found him stuck fast in the bushes of the *boma* through which for once the lion had apparently been unable to drag him. He was still alive when I saw him next morning, but so terribly mauled that he died before he could be got to the hospital.

Within a few days of this the two brutes made a most ferocious attack on the largest camp in the section, which for safety's sake was situated within a stone's throw of Tsavo Station and close to a Permanent Way Inspector's iron hut. Suddenly in the dead of night the two man-eaters burst in among the terrified workmen, and even from my *boma*, some distance away, I could plainly hear the panic-stricken shrieking of the coolies. Then followed cries of "They've taken him; they've taken him," as the brutes carried off their unfortunate victim and began their horrible feast close beside the camp. The Inspector, Mr. Dalgairns, fired over fifty shots in the direction in which he heard the lions, but they were not to be frightened and calmly lay there until their meal was finished. After examining the spot in the morning, we at once set out to follow the brutes, Mr. Dalgairns feeling confident that he had wounded one of them, as there was a trail on the sand like that of the toes of a broken limb. After some careful stalking, we suddenly found ourselves in the vicinity of the lions, and were greeted with ominous growlings. Cautiously advancing and pushing the bushes aside, we saw in the gloom what we at first took to be a lion cub; closer inspection, however, showed it to be the remains of the unfortunate coolie, which the man-eaters had evidently abandoned at our approach. The legs, one arm and half the body had been eaten, and it was the stiff fingers of the other arm trailing along the sand which had left the marks we had taken to be the trail of a wounded lion. By this time the beasts had retired far into the thick jungle where it was impossible to follow them, so we had the remains of the coolie buried and once more returned home disappointed.

Now the bravest men in the world, much less the ordinary Indian coolie, will not stand constant terrors of this sort indefinitely. The whole district was by this time thoroughly panic-stricken, and I was not at all surprised, therefore, to find on my return to camp that same afternoon (December 1) that the men had all struck work and were waiting to speak to me. When I sent for them, they flocked to my *boma* in a body and stated that they would not remain at Tsavo any longer for anything or anybody; they had come from India on an agreement to work for the government, not to supply food for either lions or "devils." No sooner had they delivered this ultimatum than a regular stampede took place. Some hundreds of them stopped the first passing train by throwing themselves on the rails in front of the engine, and then, swarming on to the trucks and throwing in their possessions anyhow, they fled from the accursed spot.

After this the railway works were completely stopped; and for the next three weeks practically nothing was done but build "lion-proof" huts for those workmen who had had sufficient courage to remain. It was a strange and amusing sight to see these shelters perched on the top of water-tanks, roofs and girders—anywhere for safety—while some even went so far as to dig pits inside their tents, into which they descended at night, covering the top over with heavy logs of wood. Every good-sized tree in the camp had as many beds lashed on to it as its branches would bear—and sometimes more. I remember that one night when the camp was attacked, so many men swarmed on to one particular tree that down it came with a crash, hurling its terror-stricken load of shrieking coolies close to the very lions they were trying to avoid. Fortunately for them, a victim had already been secured, and the brutes were too busy devouring him to pay attention to anything else.

The District Officer's Narrow Escape

Some little time before the flight of the workmen, I had written to Mr. Whitehead, the District Officer, asking him to come up and assist me in my campaign against the lions, and to bring with him any of his *askaris* (native soldiers) that he could spare. He replied accepting the invitation, and told me to expect him about dinner-time on December 2, which turned out to be the day after the exodus. His train was due at Tsavo about six o'clock in the evening, so I sent my "boy" up to the station to meet him and to help in carrying his baggage to the camp. In a very short time, however, the "boy" rushed back trembling with terror, and informed me that there was no sign of the train or of the railway staff, but that an enormous lion was standing on the station platform. This extraordinary story I did not believe in the least, as by this time the coolies—never remarkable for bravery—were in such a state of fright that if they caught sight of a hyena, or a baboon, or even a dog, in the bush, they were sure to imagine it was a lion; but I found out next day that it was an actual fact, and that both stationmaster and signalman had been obliged to take refuge from one of the man-eaters by locking themselves in the station building.

I waited some little time for Mr. Whitehead, but eventually, as he did not put in an appearance, I concluded that he must have postponed his journey until the next day, and so had my dinner in my customary solitary state. During the meal I heard a couple of shots, but paid no attention to them, as rifles were constantly being fired off in the neighbourhood of the camp. Later in the evening, I went out as usual to watch for our elusive foes, and took up my position in a crib made of sleepers which I had built on a big girder close to a camp which I thought was likely to be attacked. Soon after settling down at my post, I was surprised to hear the man-eaters growling and purring and crunching up bones about seventy yards from the crib. I could not understand what they had found to eat, as I had heard no commotion in the camps, and I knew by bitter experience that every meal the brutes obtained from us was announced by shrieks and uproar. The only conclusion I could come to was that they had pounced upon some poor unsuspecting native traveller. After a time I was able to make out their eyes glowing in the darkness, and I took as careful aim as was possible in the circumstances and fired; but the only notice they paid to the shot was to carry off whatever they were devouring and to retire quietly over a slight rise, which prevented me from seeing them. There they finished their meal at their ease.

As soon as it was daylight, I got out of my crib and went towards the place where I had last heard them. On the way, whom should I meet but my missing guest, Mr. Whitehead, looking very pale and ill, and generally dishevelled.

"Where on earth have you come from?" I exclaimed. "Why didn't you turn up to dinner last night?"

"A nice reception you give a fellow when you invite him to dinner," was his only reply.

"Why, what's up?" I asked.

"That infernal lion of yours nearly did for me last night," said Whitehead.

"Nonsense, you must have dreamed it!" I cried in astonishment.

For answer he turned round and showed me his back. "That's not much of a dream, is it?" he asked.

His clothing was rent by one huge tear from the nape of the neck downwards, and on the flesh there were four great claw marks, showing red and angry through the torn cloth. Without further parley, I hurried him off to my tent, and bathed and dressed his wounds; and when I had made him considerably more comfortable, I got from him the whole story of the events of the night.

It appeared that his train was very late, so that it was quite dark when he arrived at Tsavo Station, from which the track to my camp lay through a small cutting. He was accompanied by Abdullah, his sergeant of *askaris,* who walked close behind him carrying a lighted lamp. All went well until they were about halfway through the gloomy cutting, when one of the lions suddenly jumped down upon them from the high bank, knocking Whitehead over like a ninepin, and tearing his back in the manner I had seen. Fortunately, however, he had his carbine with him, and instantly fired. The flash and the loud report must have dazed the lion for a second or two, enabling Whitehead to disengage himself; but the next instant the brute pounced like lightning on the unfortunate Abdullah, with whom he at once made off. All that the poor fellow could say was: "*Eh, Bwana, simba*" ("Oh,

Master, a lion"). As the lion was dragging him over the bank, Whitehead fired again, but without effect, and the brute quickly disappeared into the darkness with his prey. It was, of course, this unfortunate man whom I had heard the lions devouring during the night. Whitehead himself had a marvellous escape; his wounds were happily not very deep, and caused him little or no inconvenience afterwards.

On the same day, December 3, the forces arrayed against the lions were further strengthened. Mr. Farquhar, the Superintendent of Police, arrived from the coast with a score of sepoys to assist in hunting down the man-eaters, whose fame had by this time spread far and wide, and the most elaborate precautions were taken, his men being posted on the most convenient trees near every camp. Several other officials had also come up on leave to join in the chase, and each of these guarded a likely spot in the same way, Mr. Whitehead sharing my post inside the crib on the girder. Further, in spite of some chaff, my lion trap was put in thorough working order, and two of the sepoys were installed as bait.

Our preparations were quite complete by nightfall, and we all took up our appointed positions. Nothing happened until about nine o'clock, when to my great satisfaction the intense stillness was suddenly broken by the noise of the door of the trap clattering down. "At last," I thought, "one at least of the brutes is done for." But the sequel was an ignominious one.

The bait-sepoys had a lamp burning inside their part of the cage, and were each armed with a Martini rifle, with plenty of ammunition. They had also been given strict orders to shoot at once if a lion should enter the trap. Instead of doing so, however, they were so terrified when he rushed in and began to lash himself madly against the bars of the cage, that they completely lost their heads and were actually too unnerved to fire. Not for some minutes—not, indeed, until Mr. Farquhar, whose post was close by, shouted at them and cheered them on—did they at all recover themselves. Then when at last they did begin to fire, they fired with a vengeance—anywhere, anyhow. Whitehead and I were at right angles to the direction in which they should have shot, and yet their bullets came whizzing all round us. Altogether they fired over a score of shots, and in the end succeeded only in blowing away one of the bars of the door, thus allowing our prize to make good his escape. How they failed to kill him several times over is, and always will be, a complete mystery to me, as they could have put the muzzles of their rifles absolutely touching his body. There was, indeed, some blood scattered about the trap, but it was small consolation to know that the brute, whose capture and death seemed so certain, had only been slightly wounded.

Still we were not unduly dejected, and when morning came, a hunt was at once arranged. Accordingly we spent the greater part of the day on our hands and knees following the lions through the dense thickets of thorny jungle, but though we heard their growls from time to time, we never succeeded in actually coming up with them. Of the whole party, only Farquhar managed to catch a momentary glimpse of one as it bounded over a bush. Two days more were spent in the same manner, and with equal unsuccess; and then Farquhar and his sepoys were obliged to return to the coast. Mr. Whitehead also departed for his district, and once again I was left alone with the man-eaters.

The Death of the First Man-Eater

A day or two after the departure of my allies, as I was leaving my *boma* soon after dawn on December 9, I saw a Swahili running excitedly towards me, shouting out "*Simba! Simba!*" ("Lion! Lion!"), and every now and again looking behind him as he ran. On questioning him I found that the lions had tried to snatch a man from the camp by the river, but being foiled in this had seized and killed one of the donkeys, and were at that moment busy devouring it not far off. Now was my chance.

I rushed for the heavy rifle which Farquhar had kindly left with me for use in case an opportunity such as this should arise, and, led by the Swahili, I started most carefully to stalk the lions, who, I devoutly hoped, were confining their attention strictly to their meal. I was getting on splendidly, and could just make out the outline of one of them through the dense bush, when unfortunately my guide snapped a rotten branch. The wily beast heard the noise, growled his defiance, and disappeared in a moment into a patch of even thicker jungle close by. In desperation at the thought of his escaping me once again, I crept hurriedly back to the camp, summoned the available workmen and told them to bring all the tom-toms, tin cans and other noisy instruments of any kind that could be found. As quickly as possible I posted them in a half-circle round the thicket, and gave the head *jemadar* instructions to start a simultaneous beating of the tom-toms and cans as soon as he judged that I had had time to get round to the other side. I then crept round by myself and soon found a good position and one which the lion was most likely to retreat past, as it was in the middle of a broad animal path leading straight from the place where he was concealed. I lay down behind a small ant hill, and waited expectantly. Very soon I heard a tremendous din being raised by the advancing line of coolies, and almost immediately, to my intense joy, out into the open path stepped a huge maneless lion. It was the first occasion during all these trying months upon which I had had a fair chance at one of these brutes, and my satisfaction at the prospect of bagging him was unbounded.

Slowly he advanced along the path, stopping every few seconds to look round. I was only partially concealed from view, and if his attention had not been so fully occupied by the noise behind him, he must have observed me. As he was oblivious to my presence, however, I let him approach to within about fifteen yards of me, and then covered him with my rifle. The moment I moved to do this, he caught sight of me, and seemed much astonished at my sudden appearance, for he stuck his forefeet into the ground, threw himself back on his haunches and growled savagely. As I covered his brain with my rifle, I felt that at last I had him absolutely at my mercy, but . . . never trust an untried weapon! I pulled the trigger, and to my horror heard the dull snap that tells of a misfire.

Worse was to follow. I was so taken aback and disconcerted by this untoward accident that I entirely forgot to fire the left barrel, and lowered the rifle from my shoulder with the intention of reloading—if I should be given time. Fortunately for me, the lion was so distracted by the terrific din and uproar of the coolies behind him that instead of springing on me, as might have been expected, he bounded aside into the jungle again. By this time I had collected my wits, and just as he jumped I let him have the left barrel. An answering angry growl told me that he had been hit; but nevertheless he succeeded once more in getting clear away, for although I tracked him for some little distance, I eventually lost his trail in a rocky patch of ground.

Bitterly did I anathematise the hour in which I had relied on a borrowed weapon, and in my disappointment and vexation I abused owner, maker, and rifle with fine impartiality. On extracting the unexploded cartridge, I found that the needle had not struck home, the cap being only slightly dented; so that the whole fault did indeed lie with the rifle, which I later returned to Farquhar with polite compliments. Seriously, however, my continued ill-luck was most exasperating; and the result was that the Indians were more than ever confirmed in their belief that the lions were really evil spirits, proof against mortal weapons. Certainly, they did seem to bear charmed lives.

After this dismal failure there was, of course, nothing to do but to return to camp. Before doing so, however, I proceeded to view the dead donkey, which I found to have been only slightly devoured at the quarters. It is a curious fact that lions always begin at the tail of their prey and eat upwards towards the head. As their meal had thus been interrupted evidently at the very beginning, I felt pretty sure that one or other of the brutes would return to the carcase at nightfall. Accordingly, as there was no tree of any kind close at hand, I had a staging erected some ten feet away from the body. This *machan* was about twelve feet high and was composed of four poles stuck into the ground and inclined toward each other at the top, where a plank was lashed to serve as a seat. Further, as the nights were still pitch dark, I had the donkey's carcase secured by strong wires to a neighbouring stump, so that the lions might not be able to drag it away before I could get a shot at them.

At sundown, therefore, I took up my position on my airy perch, and much to the disgust of my gun-bearer, Mahina, I decided to go alone. I would gladly have taken him with me, indeed, but he had a bad cough, and I was afraid lest he should make any involuntary noise or movement which might spoil all. Darkness fell almost immediately, and everything became extraordinarily still. The silence of an African jungle on a dark night needs to be experienced to be realised; it is most impressive, especially when one is absolutely alone and isolated from one's fellow creatures, as I was then. The solitude and stillness, and the purpose of my vigil, all had their effect on me, and from a condition of strained expectancy I gradually fell into a dreamy mood which harmonised well with my surroundings. Suddenly I was startled out of my reverie by the snapping of a twig; and, straining my ears for a further sound, I fancied I could hear the rustling of a large body forcing its way through the bush. "The man-eater," I thought to myself; "surely to-night my luck will change and I shall bag one of the brutes." Profound silence again succeeded; I sat on my eyrie like a statue, every nerve tense with excitement. Very soon, however, all doubt as to the presence of the lion was dispelled. A deep long-drawn sigh—sure sign of hunger—came up from the bushes, and the rustling commenced again as he cautiously advanced. In a moment or two a sudden stop, followed by an angry growl, told me that my presence had been noticed; and I began to fear that disappointment awaited me once more.

But no; matters quickly took an unexpected turn. The hunter became the hunted; and instead of either making off or coming for the bait prepared for him, the lion began stealthily to stalk *me!* For about two hours he horrified me by slowly creeping round and round my crazy structure, gradually edging his way nearer and nearer. Every moment I expected him to rush it; and the staging had not been constructed with an eye to such a possibility. If one of the rather flimsy poles should break, or if the lion could spring the twelve feet which separated me from the ground . . . the thought was scarcely a pleasant one. I began to feel distinctly "creepy," and heartily repented my folly in having placed myself in such a dangerous position. I kept perfectly still, however, hardly daring even to blink my eyes: but the long continued strain was telling on my nerves, and my feelings may be better imagined than described when about midnight suddenly something came flop and struck me on the back of the head. For a moment I was so terrified that I nearly fell off the plank, as I thought that the lion had sprung on me from behind. Regaining my senses in a second or two, I realised that I had been hit by nothing more formidable than an owl, which had doubtless mistaken me for the branch of a tree—not a very alarming thing to happen in ordinary circumstances, I admit, but coming at the time it did, it almost paralysed me. The involuntary start which

I could not help giving was immediately answered by a sinister growl from below.

After this I again kept as still as I could, though absolutely trembling with excitement; and in a short while I heard the lion begin to creep stealthily towards me. I could barely make out his form as he crouched among the whitish undergrowth; but I saw enough for my purpose and before he could come any nearer, I took careful aim and pulled the trigger. The sound of the shot was at once followed by a most terrific roar, and then I could hear him leaping about in all directions. I was no longer able to see him, however, as his first bound had taken him into the thick bush; but to make assurance doubly sure, I kept blazing away in the direction in which I heard him plunging about. At length came a series of mighty groans, gradually subsiding into deep sighs, and finally ceasing altogether; and I felt convinced that one of the "devils" who had so long harried us would trouble us no more.

As soon as I ceased firing, a tumult of inquiring voices was borne across the dark jungle from the men in camp about a quarter of a mile away. I shouted back that I was safe and sound, and that one of the lions was dead: whereupon such a mighty cheer went up from all the camps as must have astonished the denizens of the jungle for miles around. Shortly I saw scores of lights twinkling through the bushes: every man in camp turned out, and with tom-toms beating and horns blowing came running to the scene. They surrounded my eyrie, and to my amazement prostrated themselves on the ground before me, saluting me with cries of "*Mabarak! Mabarak!*" which I believe means "blessed one" or "saviour." All the same, I refused to allow any search to be made that night for the body of the lion, in case his companion might be close by; besides, it was possible that he might be still alive, and capable of making a last spring. Accordingly we all returned in triumph to the camp, where great rejoicings were kept up for the remainder of the night, the Swahili and other African natives celebrating the occasion by an especially wild and savage dance.

For my part, I anxiously awaited the dawn; and even before it was thoroughly light I was on my way to the eventful spot, as I could not completely persuade myself that even yet the "devil" might not have eluded me in some uncanny and mysterious way. Happily my fears proved groundless, and I was relieved to find that my luck—after playing me so many exasperating tricks—had really turned at last. I had scarcely traced the blood for more than a few paces when, on rounding a bush, I was startled to see a huge lion right in front of me, seemingly alive and crouching for a spring. On looking closer, however, I satisfied myself that he was really and truly stone-dead, whereupon my followers crowded round, laughed and danced and shouted with joy like children, and bore me in triumph shoulder-high round the dead body. These thanksgiving ceremonies being over, I examined the body and found that two bullets had taken effect—one close behind the left shoulder, evidently penetrating the heart, and the other in the off hind leg. The prize was indeed one to be proud of; his length from tip of nose to tip of tail was nine feet eight inches, he stood three feet nine inches high, and it took eight men to carry him back to camp. The only blemish was that the skin was much scored by the *boma* thorns through which he had so often forced his way in carrying off his victims.

The news of the death of one of the notorious man-eaters soon spread far and wide over the country: telegrams of congratulations came pouring in, and scores of people flocked from up and down the railway to see the skin for themselves.

The Death of the Second Man-Eater

It must not be imagined that with the death of this lion our troubles at Tsavo were at an end; his companion was still at large, and very soon began to make us unpleasantly aware of the fact. Only a few nights elapsed before he made an attempt to get at the Permanent Way Inspector, climbing up the steps of his bungalow and prowling round the verandah. The Inspector, hearing the noise and thinking it was a drunken coolie, shouted angrily "Go away!" but, fortunately for him, did not attempt to come out or to open the door. Thus disappointed in his attempt to obtain a meal of human flesh, the lion seized a couple of the Inspector's goats and devoured them there and then.

On hearing of this occurrence, I determined to sit up the next night near the Inspector's bungalow. Fortunately there was a vacant iron shanty close at hand, with a convenient loophole in it for firing from; and outside this I placed three full-grown goats as bait, tying them to a half-length of rail, weighing about 250 lbs. The night passed uneventfully until just before daybreak, when at last the lion turned up, pounced on one of the goats and made off with it, at the same time dragging away the others, rail and all. I fired several shots in his direction, but it was pitch dark and quite impossible to see anything, so I only succeeded in hitting one of the goats. I often longed for a flashlight on such occasions.

Next morning I started off in pursuit and was joined by some others from the camp. I found that the trail of the goats and rail was easily followed, and we soon came up, about a quarter of a mile away, to where the lion was still busy at his meal. He was concealed in some thick bush and growled angrily on hearing our approach; finally, as we got closer, he suddenly made a charge, rushing through the bushes at a great pace. In an instant, every man of the party scrambled hastily up the nearest tree, with the exception of one of my assistants, Mr. Winkler, who stood steadily by me throughout. The brute, however, did not press his charge home: and on throwing stones into the bushes where we had last seen him, we guessed by the silence that he had slunk off. We therefore advanced cautiously, and on getting up to the place discovered that he had indeed escaped us, leaving two of the goats scarcely touched.

Thinking that in all probability the lion would return as usual to finish his meal, I had a very strong scaffolding put up a few feet away from the dead goats, and took up my position on it before dark. On this occasion I brought my gun-bearer, Mahina, to take a turn at watching, as I was by this time worn out for want of sleep, having spent so many nights on the look-out. I was just dozing off comfortably when suddenly I felt my arm seized, and on looking up saw Mahina pointing in the direction of the goats. "*Sher!*" ("Lion!") was all he whispered. I grasped my double smooth-bore, which I had charged with slug, and waited patiently. In a few moments I was rewarded, for as I watched the spot where I expected the lion to appear, there was a rustling among the bushes and I saw him stealthily emerge into the open and pass almost directly beneath us. I fired both barrels practically together into his shoulder, and to my joy could see him go down under the force of the blow. Quickly I reached for the magazine rifle, but before I could use it, he was out of sight among the bushes, and I had to fire after him quite at random. Nevertheless I was confident of getting him in the morning, and accordingly set out as soon as it was light. For over a mile there was no difficulty in following the blood-trail, and as he had rested several times I felt sure that he had been badly wounded. In the end, however, my hunt proved fruitless, for after a time the traces of blood ceased and the surface of the ground became rocky, so that I was no longer able to follow the spoor.

About this time Sir Guilford Molesworth, K.C.I.E, late Consulting Engineer to the Government of India for State Railways, passed through Tsavo on a tour of inspection on behalf of the Foreign Office. After examining the bridge and other works and expressing his satisfaction, he took a number of photographs, one or two of which he has kindly allowed me to reproduce in this book. He thoroughly sympathised with us in all the trials we had endured from the man-eaters, and was delighted that one at least was dead. When he asked me if I expected to get the second lion soon, I well remember his half-doubting smile as I rather too confidently asserted that I hoped to bag him also in the course of a few days.

As it happened, there was no sign of our enemy for about ten days after this, and we began to hope that he had died of his wounds in the bush. All the same we still took every precaution at night, and it was fortunate that we did so, as otherwise at least one more victim would have been added to the list. For on the night of December 27, I was suddenly aroused by terrified shouts from my trolley men, who slept in a tree close outside my *boma* to the effect that a lion was trying to get at them. It would have been madness to have gone out, as the moon was hidden by dense clouds and it was absolutely impossible to see anything more than a yard in front of one; so all I could do was to fire off a few rounds just to frighten the brute away. This apparently had the desired effect, for the men were not further molested that night; but the man-eater had evidently prowled about for some time, for we found in the morning that he had gone right into every one of their tents, and round the tree was a regular ring of his footmarks.

The following evening I took up my position in this same tree, in the hope that he would make another attempt. The night began badly, as while climbing up to my perch I very nearly put my hand on a venomous snake which was lying coiled round one of the branches. As may be imagined, I came down again very quickly, but one of my men managed to despatch it with a long pole. Fortunately the night was clear and cloudless, and the moon made every thing almost as bright as day. I kept watch until about 2 A.M., when I roused Mahina to take his turn. For about an hour I slept peacefully with my back to the tree, and then woke suddenly with an uncanny feeling that something was wrong. Mahina, however, was on the alert, and had seen nothing; and although I looked carefully round us on all sides,

I too could discover nothing unusual. Only half satisfied, I was about to lie back again, when I fancied I saw something move a little way off among the low bushes. On gazing intently at the spot for a few seconds, I found I was not mistaken. It was the man-eater, cautiously stalking us.

The ground was fairly open round our tree, with only a small bush every here and there; and from our position it was a most fascinating sight to watch this great brute stealing stealthily round us, taking advantage of every bit of cover as he came. His skill showed that he was an old hand at the terrible game of man-hunting: so I determined to run no undue risk of losing him this time. I accordingly waited until he got quite close—about twenty yards away—and then fired my .303 at his chest. I heard the bullet strike him, but unfortunately it had no knock-down effect, for with a fierce growl he turned and made off with great long bounds. Before he disappeared from sight, however, I managed to have three more shots at him from the magazine rifle, and another growl told me that the last of these had also taken effect.

We awaited daylight with impatience, and at the first glimmer of dawn we set out to hunt him down. I took a native tracker with me, so that I was free to keep a good look-out, while Mahina followed immediately behind with a Martini carbine. Splashes of blood being plentiful, we were able to get along quickly; and we had not proceeded more than a quarter of a mile through the jungle when suddenly a fierce warning growl was heard right in front of us. Looking cautiously through the bushes, I could see the man-eater glaring out in our direction, and showing his tusks in an angry snarl. I at once took careful aim and fired. Instantly he sprang out and made a most determined charge down on us. I fired again and knocked him over; but in a second he was up once more and coming for me as fast as he could in his crippled condition. A third shot had no apparent effect, so I put out my hand for the Martini, hoping to stop him with it. To my dismay, however, it was not there. The terror of the sudden charge had proved too much for Mahina, and both he and the carbine were by this time well on their way up a tree. In the circumstances there was nothing to do but follow suit, which I did without loss of time: and but for the fact that one of my shots had broken a hind leg, the brute would most certainly have had me. Even as it was, I had barely time to swing myself up out of his reach before he arrived at the foot of the tree.

When the lion found he was too late, he started to limp back to the thicket; but by this time I had seized the carbine from Mahina, and the first shot I fired from it seemed to give him his quietus, for he fell over and lay motionless. Rather foolishly, I at once scrambled down from the tree and walked up towards him. To my surprise and no little alarm he jumped up and attempted another charge. This time, however, a Martini bullet in the chest and another in the head finished him for good and all; he dropped in his tracks not five yards away from me, and died gamely, biting savagely at a branch which had fallen to the ground.

By this time all the workmen in camp, attracted by the sound of the firing, had arrived on the scene, and so great was their resentment against the brute who had killed such numbers of their comrades that it was only with the greatest difficulty that I could restrain them from tearing the dead body to pieces. Eventually, amid the wild rejoicings of the natives and coolies, I had the lion carried to my *boma*, which was close at hand. On examination we found no less than six bullet holes in the body, and embedded only a little way in the flesh of the back was the slug which I had fired into him from the scaffolding about ten days previously. He measured nine feet six inches from tip of nose to tip of tail, and stood three feet eleven and a half inches high; but, as in the case of his companion, the skin was disfigured by being deeply scored all over by the *boma* thorns.

The news of the death of the second "devil" soon spread far and wide over the country, and natives actually travelled from up and down the line to have a look at my trophies and at the "devil-killer," as they called me. Best of all, the coolies who had absconded came flocking back to Tsavo, and much to my relief work was resumed and we were never again troubled by man-eaters. It was amusing, indeed, to notice the change which took place in the attitude of the workmen towards me after I had killed the two lions. Instead of wishing to murder me, as they once did, they could not now do enough for me, and as a token of their gratitude they presented me with a beautiful silver bowl, as well as with a long poem written in Hindustani describing all our trials and my ultimate victory. As the poem relates our troubles in somewhat quaint and biblical language, I have given a translation of it in the appendix. The bowl I shall always consider my most highly prized and hardest won trophy. The inscription on it reads as follows:—

Sir,—We, your Overseer, Timekeepers, Mistaris *and Workmen, present you with this bowl as a token of our gratitude to you for your bravery in killing two man-eating lions at great risk to your own life, thereby saving us from the fate of being devoured by these terrible monsters who nightly broke into our tents and took our fellow-workers from our side. In presenting you with this bowl, we all add our prayers for your long life, happiness and prosperity. We shall ever remain, Sir, Your grateful servants,*

Baboo Purshotam Hurjee Purmar, *Overseer and Clerk of the Works, on behalf of your Workmen.*

Dated at Tsavo, *January* 30, 1899.

Before I leave the subject of "The Man-Eaters of Tsavo," it may be of interest to mention that these two lions possess the distinction, probably unique among wild animals, of having been specifically referred to in the House of Lords by the Prime Minister of the day. Speaking of the difficulties which had been encountered in the construction of the Uganda Railway, the late Lord Salisbury said:—

"The whole of the works were put a stop to for three weeks because a party of man-eating lions appeared in the locality and conceived a most unfortunate taste for our porters. At last the labourers entirely declined to go on unless they were guarded by an iron entrenchment. Of course it is difficult to work a railway under these conditions, and until we found an enthusiastic sportsman to get rid of these lions, our enterprise was seriously hindered."

Also, *The Spectator* of March 3, 1900, had an article entitled "The Lions that Stopped the Railway," from which the following extracts are taken:—

> *"The parallel to the story of the lions which stopped the rebuilding of Samaria must occur to everyone, and if the Samaritans had quarter as good cause for their fears as had the railway coolies, their wish to propitiate the local deities is easily understood. If the whole body of lion anecdote, from the days of the Assyrian Kings till the last year of the nineteenth century, were collated and brought together, it would not equal in tragedy or atrocity, in savageness or in sheer insolent contempt for man, armed or unarmed, white or black, the story of these two beasts. . . .*
>
> *"To what a distance the whole story carries us back, and how impossible it becomes to account for the survival of primitive man against this kind of foe! For fire—which has hitherto been regarded as his main safeguard against the carnivora—these cared nothing. It is curious that the Tsavo lions were not killed by poison, for strychnine is easily used, and with effect.* Poison may have been used early in the history of man, for its powers are employed with strange skill by the men in the tropical forest, both in American and West Central Africa. But there is no evidence that the old inhabitants of Europe, or of Assyria or Asia Minor, ever killed lions or wolves by this means. They looked to the King or chief, or some champion, to kill these monsters for them. It was not the sport but the duty of Kings, and was in itself a title to be a*

ruler of men. Theseus, who cleared the roads of beasts and robbers; Hercules, the lion killer; St. George, the dragon-slayer, and all the rest of their class owed to this their everlasting fame. From the story of the Tsavo River we can appreciate their services to man even at this distance of time. When the jungle twinkled with hundreds of lamps, as the shout went on from camp to camp that the first lion was dead, as the hurrying crowds fell prostrate in the midnight forest, laying their heads on his feet, and the Africans danced savage and ceremonial dances of thanksgiving, Mr. Patterson must have realised in no common way what it was to have been a hero and deliverer in the days when man was not yet undisputed lord of the creation, and might pass at any moment under the savage dominion of the beasts."

(*I may mention that poison *was* tried, but without effect. The poisoned carcases of transport animals which had died from the bite of the tsetse fly were placed in likely spots, but the wily man-eaters would not touch them, and much preferred live men to dead donkeys.)

Well had the two man-eaters earned all this fame; they had devoured between them no less than twenty-eight Indian coolies, in addition to scores of unfortunate African natives of whom no official record was kept.

Some Tiger Stories

Sir Richard Dane

I SHOT MY FIRST TIGER IN THE KANKER STATE IN THE CENTRAL Provinces in January, 1900, under the wing of a gentleman who had shot many tigers and had had much experience of the sport. The lesson, which I had taken most to heart, was that a long shot taken in the direction of the beat might drive the tiger back into the beat and lead to a casualty among the beaters. There were three tigers in the beat, a tigress and two three-quarter grown cubs. My machan had been tied in front so as to give me the first chance of a shot, and my mentor sat in a machan behind me, so as to shoot any animal which might escape me. My machan was badly tied, especially for a man shooting, as I do, from the left shoulder. The string bed, which formed it, was tied with one end facing the beat, and along the left of the machan there were tree trunks. On this side, therefore, I could fire only straight in front of me, but I was too inexperienced to recognise fully the unsatisfactory nature of the position, and settled myself in the machan without making any objection. As the beat proceeded the tigress appeared and stood on my left front, looking up apparently at one of the stops. She gave me as good a shot as I have ever had in a beat, as she was broadside on and quite motionless; but the distance was over 100 yards, and, being very anxious not to be the cause of any mishap, I decided to allow her to approach. Suddenly, with a "Wouf," she started off at a gallop to the left, passed instantly out of my fire zone, and I was compelled to look on helplessly as she passed the machan. She was fired at but missed by my mentor, and got clean away. One of the cubs followed, and I got in a shot at it, as it passed, but missed. The other cub gave me an easy shot, and I killed it. If I had shot the tigress we should probably have bagged all three, but I had correctly carried out instructions, and the instructions were absolutely sound. The line between success and failure, in big-game shooting, is a very narrow one.

I then shot a fine tiger in a beat in the Bustar State, killing him with a single shot as he walked fast through the bushes. I also killed a fine panther by moonlight, when sitting up over a kill, though the body was unfortunately not found until the skin was spoiled. On the whole, therefore, I did pretty well for a beginner in this expedition . . .

I then took part in a tiger-shoot with elephants in the Terai on the border of the Bahraich district of Oudh, in April, 1900, and my companions were Mr. Harrison, the Collector of the district, and Mr. A. Wood, the Manager of the Kapurthala Estates in Oudh. I had the elephant Chainchal on this occasion, and did pretty well. It was, I think, established that I put the first bullet into a tigress, which was subsequently killed by Harrison; but I made no claim for the skin, as the tigress was unquestionably knocked over and killed by him.

We then had a beat for a tiger which was fired at by both Harrison and myself, and badly wounded, and was eventually finished off by Wood. Both Harrison and myself were using black powder .500 Express rifles, but fortunately he had only wax in his bullets, and I had copper-tubes in mine. We both claimed the shot; and, as the result of a friendly discussion, it appeared probable that the successful shot was Harrison's. I therefore resigned the tiger with the best grace possible, and we were all round the carcass during the skinning operation, when Harrison's servant, who was groping in the inside of the tiger, held up something, saying, "What is this?" Examination showed that it was the copper tube of my bullet, making it clear that mine had been the successful shot, and the ownership of the tiger was accordingly transferred.

This tiger broke out of the beat and might have gone clear away before he was fired at; but the Maila nullah which we were beating, with its cool, shady trees and dense cane brake and a stream of water in the centre, was a favourite place for tigers in the hot weather, and the animal, sooner than face the burning heat of the sun at midday, returned to the nullah further on, and met with his death in consequence.

It is sometimes very difficult to decide who has fired the first successful shot, but, if the contending sportsmen are required to describe accurately the position of the tiger when they fired, a carefully conducted post-mortem examination, after removal of the skin, will generally disclose the truth. The excitement of a tiger-shoot is not, however, conducive to the frame of mind which is required for a judicial investigation, and heated arguments and disputes often result.

I shot a fine panther in the same beat as the tiger, and Harrison also shot a female panther. Two or three days afterwards Wood shot a good tigress. The bag, therefore, was very evenly distributed on this occasion.

My next tiger-hunt was in January, 1901, in the Patna State, which was, at the time, in the Central Provinces, but has now been transferred to Bengal. I had a female elephant to ride and a good native shikari with me, but no European companion, and the country we were hunting contained buffaloes as well as tigers. The first tiger we heard of was said to have eaten a certain number of bullocks and buffaloes and two men, and the Uriya villagers, who had suffered from his depredations, were naturally very anxious to have him killed. The first bullock we tied out was completely devoured, and the tiger was not in the beat. He killed again the following night, however, and dragged the carcass of the bullock from the road on which it was tied to a place within a few yards of the edge of the jungle in the direction of the village, and there lay up with it. A machan was tied for me, and the beat was lined up in the rice-fields, within a few yards—as appeared from a subsequent examination—of the tiger's resting-place. The first yell given by the beaters evidently startled the tiger, and before the beat had well started I saw him emerging from the jungle on my right at a fast trot. The stop either did not see him or was seized with panic, as he made no attempt to check him. I turned quickly on the machan and fired, and the tiger broke into a gallop and disappeared. Examination showed that the shot had passed under the tiger and struck the ground well beyond the place where he had broken into a gallop.

It missed him, therefore, by a few inches only. The direction was good, and the elevation only was wrong.

This was a serious disappointment, but in the night the tiger, who was evidently a very ravenous brute, returned to the kill and dragged the remains to another hiding-place in the same jungle. The shikari wanted me to sit up for him, but I decided to have another beat. On this occasion the tiger emerged at a fast walk and gave me an easy shot, but on my wrong side. I hit him with the first barrel low down in the stomach. He gave a tremendous "Wouf," and went off at a gallop. I swung round on the machan and, as he was galloping off, made a good shot with the second barrel, and put a bullet into the centre of his back. When the beaters came up I descended and we began to look for blood. I knew that I had hit him with the first barrel, and the stop on my left said that he had answered to the second shot also. There was no blood, however, and a small piece of fat about the size of my little fingernail was the only trace of the tiger which could be found near the machan. The ground was most unfavourable, with clumps of bamboos at intervals and scrub jungle, as high as a man's waist, in between. There were, however, some trees. I sent for the riding elephant, and we advanced together, the elephant being a few paces in front, and I following on foot and keeping, as far as possible, a tree between me and the elephant, as I was doubtful of her staunchness. Before we had gone far the mahout declared that he heard the tiger growling, but I urged him to proceed, and we advanced a few paces farther. Then there was a roar, and the elephant swung round and bolted. I have never seen an elephant travel as she did on that occasion, and the mahout said afterwards that she had actually twisted his neck by the rapidity with which she swung round. It was, however, a case of "eyes front," and I stood waiting for the attack. Fortunately for me, the tiger did not charge, but retreated, attempting to escape.

The demonstration caused a general stampede, but after some time my attendants were reassured and returned. Mihtab Khan had, as he explained, laid hold of the shikari as he was retreating, but the shikari said that he had recently married a wife and was therefore obliged to take care of himself.

A protracted reconnaissance made from trees disclosed the fact that the tiger had gone, and in the bamboo clump, in which he was lying, there was a great pool of blood. The wounds had not bled until he lay down on the ground. This encouraged us all, and we started in pursuit, tracking the tiger by the blood which was now flowing. We followed him for a considerable distance into the open country, and there in a clump of bushes at the foot of a tree he lay up again. The Uriyas, as Indians often do, passed from panic to over-confidence, and I had the greatest difficulty in keeping them behind me. I had placed Mihtab Khan on the elephant, which followed along behind us, to give confidence to the mahout; and from the elephant Mihtab Khan and the mahout saw the tiger's ear move, as he lay in the clump of bushes. The shikari and I had passed within a few yards of him. We drew back and held a council of war. I had the black powder .500 Express, with which I had shot the other four tigers, and the shikari had a Lee-Metford. My idea was to give the Lee-Metford to Mihtab Khan and allow him to fire from the back of the elephant, and to shoot the tiger, as he rose, with the .500; but the mahout urged me to mount the elephant and shoot, and, as she was then standing very quietly, I decided to try this. The elephant, as I afterwards heard, would not stand a shot-gun; but, when drawn back from the proximity of the tiger, she allowed me to mount without difficulty and then, under pressure from the mahout, she advanced and stood within 30 yards of the bushes. After some time I made out the outline of the tiger crouching in the bushes, and the elephant allowed me to take a steady aim. As soon as I fired, however, she swung round with amazing quickness; and, seeing that I must be thrown off, as I was merely sitting on the pad and my hands were engaged with the rifle, I jumped and landed on my feet, but fell back, cracking the stock of my rifle. I sprang to my feet with very creditable rapidity, but fortunately for me the tiger was done for. He staggered to his feet but did not leave the bushes, and a shot by the shikari finally laid him low. My shot from the elephant merely passed through the forearm and did him no appreciable injury, but the shot in the back, as he galloped off, had inflicted a mortal wound. The shot in the lower part of the belly also caused serious internal injury.

He was a young tiger, with a very good coat. The shikari thought he was too young to have commenced man-eating, but there did not appear to be any other tiger in the neighbourhood, and he was a very voracious animal. The view that only old or crippled tigers become man-eaters is only partly correct. Cubs, which have been brought up on human flesh, and which have repeatedly seen their mother attacking and killing human beings, must frequently take to the business when they begin hunting on their own account, especially if game is scarce in the place in which they reside, as was the case in the Patna State. Altogether, this tiger provided three successive days' entertainment. The rifle, though damaged, was not completely unserviceable, and I was able to go on shooting.

For some days after this excitement the elephant was decidedly mischievous. On the day following the death of the tiger she tried to catch hold of a native with her trunk as he ran past her; and on another occasion, after the mahout's wife had given her some bananas, she seized the woman round the waist with her trunk and lifted her up, but did not actually injure her. I was in the tent when this occurred, but, hearing a row, I came out and found the mahout abusing the elephant as only an Indian can.

She was, I think, the fastest and most comfortable elephant I have ever ridden, but she had a temper and was said to have killed several people. The mahout managed her well, but he told me that she had been the favourite riding elephant of the Raja of Bustar, and that, on one occasion, when the Raja had gone down to the river to bathe and had dismounted from the elephant, she suddenly seized a man and tore him in two. The Raja, as was said, fell off his chair with fright, and after this, not unnaturally, parted with the elephant. The mahout said that she had killed five or six people at different times after this, but that he had succeeded in reducing her to submission. On one occasion, as he said, he had tied her up for the night and lain down to sleep at a safe distance, but had omitted to remove out of her reach the lance, which is used to subdue a refractory elephant. In the night he felt something in his hair, and, after brushing at it ineffectually, awoke to find that the elephant had got hold of the lance, broken it in two, and was trying to twist one of the broken pieces into his hair so that she might be able to pull him over to her. I am not prepared to vouch for the truth of this story; but, if it were a lie, it was exceedingly well told, and I saw no reason at the time to doubt the man. He became quite excited at the reminiscence. He was certainly a good mahout, and behaved well on the day when the tiger was shot.

On any occasion on which I was left alone on the back of the elephant, after hearing these stories, I was always glad to see the mahout return; but my personal relations with the elephant were very satisfactory.

We then started to hunt a man-eating family, which were said to have eaten over twenty people between August and the time of my visit in January. There were a tigress and two well-grown cubs, and a tiger was said to join the party occasionally. These tigers had created a scare, and we had to tie out our own buffaloes. It was rather creepy work, but the shikari did this bravely enough. The last kill had occurred about eight days before we arrived on the scene, and the villagers had been too frightened to visit the place. I went there with the old man, who had been with the victim when he was killed, and saw the two bundles of wood which they were tying up at the time. Death appeared to have been instantaneous, as his companion said that the man, when seized, did not utter a cry. The drag was clearly visible in the grass, and, after following it for a few yards, we found the man's loin-cloth, and, farther on, the place where he had been eaten. We hunted for some days and tied out baits, but saw nothing of the tigers, which had for some reason or other left the neighbourhood . . .

In April, 1901, I had another tiger-hunt in the Terai, on the border of the Bahraich district, with Mr. Faunthorpe, I.C.S., who was then the Collector, and Mr. A. Wood. We got no tigers in Nepal, and the expedition was in danger of being a complete failure, when we received news of a tigress which had killed in one day three head of cattle in a village in the Bahraich district, near the border. We moved camp to this place, and we found that the cover in which the tigress was lying, consisted of a triangular patch of high reeds on the border of a small lagoon. The line of elephants was formed at the base of the triangle, and the beat was a pretty and exciting one. Wood was with the line; I had the next position in front of the beat, and Faunthorpe was beyond me. The tigress was soon on the move, and we could hear her splashing in the reeds as she moved along the edge of the lagoon. When the line was half-way through the patch of reeds she charged the elephants with a roar and threw the line into confusion. With a little more courage she could have broken through and escaped, but her heart failed her and she retreated until she was pushed up into the very apex of the triangle. She might have escaped across the water, as this side of the beat was unprotected; but she would not face the open. At last, when driven into the extreme corner of the reeds, she rushed out on the side where we were all standing. Wood had a shot at her but missed, and she came straight for my elephant. Seeing the elephant, she declined the encounter, and swung round, and as she swung round I fired. A second later Faunthorpe's shot rang out. Our shots were so nearly simultaneous that he did not hear my shot, but I heard his. Two more shots were fired by Wood and myself at the tigress, as she was struggling in the grass; but these were misses. My shot struck the tigress in the heart, and Faunthorpe's shot struck her in the back near the shoulder as she was end on to him. I was using an Express and firing shell, and the others fired solid bullets; there was, therefore, no difficulty in identifying the different shots on this occasion. Our two shots were fired almost simultaneously, but Faunthorpe, seeing that my shot had killed the tigress, did not make any claim. I rode an elephant belonging to the Maharajah of Balrampur on this occasion, and she stood staunchly when the shots were fired though she was not highly tried.

In 1903–4, I had a run of ill-luck, taking part in three expeditions to the Terai, in the course of which no less than nine tigers and tigresses and two cubs were shot, and the only animal which fell to my lot was a large panther, which I shot over a kill.

On the first occasion, in April, 1903, the party consisted of Mr. A. Wood, the late Major Lumsden, I.M.S., Mr. Channer, the Divisional Forest Officer, and myself, and we hunted a portion of the Terai at some distance from the ground which we hunted during my first two expeditions. Major Lumsden rode the elephant Chainchal, and I was riding an elephant which was lent me by the Maharajah of Balrampur. Shortly after our arrival on the ground a good tiger was marked down in a very small patch of thick jungle on the bank of a small deep nullah, or stream, which was overhung with trees. The tiger had killed a chital, and dragged the carcass into the cover, and it was therefore a sure find. Lumsden was with the beat; Wood had the best place on the bank of the nullah at the end of the patch of cover; and Channer and I were among the trees on the opposite side of the nullah. The guns were, therefore, roughly speaking, at the four corners of a square with the corner, at which Wood was posted, projecting. The patch of jungle was very thick, and Lumsden was not thought to have any chance. Chainchal's mahout, however (Karim by name), was a very plucky, intelligent fellow, with very good vision, and while the elephants were trying to force their way into the patch of jungle, he saw the tiger standing in thick cover. Lumsden failed to see him until he moved. He then fired both barrels, but he had missed his chance, and the tiger rushed from the thicket and plunged into the water with a tremendous splash, swimming straight across to where I was posted among the trees on the other bank. An overhanging branch obscured my vision at the particular point at which the tiger was crossing; and, though I could see the water moving as he swam, I could not actually see his head. He was, however, making for the bank very near the place where my elephant was standing; and the shikari in the howdah behind me, who perhaps saw the animal, was adjuring me to shoot. Very unwisely, therefore, I fired. The tiger answered to the shot with a roar, and the bullet evidently struck the water very near him. My elephant then swung round so that I could not fire again, and, looking backwards, I could just see the tiger climb the bank behind me. Wood had a shot at him as he ascended the bank, but missed. The tiger then made off along the bank and ran right into Channer. Thinking he was trapped, he turned with a roar and plunged with another splash into the water, and swam back to the thicket in which he was lying at the outset. Owing to the overhanging trees, he was not visible after he sprang into the water until he reached cover. After some time he was beaten out again, and this time took the line he was expected to take, giving Wood a good chance. A shot near the head stopped him, and a second bullet finished him off. My shot was thought to have been a hit, but examination showed that it was Wood's tiger. This is the only occasion I can remember in which every member of a party had a fair chance in turn at a tiger. The beat also was one of the prettiest and most exciting in which I have ever taken part.

After this the shikaris reported that there were no other tigers in the vicinity of the camp, and went to some place at a considerable distance to look for tracks. We were reconciling ourselves to some hot days of waiting, but very soon after the shikaris had gone some herdsmen came in and said that a tiger had killed one of their buffaloes. We went to the place and found a recently killed buffalo; but the only patch of forest which was near the place had been fired, and, although it had apparently been too damp to burn well, some fallen trees were actually on fire. We tried a beat, and the tiger was there right enough. In shooting with elephants, there is very little danger to the beaters, and, as everyone is anxious to put the first bullet into the tiger, there is often some rather wild shooting. As the line advanced both Wood and I had shots. I fired without success at a movement in the high grass; and then the tiger, which was fairly cornered, broke with a roar into the open, a little to my left front. It was a grand spectacle, as the tiger showed up magnificently on the short green grass. With Chainchal, I should probably have got that tiger; but my elephant was not a good one, and I tried her rather severely. Leaning well out of the howdah, I waited until the tiger was close up so as to make sure of the shot; but, just as I was pulling the trigger, the elephant funked and swung round with a jerk, and the rifle went off in the air. By the time the elephant had been turned round the tiger had galloped some distance; shots fired at his tail by Wood and myself were unsuccessful, and he got clean away. It was very disappointing; but it was partly my fault, as I ought to have made allowance for the possibility of the elephant funking, and fired as soon as the tiger appeared.

The Terai, or moist alluvial land, lying between the branches of the mighty Gagra River, provides grazing in the hot weather for large herds of cattle and buffaloes. The grass is burnt in the spring, and at the end of April, the land is covered with short green grass. Tigers still abound in this part of India, and toll is taken of the herds. These grazing buffaloes will, as one of the herdsmen informed me, respond to a particular call announcing the advent of a tiger, and will charge *en masse* and drive the animal away; but young buffaloes, when detached from the herd, are not infrequently attacked and killed.

A tigress with three small cubs was then marked down in a dry ravine near a village. The tigress was in poor condition, and evidently found a difficulty in feeding her numerous progeny; and apparently she had taken up her quarters in the ravine on the chance of killing one of the village cattle, as there was no game in the vicinity. Wood was with the line of elephants on this occasion; Lumsden was on the left bank, and Channer and I were on the right bank of the ravine. The beat was up the ravine. Shortly after the beat started Wood, whose elephant was moving along the bed of the ravine, saw the tigress crouching on the sand, facing him at a short distance. He fired at her with a shotgun loaded with ball, and the shot passed through one of her ears, which was evidently cocked forward. Subsequent examination showed that the bullet drilled a small round hole, the edges of which were not even reddened with blood. It was a close shave, but the animal was quite uninjured and blood was not drawn. The tigress then appeared near Lumsden, who fired, and, as he subsequently said, knocked her over into the ravine. Very shortly after this she appeared on my side of the ravine. She walked quietly and quickly round a bush, and did not appear to be wounded, and I fired, hitting her with my Express on the near side, but rather far back. She disappeared into the ravine and wandered about there for a little time. Then Channer, who was shooting with a small-bore, high-velocity rifle, saw her and fired, and shortly after, she was seen to be dead. Two bullet-holes were visible in the skin, one a small one in the back near the neck, and the other a large one in the near side. Lumsden was quite confident that he had hit the tigress and knocked her over, and suggested that the large hole in the side was the hole of exit of his bullet. Both the other sportsmen thought that the tiger was Lumsden's, and Channer did not claim a hit. There was much blood in the ravine, but it was impossible to say from which wound it proceeded, and I therefore contented myself with pointing out that the hole in the side was the hole of my bullet, and did not claim the tigress and was not present at the post-mortem. The natives who skinned and cut up the tigress were told to produce the bullets, and mine was duly produced, and was admitted by Major Lumsden to be not his. His bullet, which was also an expanding one, was not found. On the following morning, when we were looking at the skin, Lumsden himself noticed a small round hole in the skin of the belly, but he was so convinced that he had shot the tigress that he did not give the matter much attention. I said nothing, but thought a good deal. It was clear to me that Lumsden had missed the tigress, and that I had put the first bullet into her, and that she had then been killed by Channer, whose bullet had entered the back and come out through the belly. I kept my conclusions, however, to myself, merely resolving that I would always be present at a post-mortem in the future. Poor Lumsden was a good sportsman, and was perfectly convinced that he had shot the tigress; but, as already said, a painstaking investigation is often necessary before it can be determined who has scored the first hit.

A forest officer of my acquaintance told me that on one occasion he had arranged a tiger-shoot for two military officers. One had, if I remember right, shot a tiger before, and the other had not. The tiger went first to the more experienced sportsman of the two, who fired at it. The tiger then went to the other man, who fired at it and killed it. Overjoyed at his good fortune, he chaffed his friend about his bad shot, and the other accepted the chaff. The forest officer, from curiosity, went along the route by which the tiger had approached the second machan, and found blood all along the track. But, where ignorance is bliss, it is folly to be wise; both the sportsmen were satisfied, and he left them in blissful ignorance of his discovery.

Major Lumsden shot two of the small cubs. The third must also have died, as they were much too young to hunt for themselves.

Our next hunt was an exciting one. A tiger was marked down in a thick bed of reeds in a swampy clearing in the middle of sal forest. We posted ourselves round the reeds, and the tiger broke out near the place where Channer was posted; but, as well as I remember, he did not, owing to some difficulty with his elephant, get a shot. As the tiger was disappearing into the forest Lumsden fired and put a bullet into him. There was very little blood, and it was uncertain how far the tiger had gone; but we formed a long line in the forest, with the elephants about 50 yards apart, and drove forward in the hope of rounding him up. I was on the extreme right of the line, and before we had gone far the mahout said that he heard the tiger growling. I heard him also and ought, perhaps, to have called a halt and sent for the others. I was afraid, however, that the tiger might escape, as he did not appear to be badly wounded, and was also, it must be admitted, very anxious to see a fine charge. The prospect of an encounter, therefore, was not unwelcome. I accordingly encouraged the mahout to proceed; and, as soon as we advanced, the tiger burst from some bushes at the foot of a tree in which he was lying and charged.

I have heard it said that a tiger always charges at a fast run. This one charged at a gallop. He was in the middle of a spring, with his forelegs stretched out in front and the hind-legs stretched out straight behind him, when I fired. Directly I fired, the elephant swung round so that I could not fire the second barrel, and the tiger pushed home the charge and seized her by the middle of the thigh. In the struggle that ensued I received a severe bruise on the forearm, but was not otherwise injured, though I was in great danger of being crushed, as the howdah was in constant collision with a tree or trees. The howdah, which was very strongly built, was much damaged. I was quite unable to shoot, and got down into the howdah and trusted for safety to the elephant. Presently she flopped down, and I thought the tiger had pulled her over, but apparently she sat down so as to pinch the tiger's head and make him let go. The manœuvre succeeded, as she shook him off, and then got up and bolted. She did not, however, go far, and the mahout recovered control and stopped her. Mihtab Khan, who was behind me in the howdah, seized a bough in the struggle, and, being a powerful man, swung himself up into a tree. He had a Lee-Metford rifle in one hand, and it was a fine acrobatic performance; but he made no attempt to fire at the tiger.

I then sent for the others, and Wood and Lumsden joined me. The tiger had retreated to the bushes from which he had charged, and lay there growling. We all advanced upon him together, but my elephant was badly shaken and would not keep in line with the other two. Wood saw, or thought he saw, the tiger, and fired the first shot, but the tiger made no response and continued his low growling. Lumsden then pushed forward on Chainchal, and saw the tiger lying on the ground, and put a bullet into his brain. There were two bullet-holes in his side, and his hind-leg was broken to pieces below the hock. My bullet had struck him in the flank and run down his hind-leg, as it was stretched out behind him in the gallop. But for this he would probably have sprung on top of the elephant, and might have pulled one of us out of the howdah, as he was in no way crippled and made a most determined charge. The elephant was badly mauled, but recovered under treatment. If she had not turned round, I might have finished off the tiger without difficulty with the second barrel.

This was the best tiger-shoot in which I ever took part, though in the matter of the bag I personally came off badly. My elephant did not serve me well, but in the first beat I made a bad error of judgment. I think, however, that I put the first bullet into one of the three full-grown tigers which were killed, and contributed materially to the death of another. I may possibly have transposed the order of one or two of the hunts, but the different events and scenes are still fresh in my memory.

On the next expedition the party consisted of Mr. Wood, Major Lumsden, and myself. Wood shot a tigress and a young tiger in a beat in which we were seated in machans, but I think these were the only two shots which were fired at tigers in the course of the expedition, which was comparatively unsuccessful and uneventful. . . .

On the next occasion on which I visited the Terai, the party consisted of Major Lumsden, Mrs. Lumsden, and myself; and Mrs. Lumsden, who was a very good shot, killed a tiger in fine style. The tiger had killed in a sandy nullah, and lain up with the kill in a small patch of thick cover under the high bank of the nullah. We were all posted in the forest facing the high bank in question, Lumsden on the right, Mrs. Lumsden, who was on Chainchal, in the centre, and I on the left. We took up our positions just in time, as the tiger, scenting trouble, tried to slink away before the beat commenced. He came towards Mrs. Lumsden, who hit him with her first shot with the Rigby-Mauser she was using, but missed him with the second, as he turned and dashed back into the beat. He soon appeared again on the same line, and Mrs. Lumsden fired, hitting him in the mouth. The bullet, however, merely broke one of the canine teeth, and was diverted. A shot in the head is often a very unsatisfactory one. The tiger then tried to slink out on the right, and Lumsden had two shots at him, hitting him with one and turning him back into the beat, but missing him with the other. He then broke out at a gallop between Major and Mrs. Lumsden; and the latter, with a well-placed shot, rolled him over. I was on lower ground, and, although I was not more than 100 yards distant from Mrs. Lumsden, I could not see what was going on.

The tiger had rather a small head, and was certainly wanting in spirit, as he made no attempt to take the offensive; but he was the largest tiger that I have ever seen shot, measuring between pegs fixed in the ground, at the head and tail, 9 feet 8 inches.

A day or two after this we had a beat for two young tigers in the very place in which Wood had shot the two tigers on the previous expedition; and, as before, we were posted in machans. Mrs. Lumsden had shots at the tigers, as they broke, but failed to stop them. We then formed a long line, and hunted them through the sal forest for some hours. Lumsden had a shot at one of them, a young tigress, which then passed me at a gallop. The distance, when I fired, was considerable, but the tigress passed me apparently unwounded. One of the two shots, however, was evidently a hit, as the tigress was seen shortly afterwards lying up behind a tree. I had a staunch but very slow elephant, and Lumsden reached the place before me and put a bullet into the tiger. One or two more shots were then fired to finish her off. I made no claim, as the tigress may possibly have been wounded by Lumsden's first shot, and he certainly gave her the *coup de grâce;* but the idea among the men was that I had put a bullet into her.

After the death of the tigress we sat unsuccessfully over two kills which had occurred in the forest until a late hour, and then had a long elephant-ride back to camp, arriving there long after dark. It was hot weather, and, for a lady, it was a wonderful exhibition of endurance. We got no more tigers; but I shot the panther already referred to in the course of this expedition.

I had also an interesting but most exasperating experience, when sitting up over a kill for a tiger. One of our buffaloes had been killed, and we had beaten the ground, but the beat was blank. It was decided, therefore, that I should sit up for the tiger on the chance of his returning to the kill. A machan was constructed, and a local shikari, who was with us, climbed into it. I ordered him out, but he pleaded very hard to be allowed to remain; and, as the kill was lying among bushes, I unfortunately thought that his hearing might be of use, and allowed him to sit with me. Before it was dark the tiger came, and the shikari, suddenly seeing him standing on some rising ground above the level of the machan, completely lost his nerve. He stammered out that the tiger had come, and threw his arms round me to turn me around to have a shot at it. The tiger of course saw the movement, or heard the noise and was off. I have always regarded it as creditable to my forbearance that I did not lay a hand on the shikari . . .

In April, 1905, I made my last expedition to the Terai. The party on this occasion consisted of Mr. W. B. M. Bird, Mr. A. Wood, and myself. Major Fullerton, who had succeeded Major Lumsden as Civil Surgeon of Bahraich, was also with us during part of the time. On this occasion I rode the elephant Chainchal, and had better fortune. Our shooting-camp was on the bank of the Rapti River; and we reached the camp on the 20th of April. In the afternoon of that day and on the 21st, we hunted without any definite information and without success, but on the 22nd, a tigress was marked down in some very thick cover. The first beat we had for her was unsuccessful, but she did not leave the place, and we beat the cover again on the following day from a different direction. I was on one side of the cover a little in advance of the line of elephants, and when the line had advanced for some distance the tigress came along the edge of the cover, quite near the elephant. She was not properly visible, and I was doubtful about firing; but the mahout, Karim, pointed in the direction in which the bushes were moving and urged me to shoot. I decided, therefore, to chance a shot and fired. The shot, by good fortune, struck the tigress near the root of the tail, and she turned and rushed in the direction of the beaters outside the edge of the jungle. Chainchal stood staunchly, and with the second barrel I broke the tigress's left shoulder as she charged past me. She then lay up under a bush in the cover, and with some difficulty

I made her out from the howdah and finished her off. This tigress had a very beautifully marked skin, which makes a very handsome trophy.

On the next day a good tiger was marked down, and, having shot the tigress, I was put in what was supposed to be the worst place, at the end of the beat, Wood having the position on the side of the beat, while Bird was covering him. But fortune favoured me, and, as the line of elephants advanced, I saw the tiger's head in the jungle about 80 yards away. He was standing broadside on the Wood, and at no great distance, but was hidden from him by the bushes. Momentarily I expected to hear his rifle, but he did not fire, and the tiger remained standing with his head slightly turned, listening to the advancing elephants. I accordingly fired from a standing position in the howdah, aiming between the eyes. I made a good shot, the bullet striking the tiger between the nose and the left eye. Subsequent examination showed that the bullet, which was a shell from a .500 black powder Express, broke the palate, nearly severed the tongue, and tore off two big molar teeth, one in the upper and one in the lower jaw. The tiger probably would have died, but for the time being he was in no way crippled. For some seconds, however, he was knocked out of time; and, as nothing was visible, I hoped that I had killed him. He then got up and dashed out of the jungle at a gallop, mad with pain and rage. I failed to stop him; but, after galloping aimlessly about for some seconds, he passed near Bird, who knocked him over and then finished him, with two well-directed shots. As already said, a shot in the head or face often gives very unsatisfactory results.

On the 26th of April, Bird got his chance and shot a fine tiger, killing it with a single shot. He was using a double-barrelled .360 bore high-velocity rifle, and the tiger, with a bullet through his heart, galloped, apparently uninjured, for at least one hundred yards. Thinking he had missed, Karim urged Chainchal to speed to cut him off, and, just as an encounter was imminent, the tiger collapsed in his gallop, and fell stone dead in a small ditch. He lay in this ditch all limp and crumpled up, like a well-shot rabbit.

On the 28th, Bird shot a bear, which was marked down by the shikaris in a clump of bushes; and on the 30th of April, he shot a second tiger.

This tiger had apparently had a fight with another tiger, or with a bear, and had come off second best. He had lost one eye and was badly clawed about the body. When beaten out of the cover, in which he was lying, he broke at a gallop; but his blind eye prevented him from seeing Bird, whose elephant was standing in a fairly open place. The tiger therefore passed close to him, and was killed by a single well-placed shot.

On the 1st of May, Bird and I had a very interesting but unsuccessful sit for another tiger. The tiger had killed and eaten two or three of our buffaloes, but could not be located for the purposes of a beat. He was, evidently, a very cunning brute. One day the shikaris returned full of confidence, having marked him down in a very favourable locality, but he cleared out before we arrived and the beat was blank. We decided, therefore, to sit up over a live buffalo, which was tied upon the road upon which the other buffaloes had been killed. Our machan was well screened, having been tied in a thick leafy tree, but we could see only to our front, and could neither shoot nor see anything up the road behind us. The buffalo was tied about 20 paces from us down the road. There was no moon, but the night was clear, and the tiger came at about ten o'clock. I was dozing at the time, but Bird was watchful and heard him, and, at a touch from him, I took in the situation. The tiger stood for some time on the road to the rear of the machan, watching the buffalo, and then, as could be seen in the morning, lay down in the grass to our right, nearly parallel to the machan. Then he got up and walked round the buffalo, without showing himself; but apparently he was suspicious of a trap, and made no attack. The buffalo did not appear to be particularly alarmed, but kept head on to the tiger, and, as the tiger moved, the buffalo's head followed it round. After an hour or so, the tiger departed, and we sat there until the dawn without any further excitement. We heard spotted deer calling in the distance, and the tiger was apparently in pursuit of them.

I have heard it said, more than once, that a tiger will not kill readily a buffalo with a white blaze on his forehead. The one tied out had a white blaze, and this may have been the reason why the tiger would not attack. There certainly was no other cause apparent. I do not think the tiger could possibly have detected our presence, as we both sat very still and quiet, and the machan was well hidden.

Some days of waiting and unsuccessful hunting followed, but on the 6th of May, a tigress was marked down in the same cover in which I had shot the tiger on the 24th. Fullerton was given the best place, and had a good shot at the tigress, but unfortunately missed. I had two shots at her as she galloped away, but she broke out of the cover to my right and at some distance from me, and I failed to stop her.

This ended the hunt, and on the 7th of May, we struck our tents and started for Nipal Ganj on our return journey to Bahraich.

The Gentle Art of Tiger-Hunting

From **The Blue Tiger,** *1924*

Harry Caldwell

THE METHOD RESORTED TO BY MANY EUROPEAN SPORTSMEN for hunting tigers in India would be impracticable in the mountainous regions of China. He who covets a shot at the big cat of China's wilds must be willing to forego such a vantage point as is afforded by a comfortable seat in a howdah on the back of a well-trained elephant.

There are three principal methods which are used by sportsmen in southern China when seeking a shot at one of these royal cats. Each of these has its advantages as well as disadvantages.

The method commonly used in some parts of taking a position in a tree near a recent kill and firing upon the beast as it returns is unsatisfactory and unsportsmanlike. It is unsatisfactory because very uncertain, as the tiger more often never returns to a kill, and then, too, it is difficult in the region where I have studied tigers to find a tree in the right place. I did try the tree position on a few of my first hunts, but found the thing so unsatisfactory that I abandoned it. The only advantage is that the man behind the gun is absolutely out of danger.

Since so little has been reported from first-hand observation about the habits of tigers and certain other big game, a hunter should be actuated by more than a mere desire to secure a trophy, and should note down observations concerning the life history and movements of the animal. This has been the one impelling motive with me as I have carried the study of the tiger right into its lair, and has proven far more worth while than have the several fine specimens taken.

Cave shooting has been reported on by some sportsmen in the Amoy region, but I will have to pass this up as I have had no experience of the sort.

The second method tried by me is that of staking a goat out as a bait at some point either actually in, or hard up against a lair, and then concealing myself behind a blind of grass a short distance away to await an attack.

This method has the advantage of permitting the hunter to select his position, which is of vital importance after one has learned the mode of attack, for everything depends upon the relation of the position taken to the paths and trails along which the tiger is sure to travel. From a position of this kind I have repeatedly made long studies of the movements of tigers and their mode of attack at very short distances, and have had to correct many of the ideas I had held from childhood concerning the royal cat of the jungle.

I have never seen anything to bear out the contention made by some that a tiger always attacks a large animal from the rear by springing upon its neck and bearing it down. Several attacks which I watched made upon cows proved that the tiger attacks from the side and below, fastening its fangs in the neck in the region of the jugular vein, by placing the fore paws upon the chest, breaks the neck by a sudden wrenching of the head. Examination of a number of killed cows has proven in each case that the neck was broken.

In one instance noted a medium-sized tiger stalked a water buffalo and her yearling calf. The cow was in the terraced fields, standing in about six inches of water. She kept her body between the calf and the tiger as the latter moved around following the dykes trying to get an opportunity to attack. Finally the big cat did attack from the terrace above, springing upon the back of the cow, but I have always believed this was more by way of a ruse than with any thought of harming the cow. The tiger got the worst of it, however, for the cow humped up her back as the cat struck her, and by a quick flinching movement skidded the tiger off, landing it upon its back in the mud and water. The tiger crawled out to the nearest dyke and strode away, a mud-bespattered spectacle, but yet with all the dignity of its kind.

During the month of February, 1914, I had the pleasure of trying to give an officer of the Marine Corps, at the time an attaché to the American Legation in Peking, a shot at a tiger. This was Captain Thomas Holcomb, Jr., who proved to be one of the most courageous men I have had the pleasure of being out with. A streak of luck went against us on that afternoon, else my companion would have added one of the royal cats to his long list of trophies.

Together we had beaten out an oft-frequented lair in the forenoon with no results other than to satisfy ourselves that the tiger was not there, thus rendering it doubly certain that we would connect up in the big lair in the afternoon. It is always best to eliminate just as far as possible all the wooded ravines and suitable cover adjacent to a lair before actually taking one's stand, for in this way the chances of being surprised or flanked are reduced. On two occasions I almost lost my life by ignoring this practice, in both instances the tiger succeeding in approaching to within ten feet before I detected its presence.

In the afternoon we tethered a goat on a barren terrace after making a hurried survey of the possible approaches, and then withdrew fifteen yards to conceal ourselves behind a clump of bushes. Had we taken the precaution to build a blind, we would have gotten shots, but this was not done because I suspected we were so far in the lair as to be actually within a very few tens of yards of the tiger, so did not want to make any noise cutting or breaking branches to serve as a frame for the blind.

The first indication of the presence of a tiger was the alarm call of a certain little bird a few minutes from the time the goat began to call, and not to exceed fifty yards to our left. One of the things I early learned as a result of hunting in the lair was to make careful note of the call of certain birds. Learning to interpret their language was much to my advantage in locating the exact whereabouts of a moving tiger. Thus one can have sentries stationed on all sides who will sound the alarm just as soon as any animal of the cat family begins to stir. All such helps mean much where one is hunting an animal which moves with practically no sound.

We followed the approach of the tiger across our front along a faint trail to a wild pear bush, which soon became literally full of our feathered sentinels bristling with rage and scolding vigorously. The goat saw the tiger and lunged frantically at the tether-line. From the position now taken by the cat it could look right across beyond the goat and see us on an exposed side of the clump of bushes. Instead of charging, it crouched low, not exposing itself for a shot. My companion sat rigid and waiting for the charge.

As we both began to relax a little from the tension of the moment there was a sudden crash in the lair a little to our right. We both whirled in our positions expecting the onrush of a tiger from this direction. We could see the grass swaying under the weight of some heavy body. While our attention was centered upon this disturbance there was another crash near the pear bush, accompanied by the calls of a struggling deer. What had happened soon dawned upon both of us, so we rushed forward with the hope of overtaking the first tiger before it reached the deep tangle of the lair.

The animal was moving slowly over the terraces carrying a deer in its mouth. We were just a few yards behind, following as rapidly as we could over the terraces, up which we had to climb on all fours. We followed this tiger far into the lair, until we came to the well-defined tunnels through which we could only pass by crawling. With a feeling of keen disappointment we turned and quietly retreated to a safe position in the open.

What had happened is exactly what might be expected to happen under similar circumstances in a country where so much game abounds. The first tiger had stalked the goat to within easy attacking position, but had seen us and crouched low. A second tiger responded to the bleating of the goat and was approaching along the same line of terraces. A number of little deer came along on the next lower terrace, whereupon the tiger sprang upon one from above, crushing it down in the tall grass. The remaining deer ran back along the line of terraces into the very jaws of the other waiting tiger. This animal, too, made sure its strike, bringing down one of the muntjac. This tragedy was enacted within a few yards of us, and reflected very valuable light upon the study we were making of the habits of the wild tiger.

My companion that day will never forget the moment when two tigers were at work so near at hand. He was one of the leaders of the Marines on that memorable day when a handful of Americans threw the Germans back across the Marne in France, being one of two officers out of more than thirty who survived the three days' fighting. He wrote me later from Coblenz: "Caldwell, I will never forget the thrills of our tiger hunting in Fukien. It was great, but I say to you it cannot compare with the thrill connected with chasing the Hun."

On March 25, 1914, I was called upon to dispose of an exceedingly fierce and troublesome tiger. It was my plan to lure this beast into the open near its lair so as to make certain studies as well as get a shot, as this animal was noted for its daring attacks. Not being well acquainted with the lay of the land, I did not take into account one trail leading from the lair. Instead of emerging from its lair where I had figured it would, I saw it come out on a barren ridge within one hundred yards of me, where it mused and sat like a huge tom cat, probably making a survey of its surroundings before the final charge upon the goat.

I leveled my gun for a shot, but with the sights I found there was a blur in the twilight. There remained nothing for me to do but stalk the tiger before it got too dark for me to shoot with some degree of certainty.

As soon as I moved from my hiding the tiger crouched low. I could see that the eyes of the fierce beast were following me as I hurried forward into a depression which had to be crossed, changing my course a little, for I feared the tiger would flank me as I ascended the slope.

As my head appeared above the summit of the little knoll the tiger sprang to his feet. In order to get clear of some burned-over brush it was necessary for me to advance out some twenty yards diagonally across the animal's front. While I was doing this the big cat was very nervous, twitching its tail and throwing its ears back flat upon its head. I was expecting it to charge any second, yet it was necessary for me to withhold my fire until I was clear of the bushes, which brought me to within thirty yards of the animal, which was becoming very much worked up. I saw the time had come to fire. Further delay might prove a serious matter. I was armed with the then most talked-of gun on the American market, a twenty-two Hi-power Savage rifle. The theorist had pronounced this ball of light to prove effective in big-game shooting, while, on the other sides, guides in the Rockies had reported it as being effective on both bear and big-horn sheep. The discussion I had read pro and con in the sporting magazines concerning this gun confronted me as I was brought to a place of severe test, but I dared not reflect long over these things.

I fired with great deliberation, covering as best I could my sights in the gloom, and striking the animal squarely back of the ribs. It was far too dark to undertake to pick any vital spot. The big cat lunged into the air, coming down dead. The ball entered the stomach cavity, doing terrible execution. Had the animal swallowed an explosive bomb the results could not have been more disastrous. No animal could sustain such a shock and live to do much damage.

Two observations worth mentioning were noted during the study of this tiger. It was most interesting to notice that when a tiger runs down hill it is no longer the slender, agile and graceful cat known to everyone who has visited a zoo. When making a rapid descent a tiger resembles very much a cow going down a steep place. The back is very much humped, and the body drawn up to not much more than half its ordinary length. This is in keeping with what I had always been advised by Chinese hunters, who have said that I should retreat downhill if attacked by a tiger, since the front legs were so much shorter than the hind as to cause it to travel with great difficulty down a steep grade.

Another observation was not altogether in keeping with what I had gathered out of my earlier reading about the big jungle cat. I found the stomach of this animal filled with recently devoured food, among which was a dog which had been eaten but a very short time. Instead of withdrawing to the seclusion of a quiet lair and sleeping for a full day, this animal attacked with all the vigor of a ravenously hungry one, when the facts are that it could not possibly have eaten the goat had it secured it. A tiger doubtless kills because it is its instinct to kill.

The remaining, and by far most interesting, method of hunting tigers is the so-called "still-hunt." This is the most interesting method because it reveals to the observant sportsman much concerning the home life of the tiger otherwise difficult to learn. There are rich rewards for the man who will enter the lair of a tiger with the purpose of not only finding the inmate of the home, but with a desire to make as many observations as possible which will throw light upon the domestic habits of this royal cat.

It is needless to say that still hunting is attended with many real dangers not encountered in any other method of tiger hunting. Many are the times a sound, greatly magnified by the tension of the moment, brings one to a sudden standstill with the heart pounding away well up in the throat. One often halts for a moment with attention centered upon some interesting find, when an imaginary tiger is detected stealing up under cover from the rear. While trying to locate what you now feel is certainly hiding in the bush close at hand, as the awful silence of the wilds bears down with tremendous force it is almost next to impossible to keep from breaking wildly away through the lair.

I shall never forget the struggle I have repeatedly had with that imaginary tiger which has cost me so much cold fear. Any man would rather meet all the flesh-and-blood cats in tigerdom in the open than be forced to endure that spell which sometimes comes over one when he feels himself alone in the lair of a tiger.

This is the price almost any man will have to pay for his initiation into the sport of still hunting in a tiger's lair. But all this soon passes away when one becomes hardened to the presence of both real and imaginary tigers, the silence of the wilds and all else, and really finds himself enjoying this stealing around from apartment to apartment of the lair, often connected by well-defined tunnels through which he must get down upon hands and knees and crawl for a long distance.

The most nerve-racking experience I have ever had in a tiger's lair was when I foolishly entered the lair of a tigress with three small kittens, one of which had been captured by some wood choppers the day before. The mother cat in her grief and anger had clawed great holes in the ground and attacked trees, which she had gnawed to shreds as high as she could reach. No human maniac could have torn things up any more than that enraged tigress had.

I found the remains of a pangolin which had been torn to bits and scattered about. The only thing that saved me probably from just such a fate was the fact that the lady of the place had given up hope of finding her lost child and had moved out with her remaining two.

Notwithstanding there are many real dangers attending still hunting for tigers in the tangle of their lair, still one feels richly repaid and rewarded for the risk he has run when he begins to sum up his observations. One of the most interesting finds as a result of an hour's prowling around in an oft-frequented lair is concerning the food of the cat. There are evidences a-plenty that a tiger carries its kill from long distances to devour it upon one certain terrace, or "dining table."

A sad thing happened on the 14th of April, 1914, which illustrates this point. The remains of a fifteen-year-old boy were found in a large grave in a lair but a few miles from Futsing City. No child had been reported missing in the neighborhood. Everything indicated that the child had been brought alive from a distance to this lair, as the sides of the grave were besmeared with fresh blood of the victim, indicating that the tiger had tortured the boy just as a cat tortures and plays with a mouse so long as there is life in it.

One will find on the favorite terraces the remains of prey which have been brought in. A fresh kill of a medium-sized animal shows plainly how the tiger first uses its rasplike tongue for removing most of the hair before devouring the flesh. The hair will be found in a circle around what remains of the kill.

While there is nothing to indicate that a tiger always brings its prey to one place to eat it, still there is much that would prove that this is frequently done. On a terrace of the kind one will find the skulls and bones of deer, wild hog, dog, pig, porcupine and pangolin, as well as other domestic and wild animals. The Chinese often raid a lair in order to pick up the bony scales of the pangolin, which are highly prized for medicinal properties. In addition to the larger animals, frogs, reptiles, and the like are taken when opportunity affords.

On the night of April 22, 1914, a party of frog hunters were returning from a hunt. A man carrying a sack of frogs was attacked and killed by a tiger. No attempt was made to drag the man away. It would appear that the animal was attracted by the croaking of the frogs in the sack, as it was ripped and much torn.

It is beside some trail or path in a lair where one finds the trees "marked." This is one of the first signs an experienced tiger hunter will look for. Catlike, the tiger measures its full length upon the tree. The sign is doubly interesting to sportsmen, for it serves not only the purpose of assurance of the presence of a tiger, but it gives a fair idea as to the reach of the animal as well.

One will invariably find the trails leading from a lair marked also. So frequently is this done that one would be led to suspect it is for the same purpose that a dog marks the road traveled. In this operation the tiger brushes away the grass and leaves beside the trail, and, while considerable strength must be used, the claw prints never appear. The full size of the padded foot is apparent. The way in which the debris is gathered in a heap shows plainly that the stroke is with the fore paw.

There are many more observations that reflect light upon the domestic life of a tiger which are reserved for the man who will venture to enter the lair and seek for signs which experience helps to interpret. The Chinese have had it handed down for ages that a tigress never has more than two kittens of her own kind, the third always being a leopard. It was with difficulty that I convinced the man accompanying me upon one trip, when we found a tigress with four kittens, that the handsome beast was the mother of the four.

I have learned much by studying the habits of tigers in their native habitat in China, but those observations which reflected the greatest degree of light upon the real life of the royal cat have been the results of prowling around on a still-hunt in the lair.

Wolf-Hunting in Russia

From **Hunting in Many Lands: The Book of the Boone and Crockett Club,** ***1895***

Henry T. Allen

THE ENORMOUS EXTENT AND DIVERSIFIED CONDITIONS OF THE various localities of this empire would naturally suggest a variety of sport in hunting and shooting, including perhaps something characteristic. In the use of dogs of the chase especially is this suggestion borne out by the facts, and it has been said that in no other country has the systematic working together of fox-hounds and greyhounds been successfully carried out.

Unfortunately, this sort of hunting is not now so general as prior to the emancipation of the serfs in 1861. A modest kennel for such sport consists of six to ten fox-hounds and four to six pairs of barzois,* and naturally demands considerable attention. Moreover, to use it requires the presence of at least one man with the fox-hounds and one man for each pair or each three greyhounds. To have a sufficient number of good huntsmen at his service was formerly a much less expensive luxury to a proprietor than now, and to this fact is due the decline of the combined kennel in Russia.

---

* Barzoi—long-haired greyhound, wolf-hound, Russian greyhound.

This hunt is more or less practised throughout the entire extent of the Russian Empire. In the south, where the soil is not boggy, it is far better sport than in Northern Russia, where there are such enormous stretches of marshy woods and tundra. Curiously enough, nearly all the game of these northern latitudes, including moose, wolves, hares, and nearly all kinds of grouse and other birds, seem to be found in the marshiest places—those almost impracticable to mounted hunters.

Though the distances covered in hunting, and also in making neighborly visits in Russia, are vast, often recalling our own broad Western life, yet in few other respects are any similarities to be traced. This is especially true of Russia north of the Moscow parallel; for in the south the steppes have much in common with the prairies, though more extensive, and the semi-nomadic Cossacks, in their mounted peregrinations and in their pastoral life, have many traits in common with real Americans. Nor is it true of the Caucasus, where it would seem that the Creator, dissatisfied with the excess of the great plain,* extending from the Finnish Gulf to the Black Sea, resolved to establish a counterpoise, and so heaved up the gigantic Caucasus. There too are to be found fine hunting and shooting, which merit description and which offer good sport to mountain amateurs.

The annual hunt in the fall of 1893 in the governments of Tver and Yaroslav, with the Gatchino kennels, will give a good idea of the special sport of which I have spoken. It

* The Waldeir hills, extending east and west half-way between St. Petersburg and Moscow, are the only exception.

is imperative that these hounds go to the hunt once a year for about a month, although for the most part without their owner. The master of the hunt and his assistant, with three or four guests, and oftentimes the proprietors of the lands where the hounds happen to hunt, usually constitute the party. The hunt changes locality nearly every year, but rarely does it go further from home than on this occasion, about 450 versts from Gatchino. As a rule it is not difficult to obtain from proprietors permission to hunt upon their estates, and this is somewhat surprising to one who has seen the freedom with which the fences are torn down and left unrepaired. It is true that they are not of the strongest and best type, and that peasant labor is still very cheap; yet such concessions to sport would rarely be made in America.

It was at Gatchino, on the 10th day of September, that the hunting train was loaded with men, horses, dogs, provisions and wagons. The hunt called for twenty-two cars in all, including one second-class passenger car, in one end of which four of us made ourselves comfortable, while in the other end servants found places. The weather was cold and rainy, and, as our train traveled as a freight, we had two nights before us. It was truly a picturesque and rare sight to see a train of twenty-two cars loaded with the *personnel,* material and live stock of a huge kennel. The fox-hounds, seventy in number, were driven down in perfect, close order by the beaters to the cracks of the Russian hunting whip and installed in their car, which barely offered them sufficient accommodation. The greyhounds, three sorts, sixty-seven in number, were brought down on leashes by threes, fours or fives, and loaded in two cars. Sixty saddle and draft horses, with saddles, wagons and hunting paraphernalia, were also loaded. Finally the forty-four gray and green uniformed huntsmen, beaters, drivers and ourselves were ready, and the motley train moved away amid the uttered and unuttered benedictions of the families and relatives of the parting hunt.

Our first destination was Peschalkino, in the government of Tver, near the River Leet, a tributary of the Volga, not far from the site of the first considerable check of the Mongolian advance about 1230. I mention this fact in passing to give some idea of the *terrain,* because I think that it is evident to anyone who has visited this region that the difficulty of provisioning and of transportation in these marshes must have offered a greater obstacle to an invading army than did the then defenders of their country.

We passed our time most agreeably in playing vint* and talking of hunting incidents along the route. Many interesting things were told about the habits of wolves and other game, and, as they were vouched for by two thorough gentlemen and superb sportsmen, and were verified as far as a month's experience in the field would permit, I feel authorized to cite them as facts.

The bear has been called in folk-lore the moujik's brother, and it must be conceded that there are outward points of resemblance, especially when each is clad in winter attire; moreover the moujik, when all is snow and ice, fast approximates the hibernating qualities of the bear. One strong point of difference is the

* Vint—game of cards resembling whist, boaston and *préférence.*

accentuated segregative character of the former, who always live in long cabin villages.*

But it is rather of the wolf's habits and domestic economy that I wish to speak—of him who has always been the dreaded and accursed enemy of the Russian peasant. In the question of government the wolf follows very closely the system of the country, which is pre-eminently patriarchal—the fundamental principle of the *mir.* A family of wolves may vary in number from six to twenty, and contain two to four generations, usually two or three, yet there is always one chief and one wife—in other words, never more than one female with young ones. When larger packs have been seen together it was probably the temporary marshaling of their forces for some desperate raid or the preliminaries of an anarchistic strike. The choruses of wolves and the special training of the young for them are interesting characteristics. Upon these choruses depends the decision of the hunter whether or not to make his final attack upon the stronghold of the wolves; by them he can tell with great precision the number in the family and the ages of the different members. They are to wolf-hunters what tracks are to moose- and bear-hunters—they serve to locate the game. When the family is at home they occur with great regularity at twilight, midnight and dawn.

In camp near Billings, Montana, in the fall of 1882, we heard nightly about 12 o'clock the howling of a small pack of coyotes; but we supposed that it was simply a "howling protest" against

---

* The bear is caricatured in Russian publications as a humorous, light-hearted, joking creature, conversing and making common sport with the golden-hearted moujik, his so-called brother.

the railway train, passing our camp at midnight, that had just reached that part of the world. Possibly our coyotes have also howling choruses at regular intervals, like the Russian wolves.

There was such a fascination in listening to the wolves that we went out several times solely for that purpose. The weirdness of the sound and the desolateness of the surroundings produced peculiar sensations upon the listener. To an enthusiastic lover of sport and nature these pleasurable sensations might be well compared with the effect of the Niebelungen songs upon an ardent Wagnerite. The old professional huntsmen could tell just what members of the family and how many were howling; they scarcely disagreed upon these points.

These old hunters pretended to interpret the noisy assemblies of the wolves as regards content or discontent, satisfaction or dissatisfaction.

Owing to the difficulty of securing wolves under most favorable circumstances, especially old ones, it would be considered folly to make a drive if the matinal howl had not been heard. But to make a successful drive in a large marshy forest many beaters must be employed, and, as they are gathered from far and near, considerable time is necessary to collect them; therefore it is almost essential to know that the wolves were "at home" at midnight as well as dawn.

While in the vicinity of a certain wolf family whose habitat was an enormous marshy wood, entirely impossible to mounted men, we were compelled to await for forty-eight hours the return of the old ones, father and mother. At times during this wait only the young ones, at other times the young and the intermediate ones, would sing. Not hearing the old ones, we inferred they were absent, and so they were—off on a raid, during which they killed two peasant horses ten miles from their stronghold. It was supposed that the wolves of intermediate age also made excursions during this time, as indicated by the howlings, but not to such great distances as the old ones. It was perfectly apparent, as we listened one evening, that the old ones had placed the young ones about a verst away and were making them answer independently. This seemed too human for wolves.

After one day and two nights of travel we arrived at the little station of Peschalkino, on the Bologoe-Rybinsk Railway, not far from the frontier between the two governments, Tver and Yaroslav, where we were met by two officers of the guard, a Yellow Cuirassier and a Preobiajensky, on leave of absence on their estates (Koy), sixteen versts from the rail. They were brothers-in-law and keen sportsmen, who became members of our party and who indicated the best localities for game on their property, as well as on the adjoining estates.

Peschalkino boasts a painted country tavern of two stories, the upper of which, with side entrance, we occupied, using our own beds and bed linen, table and table linen, cooking and kitchen utensils; in fact, it was a hotel where we engaged the walled-in space and the brick cooking stove. As to the huntsmen and the dogs, they were quartered in the adjacent unpainted log-house peasant village—just such villages as are seen all over Russia, in which a mud road, with plenty of mud, comprises all there is of streets and avenues. After having arranged our temporary domicile, and having carefully examined horses and dogs to see how they had endured the journey, we made ready to accept a dinner invitation at the country place of our new members. Horses were put to the brake, called by the Russians *Amerikanka* (American), and we set out for a drive of sixteen versts over a mud road to enjoy the well-known Slav hospitality so deeply engrafted in the Ponamaroff family.

I said road, but in reality it scarcely merits the name, as it is neither fenced nor limited in width other than by the sweet will of the traveler. Special mention is made of this road because its counterparts exist all over the empire. It is the usual road, and not the exception, which is worse, as many persons have ample reasons for knowing. This condition is easily explained by the scarcity of stone, the inherent disregard of comfort, the poverty of the peasants, the absence of a yeoman class, and the great expense that would be entailed upon the landed proprietors, who live at enormous distances from each other. The country in these and many other governments has been civilized many generations, but so unfinished and primitive does it all seem that it recalls many localities of our West, where civilization appeared but yesterday, and where to-morrow it will be well in advance of these provinces. The hand-flail, the wooden plow-share, the log cabin with stable under the same roof, could have been seen here in the twelfth century as they are at present. Thanks to the Moscow factories, the gala attire of the peasant of to-day may possibly surpass in brilliancy of color that of his remote ancestry, which was clad entirely from the home loom. With the exception of the white brick churches, whose tall green and white spires in the distance appear at intervals of eight to ten versts, and of occasional painted window casings, there is nothing to indicate that the colorings of time and nature are not preferable to those of art. The predominating features of the landscape are the windmills and the evenness of the grain-producing country, dotted here and there by clumps of woods, called islands. The churches, too, are conspicuous by their number, size, and beauty of architecture; school-houses, by their absence. Prior to 1861 there must have been a veritable mania here for church-building. The large and beautiful church at Koy, as well as two other pretentious brick ones, were constructed on his estates by the grandfather of our host.

Arrived at Koy, we found a splendid country place, with brick buildings, beautiful gardens, several hot-houses and other luxuries, all of which appeared the more impressive by contrast. The reception and hospitality accorded us at Koy—where we were highly entertained with singing, dancing and cards until midnight—was as bounteous as the darkness and rainfall which awaited us on the sixteen versts' drive over roadless roads back to our quarter bivouac at Peschalkino.

The following morning marked the beginning of our hunting. About 10 o'clock all was in readiness. Every hunter* had been provided with a leash, a knife and a whip; and, naturally, every huntsman with the two latter. In order to increase the number of posts, some of the huntsmen were also charged with leashes of greyhounds. I shall in the future use the word greyhound to describe all the sight hounds, in contradistinction to fox-hound; it includes barzois (Russian greyhounds), greyhounds (English)

* Hunter-gentleman, huntsman, man of the hunt—conventional terms.

and crosses between the two. The barzois numbered about 75 per cent of all the greyhounds, and were for the most part somewhat less speedy than the real greyhounds, but better adapted for wolf-hunting. They also have greater skill in taking hold, and this, even in hare coursing, sometimes gives them advantage over faster dogs. One of the most interesting features of the coursing was the matching of Russian and English greyhounds. The leash system used in the field offers practically the same fairness as is shown by dogs at regular coursing matches. The leash is a black narrow leather thong about fifteen feet long, with a loop at one end that passes over the right shoulder and under the left arm. The long thong with a slit at the end, forming the hand loop, is, when not in use, folded up like a lariat or a driving rein, and is stuck under the knife belt. To use it, the end is put through the loop-ring collars, which the greyhounds continually wear, and is then held fast in the left hand until ready to slip the hounds. Where the country is at all brushy, three dogs are the practical limit of one leash, still for the most part only two are employed. It is surprising to see how quickly the dogs learn the leash with mounted huntsmen; two or three days are sufficient to teach them to remain at the side of the horse and at a safe distance from his feet. Upon seeing this use of the leash with two dogs each, I was curious to know why it should be so; why it would not be more exciting to see half a dozen or more hounds in hot pursuit racing against each other and having a common goal, just as it is more exciting to see a horse race with a numerous entry than merely with two competitors. This could have been remedied, so I thought, by having horsemen go in pairs, or having several dogs when possible on one leash. Practice showed the wisdom of the methods actually employed. In the first place, it is fairer for the game; in the second, it saves the dogs; and finally, it allows a greater territory to be hunted over with the same number of dogs.

There are two ways of hunting foxes and hares, and, with certain variations, wolves also. These are, by beating and driving with fox-hounds, and by open driving with greyhounds alone. In the first case a particular wood (island) is selected, and the fox-hounds with their mounted huntsmen are sent to drive it in a certain direction. The various leashes of greyhounds (barzois alone if wolves be expected) are posted on the opposite side, at the edge of the wood or in the field, and are loosed the second the game has shown its intention of clearing the open space expressly selected for the leash. The mounted beaters with the fox-hounds approach the thick woods of evergreens, cottonwood, birch and undergrowth, and wait on its outskirts until a bugle signal informs them that all the greyhound posts are ready. The fox-hounds recognize the signal, and would start immediately were they not terrorized by the black *nagaika*—a product of a country that has from remotest times preferred the knout* to the gallows, and so is skilled in its manufacture and use. At the word *go* from the chief beater the seventy fox-hounds, which have been huddled up as closely as the encircling beaters could

---

* Though not pertinent to the subject, I cannot refrain from relating a curious comparison made to me by a very intelligent Russian, aide-de-camp general of the late Emperor: "Just as the scarcity of women in early American times caused them to be highly appreciated and tenderly cared for, so the relative scarcity of men in early Russia caused the Government to appreciate them and to preserve them at all hazards. Logically follows the exalted position of woman to-day in the United States and the absence of capital punishment in Russia."

make them, rush into the woods. In a few minutes, sometimes seconds, the music begins—and what music! I really think there are too many musicians, for the voices not being classified, there is no individuality, but simply a prolonged howl. For my part, I prefer fewer hounds, where the individual voices may be distinguished. It seemed to be a needless use of so many good dogs, for half the number would drive as well; but they were out for exercise and training, and they must have it. Subsequently the pack was divided into two, but this was not necessitated by fatigue of the hounds, for we hunted on alternate days with greyhounds alone.

One could well believe that foxes might remain a long time in the woods, even when pursued by such noise; but it seemed to me that the hares* would have passed the line of posts more quickly than they did. At the suitable moment, when the game was seen, the nearest leash was slipped, and when they seemed to be on the point of losing another and sometimes a third was slipped. The poor fox-hounds were not allowed to leave the woods; the moment the game appeared in the open space they were driven back by the stiff riders with their cruel whips. The true fox-hound blood showed itself, and to succeed in beating some of them off the trail, especially the young ones, required most rigorous action on the part of all. This seemed to me a prostitution of the good qualities of a race carefully bred for centuries,

* There are two varieties: the so-called white hare and the so-called red hare. The former becomes white in winter, and weighs, when full grown, ten pounds; the latter has a reddish gray coat which does not change, and weighs about one and a half pounds less than the other variety. The red hare frequents the fields less than does the white. The foxes are the ordinary red ones.

and, while realizing the necessity of the practice for that variety of hunt, I could never look upon it with complaisance.

It is just this sort of hunt* for which the barzoi has been specially bred, and which has developed in him a tremendous spring; at the same time it has given him less endurance than the English greyhound. It was highly interesting to follow the hounds with the beaters; but, owing to the thickness of the woods and the absence of trails, it was far from being an easy task either for horse or rider. To remain at a post with a leash of hounds was hardly active or exciting enough for me—except when driving wolves—especially when the hounds could be followed, or when the open hunt could be enjoyed. In the second case the hunters and huntsmen with leashes form a line with intervals of 100 to 150 yards and march for versts straight across the country, cracking the terrible *nagaika* and uttering peculiar exciting yells that would start game on a parade ground. After a few days I flattered myself that I could manage my leash fairly and slip them passably well. To two or three of the party leashes were not intrusted, either because they did not desire them or for their want of experience in general with dogs and horses. To handle a leash well requires experience and considerable care. To prevent tangling in the horse's legs, especially at the moment the game is sighted, requires that the hounds be held well in hand, and that they be not slipped until both have sighted the game.

---

* In Northern Russia, owing to the extensive forest, brush and marsh lands, every effort was made to utilize the small open spaces or clearings for the greyhounds, and this was the usual way of hunting; while in Southern Russia, where steppes predominate, the open hunt—*chasse à courre*—prevailed. This explains why the Crimean barzoi also has more endurance than the now recognized type from the north.

I much prefer the open hunt to the post system. There is more action, and in fact more sport, whether it happens that one or several leashes be slipped for the same animal. When it is not possible to know whose dogs have taken the game, it belongs to him who arrived first, providing that he has slipped his leash.

So much for the foxes and hares, but the more interesting hunting of wolves remains. Few people except wolf-hunters—and they are reluctant to admit it—know how rarely old wolves are caught with hounds. All admit the danger of taking an old one either by a dagger thrust or alive from under* barzois, however good they be. There is always a possibility that the dogs may loosen their hold or be thrown off just at the critical moment. But the greatest difficulty consists in the inability of the hounds to hold the wolf even when they have overtaken him. When it is remembered that a full-grown wolf is nearly twice as heavy as the average barzoi, and that pound for pound he is stronger, it is clear that to overtake and hold him requires great speed and grit on the part of a pair of hounds.

A famous kennel,** which two years since caught forty-six wolves by the combined system of hunting, took in that number but one old wolf—that is, three years or more old. The same kennel last year caught twenty-six without having a single old one in the number. We likewise failed to include in our captures a single old wolf. I mention these facts to correct the false impression that exists with us concerning the barzois, as evidenced by the great disappointment when two years since a pair, in one of

---

* This is the Russian phrasing, and correctly describes the idea.

** That of the Grand Duke Nicolas Nicolaievitch.

the Western States, failed to kill outright a full-grown timber wolf. At the field trials on wolves, which take place twice a year at Colomiaghi, near Petersburg, immediately after the regular field trials on hares, I have seen as many as five leashes slipped before an old wolf could be taken, and then it was done only with the greatest difficulty. In fact, as much skill depends upon the *borzatnik* (huntsman) as the dogs. Almost the very second the dogs take hold he simply falls from his horse upon the wolf and endeavors to thrust the unbreakable handle of his *nagaika* between the jaws of the animal; he then wraps the lash around the wolf's nose and head. If the hounds are able to hold even a few seconds, the skilled *borzatnik* has had sufficient time, but there is danger even to the best. I saw an experienced man get a thumb terribly lacerated while muzzling a wolf, yet he succeeded, and in an incredibly short time. On another occasion, even before the brace of hounds had taken firm neck or ear holds, I saw a bold devil of a huntsman swing from his horse and in a twinkling lie prone upon an old wolf's head. How this man, whose pluck I shall always admire, was able to muzzle the brute without injury to himself, and with inefficient support from his hounds, it is not easy to understand, though I was within a few yards of the struggle. Such skill comes from long experience, indifference to pain and, of course, pride in his profession.

Having hunted foxes and hares, and having been shooting as often as the environs of Peschalkino and our time allowed, we changed our base to a village twenty-two versts distant over the border in the government of Yaroslav. It was a village like all others of this grain and flax district, where the live stock and poultry shared the same roof with their owners. A family of eleven wolves had been located about three versts from it by a pair of huntsmen sent some days in advance; this explained our arrival. In making this change, I do not now recall that we saw a single house other than those of the peasant villages and the churches. I fancy that in the course of time these peasants may have more enlightenment, a greater ownership in the land, and may possibly form a yeoman class. At the present the change, slow as it is, seems to point in that direction. With their limited possessions, they are happy and devoted subjects. The total of the interior decorations of every house consists of icons, of cheap colored pictures of the imperial family and of samovars. In our lodgings, the house of the village *starost,* the three icons consumed a great part of the wall surface, and were burdened with decorations of various colored papers. No one has ever touched upon peasant life in Russia without mentioning the enormous brick stove (*lezanka**); and having on various hunts profited by them, I mean to say a word in behalf of their advantages. Even as early as the middle of September the cold continuous rains cause the gentle warmth of the *lezanka* to be cordially appreciated. On it and in its vicinity all temperatures may be found. Its top offers a fine place for keeping guns, ammunition and various articles free from moisture, and for drying boots;** while the horizontal abutments constitute benches well adapted to thawing out a chilled marrow, or a sleeping place for those that like that sort of thing. A generous space is also allowed for cooking

---

* *Lezanka* means something used for lying on.

** Hot oats poured into the boots were also used for drying them.

purposes. In point of architecture there is nothing that can be claimed for it but stability; excepting the interior upper surface of the oven, there is not a single curve to break its right lines. It harmonizes with the surroundings, and in a word answers all the requirements of the owner as well as of the hunter, who always preserves a warm remembrance of it.

The wolves were located in a large marshy wood and, from information of the scouts based on the midnight and dawn choruses, they were reported "at home." Accordingly we prepared for our visit with the greatest precautions. When within a verst of the proposed curved line upon which we were to take our stands with barzois, all dismounted and proceeded through the marsh on foot, making as little noise as possible. The silence was occasionally broken by the efforts of the barzois to slip themselves after a cur belonging to one of the peasant beaters, that insisted upon seeing the sport at the most aggravating distance for a sight hound. It was finally decided to slip one good barzoi that, it was supposed, could send the vexatious animal to another hunting ground; but the cur, fortunately for himself, suddenly disappeared and did not show himself again.

After wading a mile in the marshy bog, we were at the beginning of the line of combat—if there was to be any. The posts along this line had been indicated by the chief huntsman by blazing the small pine trees or by hanging a heap of moss on them. The nine posts were established in silence along the arc of a circle at distances from each other of about 150 yards. My post was number four from the beginning. In rear of it and of the adjoining numbers a strong high cord fence was put up, because it was supposed that near this part of the line the old wolves would pass, and that the barzois might not be able to stop them. The existence of such fencing material as part of the outfit of a wolf-hunter is strong evidence of his estimate of a wolf's strength—it speaks pages. The fence was concealed as much as possible, so that the wolf with barzois at his heels might not see it. The huntsmen stationed there to welcome him on his arrival were provided with fork-ended poles, intended to hold him by the neck to the ground until he was gagged and muzzled, or until he had received a fatal dagger thrust.

While we were forming the ambuscade—defensive line—the regular beaters, with 200 peasant men and women, and the fox-hounds, were forming the attack.

Everything seemed favorable except the incessant cold rain and wind. In our zeal to guard the usual crossings of the wolves, we ignored the direction of the wind, which the wolves, however, cleverly profited by. It could not have been very long after the hounds were let go before they fell upon the entire family of wolves, which they at once separated. The shouts and screams of the peasants, mingled with the noises of the several packs of hounds, held us in excited attention. Now and then this or that part of the pack would approach the line, and, returning, pass out of hearing in the extensive woods. The game had approached within scenting distance, and, in spite of the howling in the rear, had returned to depart by the right or left flank of the beaters. As the barking of the hounds came near the line, the holders of the barzois, momentarily hoping to see a wolf or wolves, waited in almost breathless expectancy. Each one was prepared with a knife to rush upon an old wolf to support his pair; but unfortunately only two wolves came to our line, and they were not two years old. They were taken at the extreme left flank, so far away that I could not even see the killing. I was disappointed, and felt that a great mistake had been made in not paying sufficient attention to the direction of the wind. Where is the hunter who has not had his full share of disappointments when all prospects seemed favorable? As often happens, it was the persons occupying the least favorable places who had bagged the game. They said that in one case the barzois had held the wolf splendidly until the fatal thrust; but that in the other case it had been necessary to slip a second pair before it could be taken. These young wolves were considerably larger than old coyotes.

So great was the forest hunted that for nearly two hours we had occupied our posts listening to the spasmodic trailing of the hounds and the yelling of the peasants. Finally all the beaters and peasants reached our line, and the drive was over, with only two wolves taken from the family of eleven. Shivering with cold and thoroughly drenched, we returned in haste to shelter and dry clothes.

The following morning we set out on our return to Peschalkino, mounted, with the barzois, while the fox-hounds were driven along the road. We marched straight across the country in a very thin skirmish line, regardless of fences, which were broken down and left to the owners to be repaired. By the time we had reached our destination, we had enjoyed some good sport and had taken several hares. The following morning the master of the imperial hunt, who had been kept at his estates near Moscow by illness in his family, arrived, fetching with him his horses and a number of his own hounds. We continued our hunting a number of days longer in that vicinity, both with and without fox-hounds, with varying success. Every day or two we also indulged in shooting for ptarmigan, black cocks, partridges, woodcocks and two kinds of snipe—all of which prefer the most fatiguing marshes.

One day our scouts arrived from Philipovo, twenty-six versts off, to report that another family of wolves, numbering about sixteen, had been located. The *Amerikanka* was sent in advance to Orodinatovo, whither we went by rail at a very early hour. This same rainy and cold autumnal landscape would be intolerable were it not brightened here and there by the red shirts and brilliant headkerchiefs of the peasants, the noise of the flail on the dirt-floor sheds and the ever-alluring attractions of the hunt.

During this short railway journey, and on the ride to Philipovo, I could not restrain certain reflections upon the life of the people and of the proprietors of this country. It seemed on this morning that three conditions were necessary to render a permanent habitation here endurable: neighbors, roads and a change of latitude; of the first two there are almost none, of latitude there is far too much. To be born in a country excuses its defects, and that alone is sufficient to account for the continuance of people under even worse conditions than those of these governments. It is true that the soil here does not produce fruit and vegetables like the Crimean coast, and that it does not, like the black belt, "laugh with a harvest when tickled with a hoe"; yet it produces, under the present system of cultivation, rye and flax sufficient to feed, clothe and pay taxes. What more could a peasant desire? With these provided his happiness is secured; how can he be called poor? Without questioning this defense, which has been made many times in his behalf, I would simply say that he is not poor as long as a famine or plague of some sort does not arrive—and then proceed with our journey.

From Orodinatovo to Philipovo is only ten versts, but over roads still less worthy of the name than the others already traveled. The *Amerikanka* was drawn by four horses abreast. The road in places follows the River Leet, on which Philipovo is situated. We had expected to proceed immediately to hunt the wolves, and nearly 300 peasant men and women had been engaged to aid the fox-hounds as beaters. They had been assembled from far and near, and were congregated in the only street of Philipovo, in front of our future quarters, to await our arrival. What a motley assembly, what brilliancy of coloring! All were armed with sticks, and carried bags or cloths containing their rations of rye bread swung from the shoulders, or around the neck and over the back. How many pairs of boots were hung over the shoulders? Was it really the custom to wear boots on the shoulders? In any case it was *de rigueur* that each one show that he or she possessed such a luxury as a good pair of high top boots; but it was not a luxury to be abused or recklessly worn out. Their system of foot-gear has its advantages in that the same pair may be used by several members of a family, male and female alike.

It was not a pleasure for us to hear that the wolves had been at home at twilight and midnight, but were not there at dawn; much less comforting was this news to those peasants living at great distances who had no place near to pass the night. The same information was imparted the following day and the day following, until it began to appear doubtful whether we could longer delay in order to try for this very migratory pack.

Our chances of killing old wolves depended largely upon this drive, for it was doubtful whether we would make an attack upon the third family, two days distant from our quarters. Every possible precaution was taken to make it a success. I was, however, impressed with the fact that the most experienced members of the hunting party were the least sanguine about the old wolves.

Some one remarked that my hunting knife, with a six-inch blade, was rather short, and asked if I meant to try and take an old wolf. My reply was in the affirmative, for my intentions at that stage were to try anything in the form of a wolf. At this moment one of the land proprietors, who had joined our party, offered to exchange knives with me, saying that he had not the slightest intention of attacking a wolf older than two years, and that my knife was sufficient for that. I accepted his offer.

At a very early hour on this cold rainy autumnal morning we set out on our way to the marshy haunts of the game. Our party had just been reinforced by the arrival of the commander of the Empress's Chevalier Guard regiment, an ardent sportsman, with his dogs. All the available fox-hounds, sixty in number, were brought out, and the 300 peasants counted off. The latter were keen, not only because a certain part of them had sportsmanlike inclinations, but also because each one received thirty copecks for participation in the drive. Besides this, they were interested in the extermination of beasts that were living upon their live stock.

The picture at the start was more than worthy of the results of the day, and it remains fresh in my mind. The greater portion of the peasants were taken in charge by the chief beater, with the hounds, while the others followed along with us and the barzois. Silence was enforced upon all. The line of posts was established as before, except that more care was exercised. Each principal post, where three barzois were held on leash, was strengthened by a man with a gun loaded with buckshot. The latter had instructions not to fire upon a wolf younger than two years, and not even upon an older one, until it was manifest that the barzois and their holder were unequal to the task.

My post was a good one, and my three dogs were apparently keen for anything. At the slightest noise they were ready to drag me off my feet through the marsh. Thanks to the *nagaika*, I was able to keep them in hand. One of the trio was well known for his grit in attacking wolves, the second was considered fair, while the third, a most promising two-year-old, was on his first wolf-hunt. Supported by these three dogs, the long knife of the gentleman looking for young wolves and the yellow cuirassier officer with his shotgun, I longed for some beast that would give a struggle. The peasants accompanying us were posted out on each flank of our line, extending it until the extremities must have been separated by nearly two miles.

The signal was given, and hunters, peasants and hounds rushed into the woods. Almost instantly we heard the screams and yells of the nearest peasants, and in a short time the faint barking of the fox-hounds. As the sounds became more audible, it was evident that the hounds had split into three packs—conclusive that there were at least three wolves. My chances were improving, and I was arranging my dogs most carefully, that they might be slipped evenly. My knife, too, was within convenient grasp, and the fox-hounds were pointing directly to me. Beastly luck! I saw my neighbor, the hunter of young wolves, slip his barzois, and like a flash they shot through the small pine trees, splashing as they went. From my point of view they had fallen upon an animal that strongly resembled one of themselves. In reality it was a yearling wolf, but he was making it interesting for the barzois as well as for all who witnessed the sight. The struggle did not last long, for soon two of the barzois had fastened their long teeth in him—one at the base of the ear, the other in the throat. Their holder hastened to the struggle, about 100 yards from his post, and with my knife gave the wolf the *coup de grace*. His dogs had first sighted the game, and therefore had the priority of right to the chase. So long as the game was in no danger of escaping no neighboring dogs should be slipped. His third barzoi, on trial for qualifications as a wolf-hound, did not render the least aid.

Part of the fox-hounds were still running, and there was yet chance that my excited dogs might have their turn. We waited impatiently until all sounds had died away and until the beaters had reached our line, when further indulgence of hope was useless. Besides the above, the fox-hounds had caught and killed a yearling in the woods; and Colonel Dietz had taken with his celebrated Malodiets, aided by another dog, a two-year-old. What had become of the other wolves and where were most of the hounds?

Without waiting to solve these problems, we collected what we could of our outfit and returned to Philipovo, leaving the task of finding the dogs to the whippers-in. The whys and wherefores of the hunt were thoroughly discussed at dinner, and it was agreed that most of the wolves had passed to the rear between the beaters. It was found out that the peasants, when a short distance in the woods, had through fear formed into squads instead of going singly or in pairs. This did not, however, diminish the disappointment at not taking at least one of the old ones.

The result of this drive logically brought up the question of the best way to drive game. In certain districts of Poland deer are driven from the line of posts, and the same can be said of successful moose-hunts of Northern Russia. Perhaps that way may also be better for wolves.

After careful consideration of the hunting situation, we were unanimous in preferring hare and fox coursing with both foxhounds and barzois, or with the latter alone, at discretion, to the uncertainty of wolf-hunting; so we decided to change our locality. Accordingly the following day we proceeded in the *Amerikanka* to the town of Koy, twenty-five versts distant. We arrived about noon, and were quartered in a vacant house in the large yard of Madam Ponamaroff. Our retinue of huntsmen, dogs, horses, ambulance and wagons arrived an hour later.

There was no more wolf-hunting.

Henry T. Allen

Wolf Chase

From Across Mongolian Plains, *1921*

Roy Chapman Andrews

For thirty-six days they had been on the road, and yet were only halfway across the desert. Every day had been exactly like the day before—an endless routine of eating and sleeping, camp-making and camp-breaking in sun, rain, or wind. The monotony of it all would be appalling to a westerner, but the Oriental mind seems peculiarly adapted to accept it with entire contentment. Long before daylight they were on the road again, and when we awoke only the smoking embers of an *argul* fire remained as evidence that they ever had been there.

Mongolia, as we saw it in the spring, was very different from Mongolia of the early autumn. The hills and plains stretched away in limitless waves of brown untinged by the slightest trace of green, and in shaded corners among rocks there were still patches of snow or ice. Instead of resembling the grassy plains of Kansas or Nebraska, now it was like a real desert and I had difficulty in justifying to Yvette and Mae my glowing accounts of its potential resources.

Moreover, the human life was just as disappointing as the lack of vegetation, for we were "between seasons" on the trail. The winter traffic was almost ended, and the camels would not be replaced by cart caravans until the grass was long enough to provide adequate food for oxen and horses. The *yurts,* which often are erected far out upon the plains away from water when snow is on the ground, had all been moved near the wells or to the summer pastures; and sometimes we traveled a hundred miles without a glimpse of even a solitary Mongol.

Ude had been left far behind, and we were bowling along on a road as level as a floor, when we saw two wolves quietly watching us half a mile away. We had agreed not to chase antelope again; but wolves were fair game at any time. Moreover, we were particularly glad to be able to check our records as to how fast a wolf can run when conditions are in its favor. Coltman signaled Mac to await us with the others, and we swung toward the animals which were trotting slowly westward, now and then stopping to look back as though reluctant to leave such an unusual exhibition as the car was giving them. A few moments later, however, they decided that curiosity might prove dangerous and began to run in earnest.

They separated almost immediately, and we raced after the larger of the two, a huge fellow with rangy legs which carried him forward in a long, swinging lope. The ground was perfect for the car, and the speedometer registered forty miles an hour. He had a thousand-yard start, but we gained rapidly, and I estimated that he never reached a greater speed than thirty miles an hour. Charles was very anxious to kill the brute from the motor with his .45 caliber automatic pistol, and I promised not to shoot.

The wolf was running low to the ground, his head a little to one side watching us with one bloodshot eye. He was giving us a great race, but the odds were all against him, and finally we had him right beside the motor. Leaning far out, Coltman fired quickly. The bullet struck just behind the brute, and he swerved sharply, missing the right front wheel by a scant six inches. Before Charles could turn the car he had gained three hundred yards, but we reached him again in little more than a mile. As Coltman was about to shoot a second time, the wolf suddenly dropped from sight. Almost on the instant the car plunged over a bank four feet in height, landed with a tremendous shock—and kept on! Charles had seen the danger in a flash, and had thrown his body against the wheel to hold it steady. Had he not been an expert driver we should inevitably have turned upside down and probably all would have been killed.

We stopped an instant to inspect the springs, but by a miracle not a leaf was broken. The wolf halted, too, and we could see him standing on a gentle rise with drooping head, his gray sides heaving. He seemed to be "all in," but to our amazement he was off again like the wind even before the car had started. During the last three miles the ground had been changing rapidly, and we soon reached a stony plain where there was imminent danger of smashing a front wheel. The wolf was heading directly toward a rocky slope which lay against the sky like the spiny back of some gigantic monster of the past.

His strategy had almost won the race. For a moment the wolf rested on the ridge, and I leaped out to shoot, but instantly he dropped behind the bowlders. Leaving me to intercept the animal, Charles swung behind the ridge only to run at full speed into a sandy pocket. The motor ceased to throb, and the race was ended.

These wolves are sneaking carrion-feeders and as such I detest them, but this one had "played the game." *For twelve long miles* he had kept doggedly at his work without a whimper or a cry of "kamerad." The brute had outgeneraled us completely, had won by strategy and magnificent endurance. Whatever he supposed the roaring car to be, instinct told him that safety lay among the rocks and he led us there as straight as an arrow's flight.

The animal seemed to take an almost human enjoyment in the way we had been tricked, for he stood on a hillside half a mile away watching our efforts to extricate the car.

Just before dark we heard the *dong, dong, dong* of a camel's bell and saw the long line of dusty yellow animals swing around a sharp earth-corner into the sandy space beside the well. Like the trained units of an army each camel came into position, kneeled upon the ground and remained quietly chewing its cud until the driver removed the load. Long before the last straggler had arrived the tents were up and a fire blazing, and far into the night the thirsty beasts grunted and roared as the trough was filled with water.

Hunting on the Turin Plain

From Across Mongolian Plains, *1921*

Roy Chapman Andrews

After ten days we left the "Antelope Camp" to visit the Turin plain where we had seen much game on the way to Urga. One by one our Mongol neighbors rode up to say "farewell," and each to present us with a silk scarf as a token of friendship and good will. We received an invitation to stop for tea at the *yurt* of an old man who had manifested an especial interest in us, but it was a very dirty *yurt,* and the preparations for tea were so uninviting that we managed to exit gracefully before it was finally served.

Yvette photographed the entire family including half a dozen dogs, a calf, and two babies, much to their enjoyment. When we rode off, our hands were heaped with cheese and slabs of mutton which were discarded as soon as we had dropped behind a slope. Mongol hospitality is whole-souled and generously given, but one must be very hungry to enjoy their food.

A day and a half of traveling was uneventful, for herds of sheep and horses indicated the presence of *yurts* among the hills. Game will seldom remain where there are Mongols. Although it was the first of July, we found a heavy coating of ice on the lower sides of a deep well. The water was about fifteen feet below the level of the plain, and the ice would probably remain all summer. Moreover, it is said that the wells never freeze even during the coldest winter.

The changes of temperature were more rapid than in any other country in which I have ever hunted. It was hot during the day—about 85° Fahrenheit—but the instant the sun disappeared we needed coats, and our fur sleeping bags were always acceptable at night.

We were one hundred and fifty miles from Urga and were still going slowly south, when we had our next real hunting camp. Great bands of antelope were working northward from the Gobi Desert to the better grazing on the grass-covered Turin plain. We encountered the main herd one evening about six o'clock, and it was a sight which made us gasp for breath. We were shifting camp, and my wife and I were trotting along parallel to the carts which moved slowly over the trail a mile away. We had had a delightful, as well as profitable, day. Yvette had been busy with her camera, while I picked up an antelope, a bustard, three hares, and half a dozen marmots. We were loafing in our saddles, when suddenly we caught sight of the cook standing on his cart frantically signaling us to come.

In ten seconds our ponies were flying toward the caravan, while we mentally reviewed every accident which possibly could have happened to the boys. Lü met us twenty yards from the trail, trembling with excitement and totally incoherent. He could only point to the south and stammer, "Too many antelope. Over there. Too many, too many."

I slipped off Kublai Khan's back and put up the glasses. Certainly there were animals, but I thought they must be sheep or ponies. Hundreds were in sight, feeding in one vast herd and in many smaller groups. Then I remembered that the nearest well was twenty miles away; therefore they could not be horses. I looked again and knew they must be antelope—not in hundreds, but in thousands.

Mr. Larsen in Urga had told us of herds like this, but we had never hoped to see one. Yet there before us, as far as the eye could reach, was a yellow mass of moving forms. In a moment Yvette and I had left the carts. There was no possibility of concealment, and our only chance was to run the herd. When we were perhaps half a mile away the nearest animals threw up their heads and began to stamp and run about, only to stop again and stare at us. We kept on very slowly, edging nearer every moment. Suddenly they decided that we were really dangerous, and the herd strung out like a regiment of yellow-coated soldiers.

Kublai Khan had seen the antelope almost as soon as we left the carts, and although he had already traveled forty miles that day, was nervously champing the bit with head up and ears erect. When at last I gave him the word, he gathered himself for one terrific spring; down went his head and he dashed forward with every ounce of strength behind his flying legs. His run was the long, smooth stride of a thoroughbred, and it sent the blood surging through my veins in a wild thrill of exhilaration. Once only I glanced back at Yvette. She was almost at my side. Her hair had loosened and was flying back like a veil behind her head. Tense with excitement, eyes shining, she was heedless of everything save those skimming yellow forms before us. It was useless to look for holes; ere I had seen one we were over or around it. With head low down and muzzle out, my pony needed not the slightest touch to guide him. He knew where we were going and the part he had to play.

More than a thousand antelope were running diagonally across our course. It was a sight to stir the gods; a thing to give one's life to see. But when we were almost near enough to shoot, the herd suddenly swerved heading directly away from us. In an instant we were enveloped in a whirling cloud of dust through which the flying animals were dimly visible like phantom figures. Kublai Khan was choked, and his hot breath rasped sharply through his nostrils, but he plunged on and on into that yellow cloud. Standing in my stirrups, I fired six times at the wraith-like forms ahead as fast as I could work the lever of my rifle. Of course, it was useless, but just the same I had to shoot.

In about a mile the great herd slowed down and stopped. We could see hundreds of animals on every side, in groups of fifty or one hundred. Probably two thousand antelope were in sight at once and many more were beyond the sky rim to the west. We gave the ponies ten minutes' rest, and had another run as unsuccessful as the first. Then a third and fourth. The antelope, for some strange reason, would not cross our path, but always turned straight away before we were near enough to shoot.

After an hour we returned to the carts—for Yvette was exhausted from excitement—and the lama took her place. We left the great herd and turned southward, parallel to the road. A mile away we found more antelope; at least a thousand were scattered about feeding quietly like those we had driven north. It seemed as though all the gazelles in Mongolia had concentrated on those few miles of plain.

The ponies were so exhausted that we decided to try a drive and leave the main herd in peace. When we were concealed from view in the bottom of a land swell I slipped off and hobbled Kublai Khan. The poor fellow was so tired he could only stand with drooping head, even though there was rich grass beneath his feet. I sent the lama in a long circle to get behind the herd, while I crawled a few hundred yards away and snuggled out of sight into an old wolf den.

I watched the antelope for fifteen minutes through my binoculars. They were feeding in a vast semicircle, entirely unconscious of my presence. Suddenly every head went up; they stared fixedly toward the west for a moment, and were off like the wind. About five hundred drew together in a compact mass, but a dozen smaller herds scattered wildly, running in every direction except toward me. They had seen the lama before he had succeeded in completely encircling them, and the drive was ruined.

The Mongols kill great numbers of antelope in just this way. When a herd has been located, a line of men will conceal themselves at distances of two or three hundred yards, while as many more get behind the animals and drive them toward the waiting hunters. Sometimes the gazelles almost step on the natives and become so frightened that they run the gantlet of the entire firing line.

I did not have the heart to race again with our exhausted ponies, and we turned back toward the carts which were out of sight. Scores of antelope, singly or in pairs, were visible on the sky line and as we rode to the summit of a little rise a herd of fifty appeared almost below us. We paid no attention to them; but suddenly my pony stopped with ears erect. He looked back at me, as much as to say, "Don't you see those antelope?" and began gently pulling at the reins. I could feel him tremble with eagerness and excitement. "Well, old chap," I said, "if you are as keen as all that, let's give them a run."

With a magnificent burst of speed Kublai Khan launched himself toward the fleeing animals. They circled beautifully, straight into the eye of the sun, which lay like a great red ball upon the surface of the plain. We were still three hundred yards away and gaining rapidly, but I had to shoot; in a moment I would be blinded by the sun. As the flame leaped from my rifle, we heard the dull thud of a bullet on flesh; at the second shot, another; and then a third. "*Sanga*" (three), yelled the lama, and dashed forward, wild with excitement.

The three gazelles lay almost the same distance apart, each one shot through the body. It was interesting evidence that the actions of working the lever on my rifle and aiming, and the speed of the antelope, varied only by a fraction of a second. In this case, brain and eye and hand had functioned perfectly. Needless to say, I do not always shoot like that.

Two of the antelope were yearling bucks, and one was a large doe. The lama took the female on his pony, and I strapped the other two on Kublai Khan. When I mounted, he was carrying a weight of two hundred and eighty-five pounds, yet he kept his steady "homeward trot" without a break until we reached the carts six miles away.

Yvette had been afraid that we would miss the well in the gathering darkness, and had made a "dry camp" beside the road. We had only a little water for ourselves; but my pony's nose was full of dust, and I knew how parched his throat must be, so I divided my supply with him. The poor animal was so frightened by the dish, that he would only snort and back away even when I wet his nose with some of the precious fluid, he would not drink.

The success of our work upon the plains depended largely upon Kublai Khan. He was only a Mongol pony but he was just as great, in his own way, as was the Tartar emperor whose name he bore. Whatever it was I asked him to do, he gave his very best. Can you wonder that I loved him?

Within a fortnight from the time I bought him, he became a perfect hunting pony. The secret of it all was that he liked the game as well as I. Traveling with the carts bored him exceedingly but the instant game appeared he was all excitement. Often he saw antelope before we did. We might be trotting slowly over the plains, when suddenly he would jerk his head erect and begin to pull gently at the reins; when I reached down to take my rifle from the holster, he would tremble with eagerness to be off.

In hunting antelope you should ride slowly toward the animals, drawing nearer gradually. They are so accustomed to see Mongols that they will not begin to run in earnest until a man is five or six hundred yards away, but when they are really off, a fast pony is the great essential. The time to stop is just before the animals cross your path, and then you must stop quickly. Kublai Khan learned the trick immediately. As soon as he felt the pressure of my knees, and the slightest pull upon the reins, his whole body stiffened and he braced himself like a polo pony. It made not the slightest difference to him whether I shot from his back or directly under his nose; he stood quietly watching the running antelope. When we were riding across the plains if a bird ran along the ground or a hare jumped out of the grass, he was after it like a dog. Often I would find myself flying toward an animal which I had never seen.

Yvette's pony was useless for hunting antelope. Instead of heading diagonally toward the gazelles he would always attempt to follow the herd. When it was time to stop I would have to put all my strength upon the reins and the horse would come into a slow gallop and then a trot. Seconds of valuable time would be wasted before I could begin to shoot. I tried half a dozen other ponies, but they were all as bad. They did not have the intelligence or the love of hunting which made Kublai Khan so valuable.

The morning after encountering the great herd, we camped at a well thirty miles north of the Turin monastery. Three or four *yurts* were scattered about, and a caravan of two hundred and fifty camels was resting in a little hollow. From the door of our tent we could see the blue summit of the Turin "mountain," and have in the foreground a perpetual moving picture of camels, horses, sheep, goats, and cattle seeking water. All day long hundreds of animals crowded about the well, while one or two Mongols filled the troughs by means of wooden buckets.

The life about the wells is always interesting, for they are points of concentration for all wanderers on the plains. Just as we pitch our tents and make ourselves at home, so great caravans arrive with tired, laden camels. The huge brutes kneel, while their packs are being removed, and then stand in a long line, patiently waiting until their turn comes to drink. Groups of ten or twelve crowd about the trough; then, majestically swinging their padded feet, they move slowly to one side, kneel upon the ground, and sleepily chew their cuds until all the herd has joined them. Sometimes the caravans wait for several days to rest their animals and let them feed; sometimes they vanish in the first gray light of dawn.

On the Turin plain we had a delightful glimpse of antelope babyhood. The great herds which we had found were largely composed of does just ready to drop their young, and after a few days they scattered widely into groups of from five to twenty.

We found the first baby antelope on June 27. We had seen half a dozen females circling restlessly about, and suspected that their fawns could not be far away. Sure enough, our Mongol discovered one of the little fellows in the flattest part of the flat plain. It was lying motionless with its neck stretched out, just where its mother had told it to remain when she saw us riding toward her.

Yvette called to me, "Oh, please, please catch it. We can raise it on milk and it will make such an adorable pet."

"Oh, yes," I said, "let's do. I'll get it for you. You can put it in your hat till we go back to camp."

In blissful ignorance I dismounted and slowly went toward the little animal. There was not the slightest motion until I tossed my outspread shooting coat. Then I saw a flash of brown, a bobbing white rump-patch, and a tiny thing, no larger than a rabbit, speeding over the plain. The baby was somewhat "wabbly," to be sure, for this was probably the first time it had ever tried its slender legs, but after a few hundred yards it ran as steadily as its mother.

I was so surprised that for a moment I simply stared. Then I leaped into the saddle and Kublai Khan rushed after the diminutive brown fawn. It was a good half mile before we had the little chap under the pony's nose but the race was by no means ended. Mewing with fright, it swerved sharply to the left and ere we could swing about, it had gained a hundred yards. Again and again we were almost on it, but every time it dodged and got away. After half an hour my pony was gasping for breath, and I changed to Yvette's chestnut stallion. The Mongol joined me and we had another run, but we might have been pursuing a streak of shifting sunlight. Finally we had to give it up and watch the tiny thing bob away toward its mother, who was circling about in the distance.

There were half a dozen other fawns upon the plain, but they all treated us alike and my wife's hat was empty when we returned to camp. These antelope probably had been born not more than two or three days before we found them. Later, after a chase of more than a mile, we caught one which was only a few hours old. Had it not injured itself when dodging between my pony's legs we could never have secured it at all.

The Forest and the Steppe

Ivan Turgenev

And slowly something began to draw him
Back to the country, to the garden dark,
Where lime-trees are so huge, so full of shade,
And lilies of the valley, sweet as maids,
Where rounded willows o'er the water's edge
Lean from the dyke in rows, and where the oak
Sturdily grows above the sturdy field,
Amid the smell of hemp and nettles rank. . . .
There, there, in meadows stretching wide,
Where rich and black as velvet is the earth,
Where the sweet rye, far as the eye can see,
Moves noiselessly in tender, billowing waves,
And where the heavy golden light is shed
From out of rounded, white, transparent clouds:
There it is good. . . .

(From a poem consigned to the flames)

The reader is, very likely, already weary of my sketches; I hasten to reassure him by promising to confine myself to the fragments already printed; but I cannot refrain from saying a few words at parting about a hunter's life.

Hunting with a dog and a gun is delightful in itself, *für sich,* as they used to say in old days; but let us suppose you were not born a hunter, but are fond of nature and freedom all the same; you cannot then help envying us hunters. . . . Listen.

Do you know, for instance, the delight of settling off before daybreak in spring? You come out on to the steps. . . . In the dark-grey sky stars are twinkling here and there; a damp breeze in faint gusts flies to meet you now and then; there is heard the secret, vague whispering of the night; the trees faintly rustle, wrapt in darkness. And now they put a rug in the cart, and lay a box with the samovar at your feet. The trace-horses move restlessly, snort, and daintily paw the ground; a couple of white geese, only just awake, waddle slowly and silently across the road. On the other side of the hedge, in the garden, the watchman is snoring peacefully; every sound seems to stand still in the frozen air—suspended, not moving. You take your seat; the horses start at once; the cart rolls off with a loud rumble. You ride—ride past the church, downhill to the right, across the dyke. . . . The pond is just beginning to be covered with mist. You are rather chilly; you cover your face with the collar of your fur cloak; you doze. The horses' hoofs splash sonorously through the puddles; the coachman begins to whistle. But by now you have driven over four versts . . . the rim of the sky flushes crimson; the jackdaws are heard, fluttering clumsily in the birch-trees; sparrows are twittering about the dark hayricks. The air is clearer, the road more distinct, the sky brightens, the clouds look whiter, and the fields look greener. In the huts there is the red light of flaming chips; from behind gates comes the sound of sleepy voices. And meanwhile the glow of dawn is beginning; already streaks of gold are stretching across the sky; mists are gathering in clouds over the ravines; the larks are singing musically; the breeze that ushers in the dawn is blowing; and slowly the purple sun floats upward. There is a perfect flood of light; your heart is fluttering like a bird. Everything is fresh, gay, delightful! One can see a long way all round. That way, beyond the copse, a village; there, further, another, with a white church, and there a birch-wood on the hill; behind it the marsh, for which you are bound.... Quicker, horses, quicker! Forward at a good trot! ... There are three versts to go—not more. The sun mounts swiftly higher; the sky is clear. It will be a glorious day. A herd of cattle comes straggling from the village to meet you. You go up the hill.... What a view! The river winds for ten versts, dimly blue through the mist; beyond it meadows of watery green; beyond the meadows sloping hills; in the distance the plovers are wheeling with loud cries above the marsh; through the moist brilliance suffused in the air the distance stands out clearly ... not as in the summer. How freely one drinks in the air, how quickly the limbs move, how strong is the whole man, clasped in the fresh breath of spring! ...

And a summer morning—a morning in July! Who but the hunter knows how soothing it is to wander at daybreak among the underwoods? The print of your feet lies in a green line on the grass, white with dew. You part the drenched bushes; you are met by a rush of the warm fragrance stored up in the night; the air is saturated with the fresh bitterness of wormwood, the honey sweetness of buckwheat and clover; in the distance an oak wood stands like a wall, and glows and glistens in the sun; it is still fresh, but already the approach of heat is felt. The head is faint and dizzy from the excess of sweet scents. The copse stretches on endlessly. Only in places there are yellow glimpses in the distance of ripening rye, and narrow streaks of red buckwheat. Then there is the creak of cart wheels; a peasant makes his way among the bushes at a walking pace, and sets his horse in the shade before the heat of the day. You greet him, and turn away; the musical swish of the scythe is heard behind you. The sun rises higher and higher. The grass is speedily dry. And now it is quite sultry. One hour passes, another. . . . The sky grows dark over the horizon; the still air is baked with prickly heat. "Where can one get a drink here, brother?" you inquire of the mower. "Yonder, in the ravine's a well." Through the thick hazel bushes, tangled by the clinging grass, you drop down to the bottom of the ravine. Right under the cliff a little spring is hidden; an oak bush greedily spreads out its twigs like great fingers over the water; great silvery bubbles rise trembling from the bottom, covered with fine velvety moss. You fling yourself on the ground, you drink, but you are too lazy to stir. You are in the shade, you drink in the damp fragrance, you take your ease, while the bushes face you, glowing and, as it were, turning yellow in the sun. But what is that? There is a sudden flying gust of wind; the air is astir all about you: was not that thunder? Is it the heat thickening? Is a storm coming on? . . . And now there is a faint flash of lightning. Yes, there will be a storm! The sun is still blazing; you can still go on hunting. But the storm-cloud grows; its front edge, drawn out like a long sleeve, bends over into an arch. Make haste! over there you think you catch sight of a hay-barn . . . make haste! . . . You run there, go in. . . . What rain! What flashes of lightning! The water drips in through some hole in the thatch-roof on to the sweet-smelling hay. But now the sun is shining bright again. The storm is over; you come out. My God, the joyous sparkle of everything! the fresh, limpid air, the scent of raspberries and mushrooms! And then the evening comes on. There is the blaze of fire glowing and covering half the sky. The sun sets; the air near you has a peculiar transparency as of crystal; over the distance lies a soft, warm-looking haze; with the dew a crimson light is shed on the fields, lately plunged in floods of limpid gold; from trees and bushes and high stacks of hay run long shadows. The sun has set; a star gleams and quivers in the fiery sea of the sunset; and now it pales; the sky grows blue; the separate shadows vanish; the air is plunged in darkness. It is time to turn homewards to the village, to the hut, where you will stay the night. Shouldering your gun, you move briskly, in spite of fatigue. Meanwhile, the night comes on: now you cannot see twenty paces from you; the dogs show faintly white in the dark. Over there, above the black bushes, there is a vague brightness on the horizon. What is it?—a fire? . . . No, it is the moon rising. And away below, to the right, the village lights are twinkling already. And here at last is your hut. Through the tiny window you see a table, with a white cloth, a candle burning, supper. . . .

Another time you order the racing droshky to be got out, and set off to the forest to shoot woodcock. It is pleasant making your way along the narrow path between two high walls of rye. The ears softly strike you in the face; the corn-flowers cling round your legs; the quails call around; the horse moves along at a lazy trot. And here is the forest, all shade and silence. Graceful aspens rustle high above you; the long hanging branches of the birches scarcely stir; a mighty oak stands like a champion beside a lovely lime-tree. You go along the green path, streaked with shade; great yellow flies stay suspended, motionless, in the sunny air, and suddenly dart away; midges hover in a cloud, bright in the shade, dark in the sun; the birds are singing peacefully; the golden little voice of the warbler sings of innocent, babbling joyousness, in sweet accord with the scent of the lilies of the valley. Further, further, deeper into the forest . . . the forest grows more dense. . . . An unutterable stillness falls upon the soul within; without, too, all is still and dreamy. But now a wind has sprung up, and the tree-tops are booming like falling waves. Here and there, through last year's brown leaves, grow tall grasses; mushrooms stand apart under their wide-brimmed hats. All at once a hare skips out; the dog scurries after it with a resounding bark. . . .

And how fair is this same forest in late autumn, when the snipe are on the wing! They do not keep in the heart of the forest; one must look for them along the outskirts. There is no wind, and no sun, no light, no shade, no movement, no sound; the autumn perfume, like the perfume of wine, is diffused in the soft air; a delicate haze hangs over the yellow fields in the distance. The still sky is a peacefully untroubled white through the bare brown branches; in parts, on the limes, hang the last golden leaves. The damp earth is elastic under your feet; the high dry blades of grass do not stir; long threads lie shining on the blanched turf, white with dew. You breathe tranquilly; but there is a strange tremor in the soul. You walk along the forest's edge, look after your dog, and meanwhile loved forms, loved faces, dead and living, come to your mind; long, long slumbering impressions unexpectedly awaken; the fancy darts off and soars like a bird; and all moves so clearly and stands out before your eyes. The heart at one time throbs and beats, plunging passionately forward; at another it is drowned beyond recall in memories. Your whole life, as it were, unrolls lightly and rapidly before you; a man at such times possesses all his past, all his feelings and his powers—all his soul; and there is nothing around to hinder him—no sun, no wind, no sound. . . .

And a clear, rather cold autumn day, with a frost in the morning, when the birch, all golden like some tree in a fairy-tale, stands out picturesquely against the pale-blue sky; when the sun, standing low in the sky, does not warm, but shines more brightly than in summer; the small aspen copse is all a-sparkle through and through, as though it were glad and at ease in its nakedness; the hoar-frost is still white at the bottom of the hollows; while a fresh wind softly stirs up and drives before it the falling, crumpled leaves; when blue ripples whisk gladly along the river, lifting rhythmically the scattered geese and ducks; in the distance the mill creaks, half hidden by the willows; and with changing colours in the clear air the pigeons wheel in swift circles above it.

Sweet, too, are dull days in summer, though the hunters do not like them. On such days one can't shoot the bird that flutters up from under your very feet and vanishes at once in the whitish dark of the hanging fog. But how peaceful, how unutterably peaceful it is everywhere! Everything is awake, and everything is hushed. You pass by a tree: it does not stir a leaf; it is musing in repose. Through the thin steamy mist, evenly diffused in the air, there is a long streak of black before you. You take it for a neighbouring copse close at hand; you go up—the copse is transformed into a high row of wormwood in the boundary-ditch. Above you, around you, on all sides—mist. . . . But now a breeze is faintly astir; a patch of pale-blue sky peeps dimly out; through the thinning, as it were, steaming mist, a ray of golden-yellow sunshine breaks out suddenly, flows in a long stream, strikes on the fields and in the copse—and now everything is overcast again. For long this struggle is drawn out, but how unutterably brilliant and magnificent the day becomes when at last light triumphs and the last waves of the warmed mist here unroll and are drawn out over the plains, there wind away and vanish into the deep, softly shining heights.

Again you set off into outlying country, to the steppe. For some ten versts you make your way over cross-roads, and here at last is the highroad. Past endless trains of waggons, past wayside taverns, with the hissing samovar under a shed, wide-open gates and a well, from one hamlet to another; across endless fields, alongside green hempfields, a long, long time you drive. The magpies flutter from willow to willow; peasant women with long rakes in their hands wander in the fields; a man in a threadbare nankin overcoat, with a wicker pannier over his shoulder, trudges along with weary step; a heavy country coach, harnessed with six tall, broken-winded horses, rolls to meet you. The corner of a cushion is sticking out of a window, and on a sack up behind, hanging on to a string, perches a groom in a fur cloak, splashed with mud to his very eyebrows. And here is the little district town with its crooked little wooden houses, its endless fences, its empty stone shops, its old-fashioned bridge over a deep ravine. On, on! . . . The steppe country is reached at last. You look from a hill-top; what a view! Round low hills, tilled and sown to their very tops, are seen in broad undulations; ravines, overgrown with bushes, wind coiling among them; small copses are scattered like oblong islands; from village to village run narrow paths; churches stand out white; between willow bushes glimmers a little river, in four places dammed up by dykes; far off, in a field, in a line, an old manor house, with its outhouses, orchard, and threshing-floor, huddles close up to a small pond. But on, on you go. The hills are smaller and ever smaller; there is scarcely a tree to be seen. Here it is at last—the boundless, untrodden steppe!

And on a winter day to walk over the high snowdrifts after hares; to breathe the keen frosty air, while half-closing the eyes involuntarily at the fine blinding sparkle of the soft snow; to admire the emerald sky above the reddish forest! . . . And the first spring day when everything is shining, and breaking up, when across the heavy streams, from the melting snow, there is already the scent of the thawing earth; when on the bare thawed places, under the slanting sunshine, the larks are singing confidingly, and, with glad splash and roar, the torrents roll from ravine to ravine.

But it is time to end. By the way, I have spoken of spring: in spring it is easy to part; in spring even the happy are drawn away to the distance. . . . Farewell, reader! I wish you unbroken prosperity.